T0330091

The New Electronic Marketplace

The New Electronic Marketplace

European Governance Strategies in a
Globalising Economy

George Christou
*Department of Politics and International Relations, University of
Warwick, UK*

Seamus Simpson
*Department of Information and Communications, Manchester
Metropolitan University, UK*

Edward Elgar
Cheltenham, UK • Northampton MA, USA

Published by
Edward Elgar Publishing Limited
Glensanda House
Montpellier Parade
Cheltenham
Glos GL50 1UA
UK

Edward Elgar Publishing, Inc.
William Pratt House
9 Dewey Court
Northampton
Massachusetts 01060
USA

A catalogue record for this book
is available from the British Library

Library of Congress Control Number: 2006937960

ISBN 978 1 84542 274 5

Printed and bound in Great Britain by MPG Books Ltd, Bodmin, Cornwall

Contents

List of Tables and Figures   *vi*
Abbreviations   *vii*
Acknowledgements   *x*

1. Understanding the Governance of the Internet Economy   1
2. Internet Governance: A Historical Context   27
3. The European Union and the Governance of the
   Communications Sector   48
4. The Dot EU Top Level Domain   75
5. The EU and Internet Commerce Regulation   93
6. The Directive on E-Commerce and the National Dimension   116
7. The Global Governance of the Electronic Network Economy
   and the EU   133
8. Conclusion:The EU and the Evolving Electronic Marketplace   160

References   *175*
Index   *198*

Tables and figures

TABLES

1.1 Positive and Negative Coordination: Key Characteristics   8
1.2 Modes of Regulation in the EU   17
1.3 Typologies of EU and US Self-Regulation 'Images'   20

FIGURES

1.1 Responsive Regulation: The Enforcement and Technique
    Pyramid   12
2.1 US Green Paper   38
2.2 Principles for a New System: US White Paper   40
5.1 Main Proposed Elements of the EU's Regulatory Framework
    for E-Commerce   99

Abbreviations

ABT	Agreement on Basic Telecommunications
ADR	Alternative Dispute Resolution
AEPSI	Association of Spanish Internet Service Providers
ARPA	Advanced Research Projects Agency
BBC	British Broadcasting Corporation
B2B	Business-to-Business
ccTLD	Country Code Top Level Domain
CEPT	European Conference of Postal and Telecommunications Administrations
CERN	European Centre for Nuclear Research
DARPA	Defense Advanced Research Projects Agency
DEC	Directive on E-Commerce
DG	Directorate General
DGT	Direction Générale des Télécommunications
DNS	Domain Name System
DTI	Department of Trade and Industry
ECRF	Electronic Communications Regulatory Framework
EDI	Electronic Data Interchange
EEJ-Net	European Extra-judicial Network
ERG	European Regulators Group
ESPRIT	European Strategic Programme for Research in Information Technology
ETNO	European Telecommunications Network Operators Association
ETSI	European Telecommunications Standards Institute
EU	European Union
EuroISPA	European Internet Service Provider Association
FICORA	(Viestintävirasto) Finnish Communications Authority
FTP	File Transfer Protocol
GAC	Governmental Advisory Committee
GATS	General Agreement on Trade in Services
GATT	General Agreement on Tariffs and Trade
GBDe	Global Business Dialogue
GIC	Global Internet Council
GIP	Global Internet Project
GIPC	Global Internet Policy Council

gTLD-MoU	Generic Top-Level Domain Memorandum of Understanding
IAB	Internet Architecture Board
IAHC	International Ad Hoc Committee
IANA	Internet Assigned Numbers Authority
ICANN	Internet Corporation for Assigned Names and Numbers
ICSTIS	Independent Committee for the Supervision of Telephone Information Services
ICT	Information and Communication Technologies
IETF	Internet Engineering Task Force
IFWP	International Forum on the White Paper
IGF	Internet Governance Forum
IP	Internet Protocol
IRG	Independent Regulators Group
IS	Information Society
ISO	International Organization for Standardization
ISOC	Internet Society
ISPs	Internet Service Providers
IT	Information Technology
ITO	International Trade Organization
ITU	International Telecommunications Union
LAN	Local Area Network
LLU	Local Loop Unbundling
MFN	Most Favoured Nation
NRA	National Regulatory Authority
NSF	National Science Foundation
NSI	Network Solutions Inc
OECD	Organization for Economic Co-operation and Development
Ofcom	Office of Communications
Oftel	Office of Telecommunications
OMC	Open Method of Coordination
ONP	Open Network Provision
OSI	Open Systems Interconnect
PPR	Public Policy Rules
PSB	Public Service Broadcasting
PTT	Postal, Telephone and Telegraph administration
PTTs	Postal, Telephone and Telegraph companies
Reg TP	Regulierungsbehörde für Telekommunikation und Post
SEEM	Single European Electronic Market
SEM	Single European Market
SLD	Second Level Domain
TCP/IP	Transmission Control Protocol/Internet Protocol
TEDIS	Trade Electronic Data Interchange System
TLD	Top Level Domain
TRIMs	Agreement on Trade Related Investment Measures

TRIPs	Trade Related Aspects of Intellectual Property Agreement
UNCITRAL	United Nations Conference on International Trade Law
UNCTAD	United Nations Conference on Trade and Development
USC ISI	University of Southern California's Information Sciences Institute
VANS	Value Added Network Services
VAT	Value Added Tax
VoIP	Voice over Internet Protocol
WGIG	Working Group on Internet Governance
WICANN	World Internet Corporation for Assigned Names and Numbers
WIPO	World Intellectual Property Organization
WSIS	World Summit on Information Society
WTO	World Trade Organization
WWW	World Wide Web

Acknowledgements

The authors would like to acknowledge the support of the UK Economic and Social Research Council, which, between 2003 and 2004, funded the 'European Regulation of Internet Commerce Project' (Grant number RES-000-22-0356) which generated the research on which this monograph is based. They would like to extend thanks to those officials at the European Union, in particular from the European Commission's Directorates-General Information Society and Media, Internal Market, and Enterprise who agreed to be interviewed in the course of the project. In addition, valuable data was gathered from interviews conducted at the national level in Finland, Italy, Germany and the UK. Finally, they would like to acknowledge the input of those from the world of Internet commerce who agreed to be interviewed and participated in the European Regulation of Internet Commerce Symposium held in Brussels, 14 October, 2004. In particular, the authors would like to thank the keynote speakers at the event – Susan Pointer (Director of European Public Policy, Amazon.com) and Philip Sheppard (Public Policy Manager, AIM – the European Brands Association) – as well as European Commission and national Member State policy officials.

1. Understanding the governance of the Internet economy

Although still a relatively new phenomenon, Internet governance has become an important issue in the global political economy with a diverse range of issues at stake, making the task of defining governance models both problematic and necessary. At its most high profile, UN initiatives such as the World Summit on Information Society (WSIS) and in particular its Working Group on Internet Governance (WGIG) and the UN Information and Communications Technology (ICT) Task Force illustrate the extent to which the minds of policy-makers, as well as the business, Internet technical and civil society communities have been concentrated in recent years.

Academic work on Internet governance is in its infancy too. Despite this, there have emerged a number of important empirically and theoretically based contributions, to which this volume aims to make a significant contribution through its focus on the European Union (EU) policy context. Amongst these, some studies have provided a critical narrative on the developing system of governance for the Internet at a global level (Froomkin 2001; Weinburg 2001; Mueller 2002; von Bernstorff 2003; Hofmann 2005), affording, in the process, some treatment of the role played by the EU (e.g. Mueller 2002). Other more EU-centric work has analysed the interaction between the EU and the US in the development of the global governance regime for the Internet (Kielbiwicz 2002; Leib 2002; Werle 2002), rule-making within it (Biukovic 2002) the activities of different actors, and various often contentious policy issues including taxation (Barbet 2001; Paris 2003), privacy (Farrell 2003), and trade and intellectual property (Simpson and Wilkinson 2003a).

The literature on Internet governance has employed a variety of frameworks from legal, economic and political science based schools of thought. Here, realist or statist (Drezner 2004); international relations (regime theory Franda 2001; Mueller et al 2004), constructivist (Farrell 2003), neo-Gramscian, (Simpson 2004); economic institutionalist (Mueller 2002); self-regulation (Price and Verhulst 2000, 2005) and also more generalised 'national systems approaches' (Kogut 2002) have all been in evidence. Kleinwachter (2004) has considered the utility of creating co-regulatory networks of Internet governance to mirror the Internet's architecture, with power dispersed widely to the system's endpoints and held only relatively weakly at its core. Drake (2004) in examining the detailed mechanics of Internet governance highlights a range of essential factors, notably: institutional settings; agreement types; decision-making procedures; strength and scope (*vis*, range and interrelatedness of issues covered); domain (public, private, civil society, universal membership versus smaller groupings); compliance mechanisms and, finally, distributional bias.

With specific focus on the electronic network economy (hereafter the e-economy) which has grown as a result of the Internet's expansion, scholars have begun to explore the nature of the emergent governance arrangements for electronic commerce (e-commerce), as well as the role of transnational business in developing frameworks for Internet governance. Ibanez (2005), for instance, has presented a comparative model of 'international regime' analysis based on several criteria – the degree of system development, its structural complexity, density of norms, degree of legalisation and type of authority. According to this model, the international regime of e-commerce is characterised by a low degree of development, high complexity, high density, low legalisation and a mix of private-public control. For Ibanez the private sector has made an important contribution to the governance of the Internet, but this has not always been consistent with public interests and preferences. Accordingly, problems of accountability have arisen with the emergence of the international regime of e-commerce.

Bislev and Flyverbom (2005) have characterised Internet governance within a postmodern framework which is highly international, networked and fluid, containing a mixture of authorities and restricting and enabling technologies.[1] Through UN initiatives like the WSIS and the ICT Task Force, a modicum of stabilisation has been attempted creating a unique institutional set-up where large corporations work with the UN, certain national government agencies, business associations and a few non-governmental organisations (NGOs) in a governance network that has an undefined authority to regulate the Internet. In this framework, core post-welfare state technologies of governance are deployed, most outstandingly soft law and cultural, dialogical and discursive governance. Interests are not formally represented but validated through participation in regulation, and resources are less allocated than involved through negotiated outcomes. Bislev and Flyverbom's study highlights the intermingling of private and public, national and international actors and interests, and the difficulty of overseeing the resulting global political economy of information and communication. Venturelli (2002), in examining the underlying philosophies guiding broader ICT governance on a comparative (socio-cultural) basis has uncovered distinct differences in approach between the world's major economic regions, the US, East Asia and Europe.

This volume aims to make a contribution to the academic literature in three areas. First, whilst invaluable, none of the above contributions to the literature on the evolving political economy of the Internet have analysed in detail (i.e. research monograph length) the nature of the governance arrangements for the electronic network economy of the Internet which have been developing over approximately the last decade within the EU. Second, in addressing this important gap in the literature, the book brings together theoretical work on the 'regulatory' state (Seidman and Gilmour 1986; Moran 2002, 2003) and 'post-regulatory' state (Scott 2004) and applies relevant elements of it to key chosen aspects of the European e-economy. This theoretical model is used to characterise the *form* of the emerging governance framework in the process of development within the EU. Third, and in complement to the second aim, the book focuses on the *mechanics* of governance of the Internet e-economy within the EU dimension. In doing so, it brings together and applies work from political science on transnational network governance (Majone 2000), on the one hand, and self-regulation (Baldwin and Cave 1999; Price and Verhulst 2005) on the other.

The core explanatory claim of the book is that the emerging patterns of European regulation for Internet-based commerce can be understood in the context of changing governance forms in the international political economy. Here, globalisation has resulted in a transformation in the way in which states pursue economic governance resulting in a variety of regulatory action. Given that the Internet has expanded rapidly to become a global phenomenon of the electronic communications economy, the volume examines the extent to which EU Internet governance:

- Exemplifies the growth of European regulatory state behaviour; by now accepted as a 'classic' state response to economic globalisation in key sectors;
- Moves beyond this to embody post-regulatory state thinking;
- Demonstrates new extended forms of mixed governance.

In doing so, the book also explores the degree to which the form of governance for Internet commerce is similar to, but also different from, other patterns of European governance for the more established elements of the communications economy (in particular, see Chapter 3). The following three sections will map out the key elements of the literature on regulatory and post-regulatory state forms in their European and global dimensions. Thereafter, the chapter explores the literature on key modes of regulation in both the EU regulatory state and post-regulatory state contexts, through an analysis of trans-European network governance and 'softer' forms of regulation. The chapter concludes with an outline description of the remaining chapters in which the chosen theoretical and conceptual framework will be utilised to map out and explain the nature and mechanics of EU policy for the Internet-based e-economy.

GLOBALISATION AND THE COMPETITIVE REGULATORY STATE

Understanding the evolving governance of the Internet within the EU and international policy context can be assisted in part by reference to wider regulatory changes that have occurred because of the exigencies of economic globalisation. Here, the move from the interventionist 'positive' or 'welfare' state to the 'competitive regulatory state' witnessed from approximately the 1980s onwards has been vital. This has led to debates, on the one hand, about the role of the nation state and its policy choices in an era of globalisation, that is, whether the state has become more or less powerful, and on the other hand, about the nature of the reconfiguration of the state, how it has adapted and what forms this has taken, that is, what the competitive regulatory state is and how regulation is coordinated within it. Within the latter school a central argument has been that, at domestic level, there has been a shift to negative coordination (see Jayasuriya 2001) based on economic governance through regulation (see Scharpf 1993, 1994, 1996), with an emphasis on the role of independent (though publicly funded) agencies and institutions in ensuring credibility and a commitment to market order.

Within the former school of thought debates have been contentious to say the least, and have led to a variety of divergent views centred on the degree to which the state has been threatened in the face of increased global pressures. On the one hand, some scholars have argued that there has been a fundamental decline in the role of the state in the global political economy (Strange 1996; Ohmae 1996, 1999). On the other, alternative accounts have suggested that the state still remains a powerful actor in an era of globalisation (Boyer and Drache 1996)[2] and that it may even have become stronger (Payne, 2000). Others have moved beyond the dichotomy characterised by these approaches to a presentation of globalisation as a dialectical process that leads to a reconstitution of the state and its functions (Mann 1997; Cerny 1995, 1996, 1999, 2000a, 2000b, 2000c; Jayasuriya 2000, 2001).

The latter approaches provide a significant insight into the relationship between globalisation and the state in terms of how state structures are being reconfigured and reconstituted in the new global political economy (Jayasuriya 2000). Their elements can assist in understanding better the regulatory arrangements that can be identified in emerging EU Internet commerce policy in the regulatory state era. Cerny (1999, p.189), argues that 'Although in recent centuries the so-called "Westphalian state"(as well as the modern nation-sate...) has, along with the concomitant "states system", been the predominant (locked-in) form of governance at macrosocial level...globalization hypothetically involves the emergence of new patterns of governance...and more intricate forms of structural *complexity*' (original emphasis).

Furthermore, he argues that the process of economic globalisation has affected key characteristics on which the institutional coherence and structural effectiveness of the modern state are based, which has meant that 'to attract or retain investment, states competing in the global economy have had to develop competitive policies on a range of fronts: tax regimes, employment and social legislation and regulatory policy in a host of economic sectors' (Humphreys and Simpson 2005, p.7). The process of economic globalisation, moreover, has affected the ability of the state to perform and fulfil its commitments in the traditional manner, with the consequence that a transformation of the modern state has taken place from a national industrial and welfare state into a 'competition' state. Within the 'competition' there has been 'a shift in the focus of economic policy away from macro-economic demand management towards more targeted meso-economic and micro-economic policies, and the restructuring of the state itself through the *new public management*' [3] (Cerny 2000c, p.126). In addition there is likely to be a shift in the focal point of party and governmental politics away from the general maximisation of welfare within a nation to the promotion of enterprise, innovation and profitability in both private and public sectors.

Cerny's central assertion is that economic globalisation has led to a reconfiguration of the state. It can no longer act in the traditional sense by decommodifying or taking activities out of the market, as complex globalisation undermines and even transforms the state's structural capacity to constitute an effective arena of internal collective action and to make credible external commitments. A commodification of the state occurs aimed at making economic activities/policies located within the national territory, or which otherwise contribute to national wealth, more competitive in international and transnational terms, including regulatory policy. The consequence, in governance terms, is a more complex set of responses and relationships in which states, through commodification, marketisation and privatisation, respond to, but also reinforce, the processes of globalisation.

Importantly, however, the transformation from national industrial welfare state to the competition state (Cerny 1997) has not led to the much-projected decline or 'retreat' of the state as suggested by certain scholars, but 'the actual expansion of types of de facto state intervention and regulation in the name of competitiveness and marketisation' (Cerny 1997, p.251). In this regard, although the competition state leads to deregulation in the form of lifting old protectionist regulations, it also re-regulates (Humphreys and Simpson 2005, p.7) through the production of 'new regulatory structures that are often designed to enforce global market-rational economic behaviour on rigid and inflexible private sector actors as well as on state actors and agencies' (Cerny 1997, p.264).

Jayasuriya (2001) too argues that states have reconfigured their function in response to the challenges of the global political economy, highlighting that 'there has been a significant change in the institutional coordination of the modern state' (Jayasuriya 2001, p.103). His perspective is located in the emergent literature on the regulatory state (Seidman and Gilmour 1986; McGowan and Wallace 1996; Majone 1994, 1996) and an attempt to address the fact that globalisation affects not only the policy choices of states, but also the transformation of the institutional landscape of the state towards governance through regulation.

Whilst acknowledging the importance of the general attributes characterizing the regulatory state: an increasingly juridical economic area; more emphasis on independent regulation; greater attention to the issue of process rather than outcomes; and technocratic policy-making detached from the normal process of political accountability, Jayasuriya's argument is located more in the detail of what this represents in terms of coordination within the regulatory state. Here, the transition from positive coordination in the corporatist or developmental state, to negative coordination in the regulatory state is emphasised.

This perceived move from coordination of economic activity based on state intervention and bargaining between different interests (positive coordination) to coordination based on economic governance through sectoral regulation by independent institutions (negative coordination) draws on and extends the work of Scharpf (1993, 1994, 1996) who was interested in patterns of coordination between public sector agencies and specifically in clarifying the nature of coordination between these agencies, as well as between the state and private actors. Whilst Scharpf's work was related more to the effects of interdependence on coordination within the state rather than to globalisation, his distinction between negative and positive coordination is an invaluable one for understanding regulation as a form of governance in an era of globalisation. According to Scharpf (1994, p.38), positive coordination was an 'attempt to maximise the overall effectiveness and efficiency of government policy by exploring and utilizing the joint strategy of options of several ministerial portfolios'. In other words, positive coordination entailed a focus on outcomes, brought about by consultation, compromise and bargaining between different interests in society. Negative coordination, on the other hand, was mainly concerned with process, by establishing mechanisms to ensure institutional autonomy in order to minimize conflict between independent regulatory agencies.

Building on and modifying these concepts, using the financial sector as an example, Jayasuriya argues that the emergence of global economic trends has produced a very uncertain environment which pressurises states to aim to create domestic stability, a task problematised by their inability to coordinate bargaining between different interest groups in ways which were possible in the context of the corporate state (i.e. through positive coordination). The chosen solution, according to Jayasuriya, is policy action aiming to underpin the smooth functioning of international markets, manifest in a preoccupation with the creation of independent public regulatory institutions responsible for different economic sectors and, very importantly, a prioritisation of the tasks and procedures of these organisations to ensure their credibility (i.e. negative coordination).

Jayasuriya argues that there is no single identifiable form of negative coordination, but rather that variety exists which is contingent upon specific national values and characteristics present within nation states. In addition, given the transitional nature of the movement from positive to negative coordination, it is also acknowledged that both kinds (negative and positive coordination) may be evident simultaneously. Significant for this book's analysis of the EU's governance of the Internet economy, negative state coordination, rather than a retreat of the state, points to a '*refashioning* of the modalities of governance' where 'the role of the state is to provide the institutional foundations for the autonomy of regulatory institutions and to constitute procedures – "riding instructions" for the functioning of these institutions' (Jayasuriya 2001, p.110, original emphasis).

A defining feature of negative coordination is the role of independent institutions in ensuring credibility and a commitment to market order. In addition it is distinguished through its emphasis on process rather than outcomes in economic governance. This in turn leads to a focus on the design and implementation of the process of economic decision-making and the organisation of governance around the monitoring of institutional processes. The regulatory state, through negative coordination, acts to shape the objectives and functions of institutions and a key characteristic of this form of economic governance is 'the increasingly juridical and legalistic nature of economic policy but a legalism that is directed at the regulation of governance structures' (Jayasuriya 2001, p.112).

Given the procedural emphasis of negative coordination, issues of transparency and accountability become important, not with regard to the interests of wider civil society but in terms of institutional objectives and decision-making processes. Various methods might be used in order to address these issues including public reporting, auditing of independent institutions, bench-marking and specification of performance indicators and targets. The procedural base of negative coordination thus involves a focus on the politics of process and procedure rather than interests and bargaining.

THE EUROPEAN REGULATORY STATE

The debate on the movement or otherwise from the positive to the regulatory state and transformations in state coordination has focused strongly on changes occurring within Europe at both national and EU levels (McGowan and Wallace 1996; Majone 1994, 1996, 1997; see Thatcher 2002a).[4] Similar to those arguments made at global level, it is contended that due to the combined pressures of integration in Europe and changes in the global political economy, state functions and forms have been transformed (Thatcher 2002a, p.860).

Table 1.1 Positive and Negative Coordination: Key Characteristics

	Positive coordination	**Negative coordination**
'State' type	Corporatist/ Developmental/Positive	Regulatory State
Influence	Outcomes	Process
Method/Mode	Politics of bargaining	Politics of procedure
Accountability	Direct: various actors/interests in decision-making process	Indirect: focus on institutional objectives and decision-making processes, not citizenry
Credibility	Compensating mechanisms	Independent institutions
Objective	Ensure that 'interests' are reflected in decision-making 'outcomes' given exposure to the global market	Insulate the market order from politics. Interests and bargaining removed from the decision-making process
Actors and Institutions	Parliaments, ministerial departments, nationalised industries, political parties, civil servants, corporate/interest groups	Single issue movements, regulators, experts, judges/courts, committees, independent regulatory bodies

Certain scholars view the regulatory state as '*the* major aspect in the transformation of the governance of capitalist economies since the 1980s' (Jordana and Levi-Faur 2004, p.9, *original emphasis*). At a practical level the regulatory state has been considered as an example of an expanding part of modern government whereby in the face of globalisation, traditional command and control techniques are being replaced by more efficacious methods (Majone 1997). Such a perspective concentrates on an analysis of how new and refined regulatory forms have been utilised, and the mechanisms and institutions that have developed to operate them (Jordana and Levi-Faur 2004, p.9).

In contrast to regulatory state adherents, there are also academics that have scrutinised the claim that such a movement has occurred across all countries and sectors (see for instance special volume of *Journal of European Public Policy*, 9:6 December 2002), in particular given that many scholars have found that deeply national forms of capitalism, institutions and regulatory styles continue to exist despite integration and global pressures for change (Hall and Soskice 2001; Schmidt 2002; Crouch and Streek 1997; Vogel 1986; Thatcher 2002a). Certain scholars have gone so far as to question the notion of a regulatory state as a somewhat fictitious concept the existence of which simply allows academics, 'to speak to each other, in a world of increasingly fragmented academic professionalism' (Moran 2002, pp.411–12).[5] There has also been sustained criticism of the theory from scholars such as Grabosky (1994, 1995; see also Scott 2002; Gunningham and Grabosky 1998), who rejects its focus on state activities and the neglect of non-state governance mechanisms (e.g. those of a non-legal kind). Important studies of Japan have also challenged the idea of the all-pervading reality of the regulatory state (Schaede, 2000). Schaede (2000, p.7) suggests that self-regulatory cooperative capitalism is what is replacing the traditionally strong role of the government in regulating Japanese industry.

Whichever view of the regulatory state is subscribed to, certain caution is needed when analysing it as a phenomenon in an era of global governance, the case of the Internet e-economy in the EU being no exception. Jordana and Levi-Faur (2004, p.9), for example, argue that sectoral characteristics condition the advance of the regulatory state, and thus must be taken into account, as differentiated advancement will exist across sectors. Second, they posit that diverse modes of regulation coexist even in heavily regulated sectors and that this is due to multiple forms of control. Third, they argue that regulatory state activity is contingent on historical context and that 'it is not meant to operate as a sole source of regulatory control. At best, it can be embedded successfully in older layers of governance that were created for different purposes and in different eras' (p.9). Fourth, national traditions and institutions mean that there exist different types of regulatory state rather than merely one (see Lodge 2002, p.177; Schmidt 2002). Finally, they caution with regard to what they call the locus of the regulatory state; in other words, given the different interpretations of what the regulatory state is (global, regional, sectoral, country specific), scholars must design research that captures what they label the 'multi-levelness' of the regulations and regulatory politics.

These points are particularly salient for analysing core aspects of the governance of the Internet based e-economy in Europe. The Internet did not emerge in Europe and did not develop within the kinds of national governance traditions that affected the evolution of telecommunications. Having grown for decades within the US technical and academic communities its commercialisation and popularisation in the 1990s occurred at a time when the policies of economic liberalisation and globalisation had become paramount. Thus Internet governance was imbued with such discourses from the outset (see Chapter 2). This combined with a lack of any established tradition of regulating the Internet within the EU presented a series of new commercial opportunities and challenges. EU Internet policy, exemplified in key policy initiatives on e-commerce and the Internet Top Level Domain, dot eu, might be expected to reflect characteristic features of regulatory state behaviour given its roots in a process of globalisation. However, its relatively short history in regulatory politics, juxtaposed with strong European regulatory traditions, also suggests that there is much potential for diversity in governance. Moreover, because regulation in the Internet sector has been driven by very different factors than those influencing more established elements of the communications sector (see Chapter 3), it might be expected that diverse modes of regulation coexist within the European (national) governance space reflecting an ongoing 'refashioning of the modalities of governance' (Jayasuriya 2001, p.110).

THE POST-REGULATORY STATE

Complementing the literature on the regulatory state there are those scholars that have begun to write about the concept of the post-regulatory state (Scott 2004) whereby 'the essence of governance is its focus on governing mechanisms which do not rest on recourse to the authority and sanctions of government' (Stoker 1998, p.17). The post-regulatory state, however, is not used 'in the sense of the body politic denoted in the phrases welfare state or regulatory state', but rather should be seen as a way of 'enlarging the regulatory envelope' (Scott 2004, pp.166–7). As a theoretical construct the central question from a post-regulatory perspective is to what extent (and how) it is possible to think of regulatory governance functioning outside the bounds of state law. Where such state law is not the central regulatory mechanism, post-regulatory governance can be a way of providing an alternative to formal (that is legal) state regulation (that occurring within the regulatory state). This perspective, although seemingly a potential challenge to the dominant regulatory state paradigm (and the implied legally-based regulatory forms within that), claims to add 'variety in regulatory norms to enrich rather than challenge the idea of the regulatory state' (Scott 2004, p.146). Such post-regulatory state thinking complements other work on governance that seeks to advance alternatives to state (legal) regulation (Better Regulation Task Force, 2000) and is 'something of a mirror-image to those...arguing that the centrality of the state is too little rather than too much assumed' (Scott 2004, p.146).

Certain caution must be exercised about the utility of post-regulatory state thinking given the organisational and institutional structure of the EU. The EU's dominant form of regulatory intervention has traditionally been hierarchical and legally based (Héritier, 2002). Such a characteristic, based on historically embedded institutional dynamics and norms, makes it difficult to envisage that post-regulatory state forms of governance, with an emphasis on non-legal tools and non-state actors, will be readily embraced by European policy-makers.

Despite this, there is evidence suggesting that the EU is becoming more receptive to new governance forms and structures (see Ronit 2005, p.8; Héritier 2001, p.3), whereby more responsibility is being delegated to regulatees and national governments and where soft law mechanisms are becoming more prevalent (Eberlein and Kerwer 2004, p.125). This is in part because of recognition on the part of the EU that coercive steering, as a regulatory tool, can be problematic, both in terms of outcomes and effectiveness and with regard to questions of legitimacy.[6] To the extent that it might be possible to witness diverse (mixed) forms of regulation coexisting within the European regulatory state space, such new ways of thinking provide added explanatory value and conceptual richness. Post-regulatory state theory can be useful to the extent that it explores ways in which non-legal regulatory tools can be enmeshed within existing regulatory state capacities. Additionally, it is germane operationally to the idea and practice of self-regulation, a core feature of Internet governance developed globally.

Scott (2004), in an attempt to provide alternative conceptions of control, that is, to state law and hierarchical models of regulation, explores, amongst other theories, responsive regulation. The theory 'is very much organised around the development of hybrid forms [of control] which employ hierarchy and community as their basis, notably in the...model of enforced self-regulation' (p.164). Responsive regulation is concerned with creating institutions and processes that will stimulate existing regulatory capacities, so that conditions can be created allowing minimum regulatory intervention whilst simultaneously creating the possibility of more stringent enforcement, if required. The model prioritises an enduring role for law at the apex of a pyramid in which the dominant regulatory mechanism envisaged is persuasion (see Figure 1.1). However, below this, at the base of the pyramid, alongside incentives for regulators and regulatees to cooperate informally, there is an allowance for stricter sanctioning and escalated regulatory activity (e.g. warning letters, and then civil or criminal penalties where compliance is not forthcoming).

In addition, the role of government is to encourage businesses to self-regulate at the base of the pyramid, and where this does not occur, to deploy enforced regulatory tactics (where firms are required to create rules for themselves and whereby these are monitored and enforced by a regulatory agency) or to escalate command regulation (through discretionary and non-discretionary punishment) (Scott 2004, p.157; see also Ayres and Braithwaite 1992). This model allows governments to take a hands-off approach whilst carrying the threat of 'big stick' intervention.

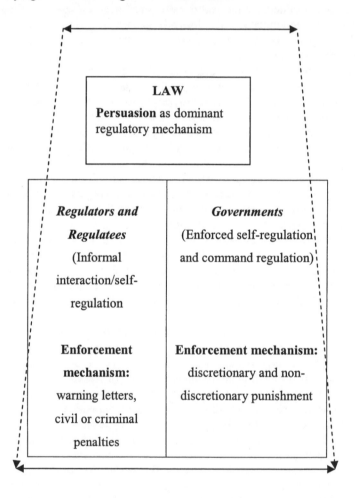

Source: Derived from Scott 2004, p.157; see also Ayres and Braithwaite 1992, p.39.

Figure 1.1 Responsive Regulation: The Enforcement and Technique Pyramid

The responsive regulation model conflates law and governance to provide an inductively reasoned model of regulating more effectively and consensually. Responsive regulation (and the pyramidal model) is underpinned by the assumption of a strong regulatory state, which although potentially problematic for post-regulatory thinking (outside the law), offers a valuable analytical tool for explaining evolving regulatory patterns in EU governance of the Internet, given the strong public policy traditions existing within Europe. It is important to note that the idea of a legal basis is still strong within the responsive regulation theory of governance, 'irrespective of whether law is actually invoked or actually perceived as a reason for cooperating with regulators or making self-regulation work' (Scott 2004, p.157). Responsive regulation and the pyramidal model within it, allows governments to employ self-regulation and gives them the potential to impose more interventionist regulatory tools if self-regulation proves ineffectual. At the higher level of sanction escalation this might include prosecutions and a revocation of any right to self-regulate.

Post-regulatory thinking also gives treatment to instruments and modes of control practised in (self) regulating activity beyond the formal legal rule-making of the regulatory state. Importantly, such mechanisms can derive their force from within a matrix of hierarchical state power. However, where the condition of 'internal legal pluralism' arises within the regulatory state, where regulatory norms coexist and overlap and communication is poor between different state institutions, a movement away from formal law is prompted. This can create alternative tools for influencing regulatory behaviour such as soft law (including contractual rules, individual and collective), standard-setting (including codes of conduct), and normalisation (practice/socialisation). Here, collectivised contractual rules 'are typically used to establish and make binding self-regulatory regimes', where 'Self-regulatory bodies are frequently much more complete regulators, in the sense that they combine rule-making, monitoring and sanctioning powers within a single organization, something which is rare for state regulatory agencies' (Scott 2004, p.163). The principles and practices for regulating rule-making are also important in post-regulatory state analysis, commonly described as meta-regulation in the literature. Meta-regulatory rule-making, in turn, results in the proceduralization of self-regulatory regimes, employing minimum requirements for particular types of standards set by individual firms or organizations, and more typically setting 'minimum standards for collective codes of conduct...through trade associations' (Scott 2004, p.163).

It is important to reiterate that even with these non-legal tools (soft law and contracts developed outside primary and secondary legislation), an essential part of their power is still derived from their location within the hierarchical state power matrix. In this sense, a post-regulatory state might look beyond...command based legal control, but, as with responsive regulation, retain in it in at least some residual form such that ends are ultimately set and determined by the sovereign state' (Scott 2004, p.168). At the same time, it must be emphasised that not all post-regulatory state tools are derived from a hierarchical state power matrix (i.e. like responsive regulation). Tools such as standard setting and codes of conduct delivered as a consequence of non-hierarchical relations – such as community and, by contrast, economic power – are more reliant on processes of socialisation and normalisation, as opposed to the threat of the (state's) 'big stick'. Within the post-regulatory state diverse modes of meta-regulation can coexist derived from differing control mechanisms, each of which has different connotations for the role of the 'state' within post-regulatory thinking. In this book, a post-regulatory state perspective, in examining the EU's governance of the e-economy, allows a consideration of the extent to which the EU's traditional hierarchical and legal regulatory model has been displaced or complemented by alternative regulatory forms and modes.

MODES OF REGULATION WITHIN THE REGULATORY AND POST-REGULATORY STATE

The debates surrounding the movement to regulatory state forms has led to a wealth of literature on the nature, style and type of regulatory activity (including implementation) occurring within the national and European dimensions.[7] A number of authors have considered typologies of regulation that have been developed in the global and European regulatory state context (Jordana and Levi-Faur 2004; Scott 2004; Knill and Lenschow 2004; Majone 2000; Eyre and Sitter 1999; Thatcher 2002b). In doing so, a nuanced analysis of how the regulatory state operates has been developed, not least within the European context, which provides examples of the regulatory state par excellence according to Majone (1994, pp.85–92). At EU level, 'a version of the regulatory model has come to characterise the EU approach to policy making' (Majone 1996, p.55; see also, McGowan and Wallace 1996, p.565; Young and Wallace 2000).

To understand the emerging operational mechanics of Internet commerce regulation in the EU in an age of regulatory governance, Majone's work on trans-European regulatory networks and regulatory agencies in Europe (1997, 2000) is an instructive starting point. A key issue in this book is the extent to which such networked arrangements are emerging. Majone developed the trans-European regulatory network concept within the specific context of the European regulatory state, with a focus on the EU dimension. He argues that the EU played a vital role in the further development of the regulatory state in Europe, through shaping its own characteristic approach to core elements of the regulatory state, notably re-regulation and liberalisation.

Here, the European Commission has emerged as a central agent of its Member States.[8]

An important aspect of Majone's work is his contention that EU regulation is undermined by a lack of sufficient administrative resources, as well as the increasingly political role played by the European Commission. He suggests that 'problems of regulatory credibility in the EC/EU arise at different levels', some of which 'are rooted in the deep structure of the founding treaties, while other problems result from the path-dependent aspects of the integration process, from institutional inertia, or from the pursuit of short-term advantages' (Majone 2000, p.273). As a solution to these sets of problems in all areas of EU economic and social regulation, he posits the creation of independent European regulatory agencies to be 'embedded in transnational networks of national regulators and international organizations' (ibid. p.274). He argues that only through networks can the requirements of subsidiarity, accountability and efficiency be met and regulatory credibility ensured.

Majone sees one of the most obvious defects of the EU regulatory system in 'the mismatch between the Community's highly complex and differentiated tasks, and the available administrative instruments'. This he posits is not a case of limited resources, but a lack of recognition that 'policy credibility depends crucially on effective implementation' (ibid. p.279). He argues that despite increased awareness by the European Commission of the importance of implementation and enforcement of rules, as well as actual rule-making, the 'administrative infrastructure at European level' is underdeveloped and is a 'serious obstacle to the completion of the internal market and thus a serious threat to the credibility of the integration project' (ibid. p.280).

Whilst highly critical of the regulatory regimes for food safety and telecommunications, Majone has argued that the kind of transnational regulatory network emerging in the pharmaceuticals sector is a particularly instructive 'path of institutional development [for] other areas of Community regulation' (ibid., p.280) with its 'network where national regulatory authorities, independent scientific experts, Members States, the Commission and European Parliament each have a role to play' (ibid.). Here, 'locals' can become 'cosmopolitans' (explained below) and qualities of independence, expertise and legitimacy, critical for ensuring credible regulation, can be developed.

For Majone, the key regulatory question is not whether independent European regulatory agencies should exist, but what they should look like, and 'how they should be designed and made accountable to their political principals' (ibid. p.290). In this, however, he recognises that policy transfer or learning is unlikely to occur in relation to the 'American model of centralised federal agencies operating independently from the regulatory authorities of the states', primarily because it would contravene the subsidiarity principle and 'aggravate, rather than ameliorate, the credibility problem' (ibid. p.295). To this end, subsidiarity and integration can adequately be dealt with by the emergence of a regulatory-networked agency model of transnational nature. Critical here is the definition of agency specified by Majone, where it is decisional autonomy rather than institutional separateness that is essential in any defined policy area. An agency is loosely specified as any kind of administrative entity which is in charge of a particular programme or activity and crucially 'may operate as part of a network including both national and European regulators...the new European agencies...are expected to become the central nodes of networks including national agencies as well as international organisations' (ibid.).

Such an inclusive and collaborative model based on transnational network interaction adds an incentive to transform locals (with a national and sub-national orientation) into cosmopolitans (likely to adopt an international reference group orientation). In this sense, Majone argues that such a structure encourages open discussion of regulatory philosophies and facilitates links between European and non-European regulatory bodies through the provision of institutional focus within the European dimension. To be successful, a transnational regulatory network needs to develop mutual trust and cooperation, high levels of professionalisation of regulators and a common regulatory philosophy.

Knill and Lenschow (2004) provide a detailed account of the EU regulatory state and its possible different modes of regulation and the steering models/mechanisms relating to them (see Table 1.2). These range from hard legalistic instruments to softer forms of regulation including self-regulation (see Héritier 2002, 2003). The latter exemplifies a regulatory mode that might be employed in the post-regulatory state. The EU has, in the past, demonstrated its willingness to experiment with multiple regulatory approaches in order to meet new governance challenges triggered by internal reform, expansion and structural changes in the global political economy. Envisioning the EU as a multidimensional governance space[9] allows the fluidity, complexity and interconnectedness of regulatory modes within and across its different policy sectors to be captured.

Knill and Lenschow posit four modes of intervention around the two regulatory dimensions of obligation and discretion and that within each different regulatory tools can be identified. The first mode of intervention, substantive and regulatory standards (which includes EU Regulations) with a high level of obligation imposed by the regulator (EU) and a low level of discretion for the domestic implementing actors, is seen as the most common and prevailing but also the most hierarchical form of regulation as it focuses on setting standards and establishing legal rules at the supranational level. This mode of intervention allows, in theory, considerable space for the Commission to play an authoritative role in steering and compliance within national and regional governance structures.

The second mode is that of new instruments (which would include EU Directives), and, like the first mode, is also based on the traditional legally embedded instruments of intervention, but includes a variety of regulatory tools and framework regulation. The level of discretion is high for the domestic implementing actors with a concomitant high level of obligation imposed by the regulator (i.e. the EU in the form of the Commission) on the implementing actor. There is a greater level of flexibility for the domestic implementing actors to adapt frameworks to local conditions and instead of an emphasis on hierarchy and control, such framework regulation places emphasis on 'participation, self-initiative and voluntarism' (Knill and Lenschow 2004, p.21).

Table 1.2 Modes of Regulation in the EU

	Coercion	**Incentive structures**	**Learning**	**Steering model**
Regulatory standards	Legally binding standards (dominant)	None	None	**Hierarchy model**
New instruments	Framework and procedural rules (relevant)	Changes of procedural and/or material opportunities (dominant)	None	**Public delegation model**
Self-regulation	Shadow of hierarchy (relevant)	Private actors influence regulatory standards (dominant)	Private network communica tion (relevant)	**Private delegation model**
OMC	Reporting and monitoring (relevant)	Peer pressure (relevant)	Best practice models (dominant)	**Radical subsidiarity model: public learning approach**

Source: Adopted from Knill and Lenschow 2004, p.122.

The final two modes identified are those of self-regulation in the shadow of the state and the Open Method of Coordination (OMC). The latter involves no formal legal mechanism or sanction: the EU, rather, provides an enabling context for national policy-makers to learn, coordinate and cooperate, whilst also affording them the space to formulate responses and solutions independently. Here, regulatory impact is dependent on tools such as bench-marking, targets, best practice dissemination and incentives such as peer review, with a move away from hierarchy towards a policy-learning networked approach.[10]

The former, self-regulation in the shadow of the state, involves a move away from formal law-making at EU level to self-responsibility on the part of national implementing actors – private and public – but always with the threat that if self-regulation fails, legal intervention is ever present as an alternative. This has resonance, too, with post-regulatory thinking, in particular within the responsive regulation model, whereby the shadow of the state is prominent as a default option in securing compliance. In turn, this highlights the extent to which post-regulatory, hierarchically derived regulatory tools can be perceived as, and conflated with, extensions of the regulatory state. According to Knill and Lenschow (2004) private self-regulation is identifiable in two basic modes in an EU context. The first entails agreement, on a voluntary basis, between the European Commission and relevant sectoral actors, whereby there is a commitment by the latter to implement certain requirements. The second (found in the field of social policy), involves consultation with corporate partners (which is a legal obligation on the part of the Commission), whereby the final agreement reached by all the partners then results in an EU directive, a traditional regulatory form (Knill and Lenschow 2004, p.21).

Knill and Lenschow's typology is heuristically helpful as a starting point for identifying and analysing core aspects of the EU's governance of the Internet e-economy though the rigidity of its typological representation does not accommodate well enough the possibility of multiple regulatory modes within the EU governance constellation. In particular, it might be extended usefully to allow for a blurring of the boundaries between traditional and non-traditional regulatory modes.

THE EU AND SELF-REGULATION

Self-regulation (Baldwin and Cave 1999; Price and Verhulst, 2000, 2005) has been an important part of the policy debate on Internet governance for at least the last decade and has become a significant part of the thinking of the EU on the governance of ICT since the mid- to late 1990s. However, despite its aforementioned receptiveness to new modes of governance the EU's perception of self-regulation is derived from well-embedded traditions of regulation based predominantly on the traditional Community method, reliant on legislation and public authority involvement (Héritier 2002). This tradition was highlighted in a speech by EU Information Society Commissioner, Erkki Liikanen (2004, p.1) where, although it was acknowledged that 'the Internet's architecture does not lend itself easily to hierarchical control', it was also stated strongly that it was not 'realistic to expect governments to take a backseat completely [where] governments clearly do have legitimate concerns'. In diametric contrast, the perspective of the Internet technical community on self-regulation is located neither in European national nor supranational governance tradition and practice (see Chapter 2). Instead, it is rooted in the philosophy of non-interference, characterised by self-management and private self-regulation.

Conceptualising self-regulation is particularly salient in the context of the EU regulatory state as it does not imply the retreat of the state, but rather that the shadow of the state still remains a critical stimulus for industry self-regulation (Scharpf 1997). Furthermore, different interpretations of self-regulation can alter 'the way the shadow of the state is cast over industries and sets states on distinct self-regulatory trajectories' (Newman and Bach 2001, p.2). It can also lead to potential clashes in regulatory styles and philosophies, resulting in new hybrid modes of regulation that seek to reconcile what seem to be contradictory approaches. Furthermore, self-regulation within the EU has implications for rule formation (primarily related to hard and soft law), transposition and implementation. In the context of the emerging governance of core elements of the Internet based e-economy covered in this book, it is important to consider the extent to which the EU has customised global regulatory principles of Internet governance related to self-regulation to fit with its own traditions of public policy practices for the communications sector.

Newman and Bach (2001), in their comparison of US and EU approaches to self-regulation, provide two ideal-type cases: legalistic self-regulation in the US and coordinated self-regulation in Europe. The model is based on four characteristics of the state/industry relationship that shape the character of self-regulation in political economies: business coordination capacity, strength of the judiciary, carrot capacity and stick capacity (see Table 1.3). Although a narrow typological focus, incorporating only the role of business and the judiciary, it is nevertheless analytically useful for understanding the core characteristics of an EU self-regulatory governance model for the Internet.

Newman and Bach (2001) find that the EU can employ a high 'carrot capacity' to the enforcement of self-regulation where the role of the EU Commission is important. The Commission uses its control over the research and development budget to forge transnational industry networks and position itself close to such networks in order to ensure support for its activities in other policy areas. The tradition of delegation to private bodies and state sanctioning of industry standards has been a long-standing one in the European political economy. Regarding its 'stick capacity', the EU is much weaker because of its lack of a central regulator (apart from in competition policy) and its slow and cumbersome legislative process (in comparison to the US). However the *sui generis* nature of EU decision-making, involving national and European levels, can give the EU considerable 'stick capacity', where policy-making is needed to avoid the costs of regulatory fragmentation at national level.

It is argued that in the EU case, 'considerable business coordination capacity combined with a relatively weak judiciary and a public sector that can offer substantial rewards but is limited in its ability to sanction sets Europe on a path towards coordinated self-regulation' where 'industry's self-image of self-regulation has a corporatist twist, that is, the public sector is accepted as a *participant* in the self-regulatory process, albeit mostly in a catalytic or facilitative role' (emphasis in original) (Newman and Bach 2001, p.9). According to Newman and Bach, the EU can employ an informal, cooperative mode of regulation with a variety of actors involved, where interests need to be organised hierarchically and connected in networks (ibid. p.10). In addition, business coordination capacity in the EU is characterised by national institutions of coordination, an increasing density of transnational networks and a tradition of coordination.

Table 1.3 Typologies of EU and US Self-Regulation 'Images'

	US	EU
Business coordination capacity	Low	Medium
Strength of the judiciary	High	Low
Carrot capacity	Low	High
Stick capacity	High	Medium

Source: Newman and Bach (2001, p.8).

Based on the above typology, the EU's idea of self-regulation is not that of out-and-out private self-regulation prominent in early international efforts to regulate the Internet. On the contrary, the EU has gone as far as to advocate what it terms a co-regulatory approach, which, in the words of the Commission, '...may be more flexible, adaptable and effective than straight forward regulation and legislation' and which 'implies an appropriate level of involvement by the public authorities...[and]...consists of cooperation between public authorities, industry and the other interested parties' (European Commission 2004b, p.6). Schulz and Held (2001) refer to this governance mode as 'regulated self-regulation'[11] sitting somewhere between private self-regulation, where the state refrains completely from the process of regulation, and command and control regulation, where the state is dominant in setting, implementing and enforcing regulatory rules and procedures. As a consequence, 'self-regulation that fits in with a legal framework or has a basis laid down in law' (2001, p.7) materialises.

The EU's interpretation of self-regulation clearly embodies a role for public authority, creating a practical blurring of the boundaries between public and private spheres. Price and Verhulst (2005, p.3) point out that in practice, self-regulation by industry rarely occurs in its purest form. Ronit (2005) notes in his analysis of self-regulation that assistance by public authority is often required to sustain private interest governance (see also Streeck and Schmitter 1985), 'otherwise, free-riding would lead to lower standards and tend to disqualify private solutions' (Ronit, p.5). He also posits that the relations between public and private authority are complex in the sense that self-regulation can be stimulated either by the public authority to restrain self-interested actors for the benefit of business and society as a whole, or business can insist on regulatory intervention by public authorities where they perceive this is necessary. The implication is that the end product is politicised regulated self-regulation.

The relationship between public and private interests within self-regulatory activity is important. 'Subcontracting' occurs where state involvement is limited to setting formal conditions for rule-making, with private actors then shaping the content. 'Concerted action' occurs where the state sets both formal and substantive conditions for rule-making. 'Incorporation' involves existing but non-official norms being inserted into statute and becoming in the process part of the legislative framework. Market-based regulation involves industry-setting, monitoring and enforcing standards in the knowledge that if it fails, state intervention could be imminent, that is, self-regulation in the shadow of the state (Self-regulation of Digital Media 2004, p.11). However, the exact nature of self-regulation requires a case by case examination and can generate numerous possible forms. New modes of regulation have gained in salience across the EU over the last few years to address new governance challenges (Eberlein and Kerwer 2004, p.122; Héritier 2001, p.3).

However, questions of their legitimacy, accountability, efficiency and effectiveness have arisen. This is particularly relevant to an analysis of the Internet based e-economy, where the central feature of its global governance is private self-regulation and where, by contrast, the EU's interpretation of self-regulation embodies a clear role for public authority. Self-regulation can be problematic from a democratic legitimacy perspective. Private market-based self-regulation outside the legal framework is susceptible to capture by the industry being regulated and thus can constrain the involvement of wider societal interests. Cutler et al. argue that private actor authority leads to decisions about 'who gets to play, what are the limits on play, and often who wins' (1999, p.369). Whilst self-regulatory practices might be legitimised indirectly through European Commission initiation and consultation, they suffer potentially in comparison to methods such as OMC,[12] or new instruments (notably framework legislation). The former receives its legitimacy within the national domain, and the latter allows at least scope for national interpretation and the democratic potential inherent within the principle of subsidiarity (Knill and Lenschow 2004, pp.233–37). Public-private hybrid regulatory forms and associated practices, however, have relatively greater legitimacy and scope for democratic participation.

Also challenging within a private self-regulatory mode of governance is the issue of accountability. This is most problematic with private forms of self-regulation, given that sanctioning powers are remote and potentially weak, and that they are not subject, most likely, to any public oversight (Eberlein and Kerwer 2004, p.124; Knill and Lenschow 2004, p.238). Private actors are neither accountable politically nor elected, which begs the question of to whom private regulators are accountable (Tsingou 2005, p.21).

A third issue concerns the ability of the EU to guarantee implementation of, and compliance with, agreed norms and practices across self-regulatory networks, problematised by the relatively weak stick capacity of the EU (Newman and Bach 2001). Since within the private self-regulatory mode the effectiveness of the carrot depends on the strength of the stick, compliance might be less forthcoming. There may exist variation in the extent to which private regulators formulate and comply with their own rules depending on the how strong the shadow of the state is perceived as being: the weaker the shadow, the less compliance is likely to occur (Baldwin and Cave 1999, p.58; Knill and Lenschow 2004, pp.227–29).

In addition to questions of legitimacy, effectiveness and accountability, there is also the question of suitability and the quality of a chosen self-regulatory mode. Here the most important factors are adjustment flexibility, responsiveness, and the predictability of regulatory outcomes (Baldwin and Cave 1999, p.43; Knill and Lenschow 2004, p.230). Self-regulatory modes of governance are much more flexible than legally binding directives which require a lengthy process of consultation and can be fairly cumbersome. The flexibility of public-private hybrid regulatory modes depends on the degree to which predefined rules and objectives build in private actor discretion. Regarding predictability in outcomes, Knill and Lenschow (2000, 2004) argue that self-regulation tends to be based on clear and substantive objectives and goals.

Thus, whilst private self-regulation can bring flexibility, responsiveness and predictability of outcomes, questions remain regarding the extent to which such a mode of regulation is legitimate, democratic and accountable and how far industrial or other regulatees can be incentivised to comply, if the shadow of the state is not present. If the shadow of the state is present then many of the problems with self-regulation can be reduced or eliminated. However, how far responsiveness, decisional autonomy and adjustment flexibility could be achieved depend on two factors: the relative strength of the shadow of hierarchy and the power relationships defined by the rules and procedures formulated by the relevant public authority.

THE STRUCTURE OF THE BOOK

This chapter has aimed to construct a framework which can be utilised to explain and understand the pattern of governance which is emerging across the EU for key aspects of the Internet based e-economy. Economic globalisation and related changes in regulatory forms and modes employed by states, of which the EU is considered one, provide the theoretical and conceptual foundation for this book's analysis of governance activity related to growing Internet-based commercial activity across the EU. The remainder of the chapters consider the key features of policy which is developing, the central actors involved, the nature of the emergent patterns of regulation and the implications of these for regulation in the wider global Internet political economy.

Chapter 2 charts the Internet's history and locates its development within the connected processes of commercialisation and the formation of the key (albeit contested) principles that emerged for its governance. It explores the growth of the Internet until the emergence of the Internet Corporation for Assigned Names and Numbers (ICANN) as a new, global level, governance organisation for key parts of the Internet. Second, it examines the brief history of the relationship between ICANN and the EU in its early stages, and illustrates in particular the limited extent to which the EU was involved in shaping the emergence of ICANN.

Chapter 3 illustrates the, in some cases well-established, in others newly embedding, communications governance context within which EU and national Member State policy-makers considered the challenges of governing the Internet as it, somewhat belatedly, became an important part of European communications policy and regulation from the mid-1990s onwards. This provides a basis for understanding the nature of recent EU policy for Internet governance, in particular Internet commerce. The chapter provides an explanatory context to appreciate the extent to which the EU would readily embrace, or by contrast baulk at and attempt to refashion, elements of the new, though contested, governance agenda of the Internet emerging principally from the US and suffusing global policy debates from the mid-1990s.

Chapter 4 explores the EU's movement into the governance of Internet Top Level Domains by focusing on policy developments related to the establishment of the dot eu TLD. The chapter considers the extent to which dot eu is representative of the EU's established regulatory *modus operandi* and how far the EU has been able to reconcile the global principles of

Internet management with its own regulated self-regulation style, distinguished by its coordinative, so-called co-regulatory approach. It explores the central characteristics of the dot eu regulatory framework and how it has developed. The core argument of this chapter is that dot eu has emerged in the form of a public-private trans-European network, with the shadow of the European Commission central to the network's functioning.

Chapter 5 provides an account of the main features of the EU's efforts to develop a regulatory framework for Internet based e-commerce. It illustrates how the Internet as a commercial phenomenon became a central part of the EU's policy portfolio aimed at creating the so-called Information Society (IS). It proceeds to describe and analyse in detail the regulatory core of the EU's Internet e-commerce policy which is argued to have three dimensions: the framework directive on e-commerce; a number of legal measures which complement the key stipulations of the directive on e-commerce in relation to the mechanics of e-commercial transactions but which also apply more widely; and, third, a series of 'backdrop' supportive legal measures which have relevance to the commercial environment within which electronic transactions take place. From this it is argued that two core contrasting regulatory modes have emerged: regulation through the well-established EU legislative process and, by contrast, private self-regulation in the shadow of the state involving the emergence of codes of conduct and alterative dispute resolution (ADR). It demonstrates how a complex and differentiated regulatory picture is emerging epitomised by a novel conjunction of 'hard' legal measures, which, paradoxically, make provision for, whilst not mandating the creation of, a series of 'soft' self-regulatory governance strategies.

Chapter 6 – drawing on empirical data gathered in three EU Member States: Finland, the UK and Germany – explores the transposition and early implementation of the EU's cornerstone piece of legislation on Internet commerce: the Directive on E-Commerce (DEC). Complementing the analysis developed in the previous chapter, it is particularly concerned with an examination of the treatment by EU Member States of those elements of the DEC which are 'post-regulatory state-like' in nature. It finds strong evidence in the DEC's transposition of acceptance by Member States of the usefulness of legally provided and protected self-regulation (and by implication post-regulatory state practices) in the European e-economy. However, it also argues that there is evidence of different interpretations of how self-regulation should be created and governed within Member States where the national intervening variable is strong in governance which exhibits extensions of the well-established regulatory state.

Chapter 7 develops the theme of the evolving global governance arrangements for the Internet and their relationship to the EU. First, it considers the relationship which has developed between the EU and ICANN since the latter's inception in 1998. Thereafter, it draws on the themes of

Chapter 5 on Internet-based commercial activity by exploring the emergence of the World Trade Organization as an institutional forum within which the global governance of e-commerce has been considered. Finally, it explores the institutional context of the United Nations – specifically the International Telecommunications Union-organised World Summit on the Information Society (WSIS) – and the role that the EU has played in the 'WSIS process'. The third line of analysis of the chapter involves an identification of the patterns of global governance which are developing for the Internet, and their implications for the EU and its Internet based e-economy. It argues that the EU has developed relatively quickly into an important actor in global Internet governance and that the model being developed for Internet governance at the global level is comparatively similar to the one the EU is developing internally for the governance of its Internet-based e-economy.

Chapter 8 aims to draw together the main themes of the book's chapters, in the process reflecting on the extent to which the EU has developed new governance approaches not hitherto employed for the communications sector. Contending that EU Internet governance is more akin to the well-established and traditional, rather than the radically new, the chapter illustrates the degree to which governance characteristic of the European regulatory state is being deployed alongside alternative forms, such as post-regulatory state governance. It examines the degree to which it is possible to discern a clear pattern of modes, or practices, of Internet commerce governance in the policy measures formulated and deployed by the EU in the areas considered in the book.

NOTES

1. Although this is not completely reflective of the reality of Internet governance – where elements of postmodern governance still often sit alongside more traditional forms, in particular within the EU dimension.
2. See Drezner (2004) for the application of a 'realist' or 'statist' argument on globalisation and the state in the context of Internet governance.
3. NPM refers to an attempt to reform the public sector through private sector techniques, especially the introduction of markets and private sector management into the delivery of public goods. In governance terms it reflected a belief that standardised systems of rules and hierarchy, which had hitherto governed the public sector, were no longer appropriate to all public services (see Smith and Richards, 2002, p.104; Minogue 2002, p.653).
4. For a review of the European experience of regulating markets see Moran (2002).
5. Alternatively, the regulatory state may exist but its character is very much contingent on national setting (Moran 2002, p.412)

6.   This is a problem that has also been recognised at the global level, where debates exist on the scope for creating distinctive, autonomous regulatory entities above the level of the nation state (Held and McGrew 2002)

7.   See for example Majone 1994, 1996, 1997, 2000; Thatcher 1999, 2001a, 2001b, 2002a, 2002b, 2004; Bartle 1999, 2002; Humphreys 2002; Humphreys and Simpson 2005; Minogue 2002; Moran 2002; Jordana 2002; Jordana and Levi-Faur 2004; Schmidt 2002; Gilardi 2002; Serot 2002; Héritier 2002, 2003; Vogel 1986.

8.   It is important to note in this context, however, that the EU Treaties delimit severely the extent to which Member States can create additional bodies with formal legal powers to undertake tasks such as regulation (Majone 1997).

9.   See Baker et al (2005) for detailed analysis of the problems with the multi-*level* governance approach as opposed to a multi-dimensional approach.

10. See Borrás and Jacobsson (2004) for an evaluation of the impact of OMC on EU policy, politics and polity. See also Eberlein and Kerwer (2004).

11. As noted by Schulz and Held (2001, pp.7–14), co-regulation is used in such a variety of circumstance that its specific meaning must be seen in the national, sectoral and temporal context in which it is used.

12. Eberlein and Kerwer (2004) argue that in reality OMC has not translated in to a more participatory style. See also Borrás and Jacobsson (2004) and Mosher (2000) for a critique of OMC.

2. Internet governance: a historical context

As is by now widely documented the Internet emerged from US government-funded research of the 1960s and 1970s, with the goal of creating interactive computing. The result was a robust system which, using common technical protocols, allowed computers operating at a distance from one another to communicate. Through the 1970s and 1980s, Internet use was centred in academic and governmental communities (see Winston 1998; Slevin 2000), though a series of key technological breakthroughs made in the early 1990s significantly increased its user-friendliness and facilitated exceptionally rapid traffic expansion rates.

The Internet's emergence as a sophisticated and fairly easy to use communications system began to convince governmental and business interests in particular of its commercial potential. Through its ability to provide a medium of information provision and exchange of many kinds (such as promotional and financial), the Internet possessed vital characteristic elements of a market. Furthermore, the digitisation of audiovisual content created the possibility of transporting and delivering information goods and services to customers. More broadly, some heralded the Internet's potential to enhance the quality of life of citizens – through creating new communities and providing new means of democratic participation – all due to its enrichment of the communications process. Thus, 'not for the first time in the history of information and communications technologies, what had initially evolved as a tool of the specialist and the enthusiast, emerged from the margins with almost unbounded commercial potential' (Simpson 2002, p.10).

Governance of the Internet has been the subject of a long process of deliberation and negotiation contested on the grounds of competing visions of regulatory appropriateness derived from important phases in the Internet's historic development. This chapter charts the Internet's history locating its progression within the processes of commercialisation and the formation of the key (albeit contested) principles that emerged for the governance of the virtual economy which has grown around the Internet. In doing this, it explores the role of the European Union (EU) in shaping the emergence of the global governance structures for the Internet and their underlying principles. More specifically it explores the growth of the Internet up to the emergence of the Internet Corporation for Assigned Names and Numbers (ICANN) as a new, global governance organisation for the management of Internet names and addresses. It examines the brief history of the relationship between

ICANN and the EU in its early stages, and illustrates in particular the limited extent to which the EU was involved in shaping the emergence of ICANN.

The focus of the chapter therefore is on the formative stages of Internet governance and the role the EU has played in influencing debates and deliberations which have taken place at the global level. To contextualise the analysis, the next section examines the foundations of the Internet and the fundamental issues which influenced the growth of the Internet economy and arguments around how it should be governed. Thereafter, it provides an overview of the deliberations between key interests on Internet governance arising from commercialisation, in particular in relation to the important issue of ownership of 'the root' (Mueller 2002 – see below). The emergence of the key principles for Internet governance are explored through an analysis of the period prior to ICANN's establishment and the roles of key political and economic actors involved. The EU's role in the formation of ICANN is considered with particular emphasis on areas of consensus and, by contrast, tension and disagreement which were evident at the time. Very importantly, these have resonated in much of the themes of the EU's policies for the Internet-based e-economy explored in the remainder of this book.

THE EMERGENCE OF THE INTERNET AS A COMMERCIAL TOOL

The history of the Internet is well documented, but nevertheless important for providing contextual basis for the sections that follow. Although there are varying accounts of where the idea of the Internet was founded (see Guice 1998), the standard and most widely accepted explanation, and an explanation propounded by the recently labelled 'father of the Internet', Vinton Cerf, is that it is the direct descendant of strategically motivated fundamental research begun in the 1960s with US federal government sponsorship (Cerf 1995).

The Internet had its origins in the circumstances of the Cold War, and the fear of nuclear attack from the Soviet Union. Although much debate has surrounded the issue of how far such a threat was 'real' or 'perceived', it led to the establishment of the Advanced Research Projects Agency (ARPA) within the US Department of Defence. ARPA's main remit was to establish and maintain a worldwide lead in science and technology and a key research programme involving the investigation of technologies for interlinking computer networks. The outcome of the research was the foundation of ARPANET – a communications network that facilitated the exchange of information between research centres involved in ARPA projects, and that allowed the various participants in the network to share computer resources (Slevin 2000, p.28).

The APRANET was based on packet switching technology, a technology that appealed particularly to the US Defense Department, since a strategically important network based on packet switching technology could potentially survive any nuclear attack[1]. It was the ARPANET that would develop into a collection of interlinked computer networks with the support and funding of the US Defense Department. However, it is important to note that ARPANET was not the Internet – the Transmission Control Protocol/Internet Protocol (TCP/IP) central for computer-to-computer communication had not yet been invented – nor had the word 'Internet' to describe it yet entered the cyberspace lexicon. The ARPANET project, however, was important, as it brought together the key actors at the epistem of the Internet's development: in the words of Milton Mueller 'ARPANET created the nucleus of an Internet technical community' (Mueller 2002, p.74).

How then did the ARPANET, with an academic and military focus, develop into the Internet, and more importantly, what were the key developments that led to the commercialisation and proliferation of the Internet? Clearly the Internet's emergence was related to the military-industrial complex rather than the logic of the free market, and thus for some time it 'continued to be housed within the secretive netherworld of the garrison state' (Schiller 1999, p.9). An important development in the movement from ARPANET to Internet was the invention in 1973, by Bob Kahn and Vinton Cerf, of the Transmission Control Protocol/Internet Protocol (TCP/IP), which allowed the internet-working of computer networks on a universal scale. Research on internet-working had gained considerable ground soon after the ARPANET was launched, and by 1973 the Defense Advanced Research Projects Agency DARPA[2] (previously ARPA) supported several other packet-based networks. These networks, however, used incompatible protocols, therefore a new internet-working protocol was needed which met local (specialised) network requirements, but also allowed distant users to communicate with each other (Mueller 2002, pp.74–75; Slevin 2000, p.32).

TCP/IP was a significant technological development that facilitated the explosive growth of the Internet and its global penetration. According to Dan Schiller, 'just deploying TCP/IP brought new forms of information sharing suddenly within reach. The Internet's astonishing versatility – its still rapidly evolving capacity to support novel as well as established forms of intercommunication – only added to its popularity' (Schiller 1999, p.9). The potential commercial viability of the Internet and its associated e-network economy only began to unfold, however, after a series of technological innovations and significant developments in the management of the 'Internet backbone', which had hitherto been the responsibility of ARPANET. In addition to this, there were important aspects of the liberalisation of the telecommunications and wider information and communications sectors that were relevant to the emergence and commercialisation of the Internet (see Chapter 3).

In terms of technological innovations, the invention of the modem in the late 1970s resulted in greater connectivity between computer networks, which had previously been excluded from connecting to ARPANET, or other backbone systems. This in its restricted way 'pointed to the existence of a wider potential demand for computer-mediated communication and to the wide range of situations in which it could be used' (Slevin 2000, p.32). Even more significant was the development of the Domain Name System (DNS) in 1982, which assigned a unique name and address to domains (Internet-connected computer networks). This was important not just for the contribution it made to the commercialisation and popularity of the Internet but for the architecture, regulation and ultimate control of such commercialisation through authority over the root zone (discussed below).

Following security concerns over the Internet backbone and the open nature of the APRANET, in 1983, it was split into a new ARPANET for academic use and MILNET for exclusive use by the military. ARPANET's role as the backbone providing the link between networks, however, was taken over by the US National Science Foundation (NSF) during the 1980s, and it was the NSF that took the Internet beyond its military capacity. A new backbone was sponsored by the NSF that enabled intercommunication between five university-based supercomputing centres (NSFNET). In addition, it permitted regional and university computer centres to utilise Internet technology to connect to this backbone (Schiller 1999, p.10). NSFNET, although restricting the use of its backbone to research and education primarily, did allow commercial use on a local and regional level through its acceptable use policy (Slevin 2000, p.33). The consequence was that traffic grew, encompassing a diverse community of users beyond that of academics, government agencies and think tanks. By 1991, 3500 users were connecting to the NSFNET backbone (Schiller 1999, p.10), and this is when the growing importance of commercialisation became emphatically evident.

The diverse range of self-funded networks connecting to the NSF backbone in the early 1990s led not only to developments in informal organisational structures in relation to Internet traffic and policy, but to innovations in interconnection and information representation on the Internet. Commercial services such as CompuServe, Prodigy, and American Online offered limited access to subscribers *primarily* through e-mail, Usenet newsgroup access, and access to data and programmes on the Internet through the File Transfer Protocol (FTP). It was also at this stage that the seeds of a market-driven approach to commercialisation became visible, although in reality they were sown much earlier. Outposts of market activity appeared in the 1970s with the liberalisation of US network development, which effectively 'freed the initial sponsors of Internet technology[3] to exploit its commercial applications' (Schiller 1999, p.11). This allowed private vendors such as Telenet to offer corporate actors in different localities with access to data services and remote access to computer facilities (ibid.).

As well as this, there was also the development of Local Area Networks (LANs) in the early 1980s which allowed the growth of the Ethernet system. The Ethernet was initially developed and commercialised by Robert Metcalfe in 1975 (a researcher at Xerox), and provided the software and hardware for linking workstations into office networks within a local area within certain technical parameters built around an open standard. The site in question had to run TCP/IP on the local network, and to set up a gateway or router between its network and the ARPANET. ARPANET also encouraged vendors, through funding, to develop products for the Ethernet, and, according to Metcalfe, there were more than 5 million Ethernet LANs in operation by the mid-1990s (see Franda 2001, p.31). Even more important was the fact that the major site for LAN applications was US business and as Schiller notes, even though 'Internet technology was not integrated on a significant scale in local area networks until the mid-1990s...Local network proliferation...comprised a critical prerequisite for the eventual takeoff of the Internet as a decentralised network of networks' (Schiller 1999, p.12).

The appearance of the World Wide Web (WWW), 'point and click' navigational devices such as Gopher in 1991 (the product of research at the University of Minnesota), and graphic browser software such as Mosaic, in 1993, clearly opened up opportunities for the commercial exploitation of the Internet. Such technological advances combined with the Domain Name System (DNS) made up a vital juncture in the transformation of the Internet from a military, academic research network into a commercial 'entity' with strong political economic implications. The growth and commercialisation of the Internet, especially the WWW, led to two mutually reinforcing effects. First, it endowed the domain name space for Internet naming and addressing with a new kind of strategic commercial and economic value. Second, this led to the increasing attentions of the economic and political actors wishing to exploit such commercial value in the emerging global Internet economy. The Internet was now displaying 'characteristic elements of the market process' (Simpson 2002, p.10) which key players from governments to the private sector wished to influence, with their vision of how Internet commerce should evolve and be governed.

Up until then the main actor involved in the technical development and management of the Internet was an informal group of engineers 'which in the course of the 1980s had grown into the most important standards organization for the Internet, the Internet Engineering Task Force [IETF]'[4] (Hofmann 2005, p.3). Perceived as key decision-makers with regard to technical innovation, they also, importantly, represented a model of governance for the Internet that was seen as informal and post-industrial, and an alternative to any governmental institutions that regulated standards. The 'IETF emerged as a prototype for new "postgovernmental" forms of coordination' (Hofman 2005, p.6). Such a model was inevitable given the academic roots of the Internet's development, where all elements of the Internet including technical standards and domain name space were seen as public goods 'to be administered in the interest of the entire academic community of users' (Hofmann 2005, p.4). The main body involved in the administration of the Internet at the time was the Internet Assigned Numbers Authority (IANA), funded by the NSF and established within the Information Sciences Institute of the University of Southern California. John Postel was the leading figure in administrating name and address space and editing standards for the Internet, his position emanating from the leading role he had played in founding the IETF.

The WWW, developed at the European Centre for Nuclear Research in Switzerland, was not the product of the US military establishment or the academic and research community. Its principal founder,[5] Tim Berners-Lee, envisaged the Internet (in a similar way to the US Internet technical community) as an open 'public' space with a decentralised universal structure and system (Franda 2001, p.31). However, commercialisation moved both the Internet and the Web to the centre of attention of governmental and business actors in the US with a vested interest in developing a 'virtual' e-economy similar to that in the capitalist commercial world. This would require a system of governance to be developed which was not necessarily shared with the Internet technical community's vision of a post-industrial and post-regulatory system of organisation.

As soon as the viability of the Internet as a commercial network became apparent, there was a distinct change of approach to its development, with the US government withdrawing its support of different Internet functions. Most significant in this was the decision to privatise and commercialise the backbone[6] of the NSF's NFSNET through selling the backbone infrastructure to US telecommunications operators Sprint, Ameritech and Pacific Bell in 1995, which forthwith became the managers and gatekeepers of its principal access points (Winston 1998, p.333). In addition to this, creation of private Internet Service Providers (ISPs), agreements between government agencies and the institutions that administered Internet Protocol (IP) addresses and domain names were also terminated (discussed below). The onset of the commercialisation of the Internet unveiled the intentions of the US government and key business players in the US: the neoliberal market-driven approach had emerged as the primary strategy for the Internet's promotion and development. It also immersed the world of politics (and governance) with the technical and administrative world of the Internet, as commercialisation, in particular in relation to domain names, brought with it questions of trademark ownership and regulatory control.

CONTESTATION OF INTERNET GOVERNANCE

Not surprisingly, the commercialisation and privatisation of the Internet and the concerns and issues emergent from it, focused on the Domain Name System (DNS). The DNS was designed in 1982, initially by Paul Mockapetris, and then Jon Postel, both of the University of Southern California's Information Sciences Institute (USC ISI). The basic function of the DNS was to match Internet Protocol (IP) addresses, which identified individual host computers on the Internet, with domain names. The DNS assigned specific names (written as unique numerical addresses) for individual machines on the network, so that being on the network required being connected to a machine that had been assigned a specific name. When a message was sent to a specific name, the message automatically went first to a DNS server, operated by Internet Service Provides (ISPs) in most cases, to find the numerical address for the name. Each of these DNS servers then went to one particular computer (the 'root') to find the numerical addresses that would enable the servers to send the message on its way (Franda 2001, p.47).[7] What is important here is the implication of such a structure: the authoritative 'root' zone file is the one that has been loaded first; the others simply copy its contents. Put another way, ownership and control over the root zone file carries with it considerable economic and political power (Mueller 2002, p. 41; Weinburg 2001, p.3, Froomkin 2001, p.10).

The transformation of domain names (following the emergence of the WWW) to endow them with economic value was clearly 'driven by rational economic concerns about visibility in an emerging global marketplace' (Mueller 2002, p.109). The supply of Internet connectivity commercially after 1995 through private ISPs, combined with the new-found commercial value of domain names, had a major effect on the demand for domain names as business interests increasingly realised their value. This, in turn, brought with it a greater significance for the management and administration of the 'root zone'. Those that controlled the DNS root server controlled the supply and visibility of domain names, and in this sense the issue of 'the root' had major implications[8] for the nature in which the commercialisation of the Internet would proceed with regard to regulation, management and governance; especially for those agents that were driving the process. Here the US government and key corporate, trademark and business actors assumed the lead roles.

Importantly from a governance perspective, the increase in demand for domain names created a conflict between economic actors and the pioneers of the Internet. There was a challenge to the free, liberal and decentralised vision for domain names held by its technical community, as the increased significance of domain names brought about demands for an effective regime for trademark protection. Trademark interests did not want to see an expansion of domain names to meet excessive demand, whereas the technical community, true to its approach to Internet governance, argued that this was a necessity to preserve the open and accessible nature of the domain name space. Such conflicts soon exposed the issue of ownership and authority with regard to making decisions about the Internet and its governance, leading to protracted debate between many competing interests that had gained a stake in 'cyberspace' (discussed below). Significantly, it shaped the debate on Internet governance and the subject of political authority on the Internet.

Historically, 'all of the major actors involved with the name space had fulfilled their responsibilities pursuant to agreements with the *US Government*' (Weinberg 2001, p.11, *original emphasis*). Initially, Jon Postel at the USC's ISI oversaw the administration of the Internet root zone and the DNS with funding from DARPA. He created IANA in order to do this, but although the Internet Society (ISOC)[9] accepted it as a constituent organisation, it did not have legal standing; and all Postel's attempts to confer it such standing failed. Subsequently, in 1994, a cooperative agreement was concluded between the NSF and Network Solutions (NSI), a private for profit organization offering registration services under .com and other TLDs (the service was called InterNIC).

Such an agreement, however, came prior to the rapid commercialisation of domain names: in other words, before the economic implications of Webification had been fully realised. According to Mueller (2002, p.110), 'Post-Web, the new registry was faced with a huge increase in volume of registrations' with almost all being 'concentrated in the *.com* top-level domain'. Figures showed that registration applications dealt with by NSI went from a mere 300 a month in 1992 to over 30,000 in 1995, with the growth of *.com* registrations alone increasing from 12,687 in 1994 to 232,004 in 1996 (Mueller 2002, p.110). Such a dramatic rise in registrations had major financial and administrative implications, not least for the NSF.

Up until this point the NSF paid for all registrations and the US government paid NSI an annual fee of $1 million in order to run the registration service. However, given the growth of registrations NSF complained, first, that it did not have a charter to support commercial registrations, and second, that it was unhappy about paying for the increasing number of registrations without the necessary administrative structures to allow adequate screening of requests (Franda 2001, pp.48–49; Mueller 2002, pp.110–11; Weinburg 2001, p.8). The upshot of this was that registration was effectively privatised – the US government had agreed to allow NSI to charge a $50 annual fee to each domain name registrant in return for its agreement that its rights to a fixed annual payment would be relinquished. This agreement was characterised by Mueller as 'a commercial beachhead in the heart of Internet administration' (cited by Franda 2001, p.49).

The NSI fee created a rivalry and rift between ISOC and the NSI, the latter clearly aggravated further by the acquisition of the InterNIC registry by the multi-billion dollar defence contractor, Science Applications International

Corporation, in 1996. There was a clear contradiction between ISOC's (academic and technical community) broad, not-for-profit approach to the Internet and domain names and the commercial, for-profit approach of the InterNIC registry. It also generated animosity towards the NSI amongst registrants who were unhappy about the NSI monopoly on the registration of the TLD addresses dot com, dot edu, dot gov, dot net and dot org. The arbitrary nature and lack of clarity in its domain name dispute policies was another source of controversy as 'it would suspend a domain name upon receiving a complaint from a trademark owner, without regard to whether the trademark owner had a superior legal claim to the name' (Weinburg 2001, p.8).

The feeling amongst the ISOC community was that it was gradually losing its grip on the supervision of a key Internet governance function to a body that held a philosophy that sat at the polar opposite of their own. This, and the fact that many within the technical community also believed that the dominance of the dot com domain in the name space was harmful, led to a proposal in 1996 from Jon Postel to authorise 150 new generic TLDs to be operated by new registries, at the expiration of NSI's contract in 1998. Whilst ISOC endorsed the proposal from Postel, however, objections soon emerged from key commercial players. Here, global business and governmental organisations were amongst those that were most vociferously opposed to such a plan.

Trademark holders complained that the expansion of the top-level domain space would lead to trademark infringement and speculation. Others such as the International Telecommunications Union (ITU) believed that IANA lacked the legitimacy and authority to impose such a plan, which, moreover, had implications for their own role in the future governance of the Internet. Postel's plan also, critically, failed to win the support of prospective domain name registration businesses despite the fact that many new registries would be authorised and operationalised, creating a more competitive environment for registration. Postel's plan thus 'began a long and contentious process in which participants debated the nature of the new TLDs and the future of Internet Governance' (Weinburg 2001, p.10).

The issue of control and ownership of the root was clearly crucial: whoever controlled the DNS 'root' would hold the vital power to determine the visibility of TLDs and which registries got to allocate names within each of the TLDs. The 'root' server and the various domain servers that interact with it have been described as the 'very heart of the Internet' and, as a 'passport without which passage across the border into cyberspace is impossible' (Post quoted by Franda 2001, p.48). The root server and DNS servers represent single controlling points and give tremendous political and economic leverage to the player(s) in control of them. Effectively, control of the root server and DNS could mean being able to deny access to the Internet: those that controlled the root were the ultimate Internet gatekeepers. In addition, such control could have implications for more routine functions through acting as a mechanism for collecting taxes, levies and fees (punished by removal or suspension of a domain name if not paid), regulating behaviour and enforcing intellectual property rules and laws (Franda 2001, p.48). Moreover, such power enabled those players that controlled the root server and DNS server to lock other actors into their ideological vision of how the Internet would be developed and governed, with the price of non-compliance or an alternative seemingly too high.[10]

The issue of root ownership, however, was not straightforward in the early stages of the debates on Internet governance, even though the US government was clearly the most powerful claimant. Seven of the twelve root servers drawing data directly from the 'root' were owned by it[11] or operated by its contractors (Froomkin 2001, p.11). A two-year debate ensued initially between ISOC and the US Government, with both putting various proposals forward claiming or contesting each other's rights to control the 'root', but gradually broadening the debate to other affected parties which had hitherto had a marginal input and influence.

In its most significant attempt to assert control over the 'root', ISOC put together an International Ad Hoc Committee (IAHC) in October 1996. This was a coalition between the technical community's governing hierarchy (ISOC/IAB[12]/IANA) and other political forces that had previously contested ISOC's claims on the 'root' (most notably the ITU and trademark owners) which aimed to develop and implement a global governance structure for the DNS. The proposal it developed, which became known as the Generic Top-Level Domain Memorandum of Understanding[13] (gTLD-MoU), incorporated a structure that straddled the boundary between private and public interests, with claims that it was agreed in the interests of the 'Internet Community'.

GOVERNANCE OF THE INTERNET: THE CREATION OF ICANN

The IAHC-MoU represented a key phase in the development of Internet governance. The US government became aware of the controversy surrounding the process of contestation related to the future governance of the Internet and entered the policy fray, becoming, in the process, a powerful and, ultimately, the most decisive and influential actor. This political intervention arose from several concerns about the ongoing deliberations. On the one hand, it was alarmed at the influence that the old telecommunications order, in the shape of the ITU, was apparently exerting on the process. For most of the 1990s it had been an open critic of what it saw as the ITU's unwillingness to reform the international telephone accounting rate system and regarded the

ITU as a significant structural impediment to the liberalisation of the global telecommunications sector.

In this, it was supported by large, pro-liberalisation, US multinational business interests in ICT, many of which initially did not consider the Internet of strategic commercial importance, but gradually became aware of its commercial potential and, simultaneously, its possible threat to their well-established intellectual property and trademark interests. The US government also noted the growing unease of the NSF at being placed at the centre of an increasingly acrimonious struggle between the gTLD-MOU constituency and NSI. It is also important to note that a range of commercial interests in the shape of alternative domain name registries and smaller Internet Service Providers (ISPs) from the US and beyond, also opposed the gTLD-MOU (Mueller 2002). As a consequence of these factors, the US government decided to directly and decisively intervene in the formative process of Internet governance.

In 1997, it publicly declared its opposition to the gTLD-MOU and charged the Department of Commerce (specifically its National Telecommunications and Information Administration) with the task of providing an alternative set of proposals. According to Hofmann (2005, p.9), 'in 1997 the US government decided to step out from the "shadow of hierarchy" and redirect further efforts to reform the domain name system'. This exercise had a very practical manifestation in the shape of, in the first instance, a discussion Green Paper (US Department of Commerce 1998a) and subsequently, a non-binding White Paper statement of policy (US Department of Commerce 1998b). The White and Green Papers generated a short period of intense and complex deliberations and negotiations as a result of which a set of governing principles emerged to underpin the creation of a new global organisation for Internet governance in the shape of the Internet Corporation for Assigned Names and Numbers (ICANN).

This period was clearly driven by the coercive entrepreneurship of the US government whose actions served to secure enough agreement to create ICANN. First, in the Green Paper, the US unambiguously declared its ultimate ownership of and authority over the facilities that underpin the IP address and TLD name system (i.e. the 'A root server') (Froomkin 2001, pp18–9). Second, it stated its intention to hand over to the international private sector the functional management of this system in the shape of an unspecified not-for-profit company. Within this regulatory system, the Green Paper proposed to create competing registries, as well as competing registrars[14] (see Figure 2.1). The paper was outstanding in its lack of recognition of the IAHC and its gTLD-MOU.

> - There is widespread dissatisfaction about the absence of competition in domain name registration.
> - Conflicts between trademark holders and domain name holders are becoming more common. Mechanisms for resolving these conflicts are expensive and cumbersome.
> - Many commercial interests, staking their future on the successful growth of the Internet, are calling for a more formal and robust management structure.
> - An increasing percentage of Internet users reside outside of the US, and those stakeholders want to participate in Internet coordination.
> - As Internet names increasingly have commercial value, the decision to add new top-level domains cannot be made on an *ad hoc* basis by entities or individuals that are not formally accountable to the Internet community.
> - As the Internet develops commercially, it becomes less appropriate for US research agencies to direct and fund these functions.

Source: http://www.choicefree.com/domainnmaeauctionsales
/governmentdomainnamepolicy1.htm
Figure 2.1 US Green Paper

Aside from the assertiveness of the US government, the Green Paper provoked a debate in which it became clear that the principles underlying the governance of the Internet within it was open to serious contestation. In particular, there was concern, on the one hand from the technical community, about the new degree of government influence in evolving Internet governance, to the extent that the original governance framework characterised by private sector leadership and self-governance was in danger of being abandoned. On the other hand, non-US governmental (notably the EU) and business interests feared that the original internationally oriented governance framework of Internet governance was also being, de facto, forsaken as part of a US-centred *fait accompli*. The European Commission considered the US proposals as a thinly veiled attempt to gain strategic control over the electronic marketplace (Halpin and Simpson 2002, p. 289). The EU feared that the US proposals would 'consolidate permanent US jurisdiction over the Internet as a whole' (European Commission 1999).

However, very importantly the Green Paper's proposals were supported by a small, but very powerful, group of elite Information and Communication Technologies business interests dominated by IBM and MCI. As Mueller (2002, pp.168–72) clearly illustrates, these companies formed a close, mutually supportive, relationship with the US Clinton administration and used their influence within a lobbying group formed in 1996 called the Global Internet Project (GIP)[15] to propound the Green Paper's agenda. A vital part of this was the process of personal negotiation that took place between the US Federal government representative Ira Magaziner, key members of the GIP and elites within the technical community. This process of negotiation gradually won acceptance by the technical community of a set of guiding principles for ICANN's governance, focused on it being a continuation of IANA; it being incorporated in US law; its management being internationally constituted and representative; and it operating through self-regulation where government would remain outside the organisation and its processes. More specifically, there was a preference that a non-state actor should be responsible for the management of the DNS regime and that 'there should be a stakeholder-based, private international organization set up for technical management' (cited in Drezner 2004, p.28). The US government then, under the influence of the above actors, indicated that it wanted to minimise the influence of both governments and intergovernmental organisations in the new regime in order to create greater flexibility and efficiency.

Further concessions were afforded to trademark interests and the EU (see below). By the time the US government followed up the Green Paper with a White Paper (see Figure 2.2) it was clear that a critical mass of interests – business, governmental and technical – broadly accepted the above series of principles upon which ICANN would be based. However, in its White Paper, the US government, recognising the problem of appearing excessively unilateralist (see Leib 2002, p.166) threw the process of finalising the details of an additional number of (what became) ICANN's regulative and prescriptive rules open to debate and resolution by what was described at the time as the Internet community, meaning; broadly, anyone or any organisation with an interest in its evolution. In particular, a call was made for a consensual decision to be reached on issues of the structure and composition of the (unnamed) new organisation (Froomkin and Lemley 2001, p.6), notably its governing board and *modus operandi*. Thus, simultaneous to the development of new ideas embodying Internet governance, another short, deliberative, non-government-organised phase in the process ensued which was given the name the International Forum on the White Paper (IFWP).

The Forum was time constrained, in that it had less than a year to come to an agreement before the point of termination in 1998 of the contract related to the management of the IP address and TLD name system between the US NSF and NSI. A series of meetings of the IFWP occurred at which a process developed through the exchange of views between different interest groups from business, technical and civil society quarters on how (a putative) ICANN should be constructed. However, the process soon gained notoriety for the conflicts it generated and the alterative agendas which were being simultaneously pursued. As Mueller (2002, pp.176–79) clearly shows, a policy axis emerged between the GIP business grouping and the IANA-led technical community to design the management board of (what became) ICANN according to a structure which would see their interests maximised ahead of those of a broader range of commercial and civil society ones. Their generally powerful position in this pathological move for control of ICANN's management structure was further assisted by the fact that they were able to deliberately infiltrate, undermine, destabilise and, ultimately, scupper the IFWP process (see also Von Bernstorff 2003, p.517).

Stability
The US government should end its role in the Internet number and name address system in a manner that ensures the stability of the Internet. The introduction of a new management system should not disrupt current operations or create competing root systems. During the transition and thereafter, the stability of the Internet should be the first priority of any DNS management system. Security and reliability of the DNS are important aspects of stability, and as a new DNS management system is introduced, a comprehensive security strategy should be developed.

Competition
The Internet succeeds in great measure because it is a decentralised system that encourages innovation and maximises individual freedom. Where possible, market mechanisms that support competition and consumer choice should drive the management of the Internet because they will lower costs, promote innovation, encourage diversity, and enhance user
choice and satisfaction.

Private, Bottom-up Coordination
Certain management functions require coordination. In these cases, responsible, private-sector action is preferable to government control. A private coordinating process is likely to be more flexible than government and to move rapidly enough to meet the changing needs of the Internet and of Internet users. The private process should, as far as possible, reflect the bottom-up governance that has characterised development of the Internet to date.

Representation
The new corporation should operate as a private entity for the benefit of the Internet community as a whole. The development of sound, fair, and widely accepted policies for the management of DNS will depend on input from the abroad and growing community of Internet users. Management structures should reflect the functional and geographic diversity of the Internet and its users. Mechanisms should be established to ensure international participation in decision-making.

Source: http://www.ntia.doc.gov/ntiahome/domainname/6_5_98dns.htm
Figure 2.2 Principles for a New System: US White Paper

The final major negotiating hurdle to be overcome was to reach agreement with NSI, which viewed the process to this point with concern, fearing a diminution of its dominant position in the TLD name registration business. The question of NSI participation, however, was more complex with regard to ICANN. It had been excluded by the dominant coalition which saw it as an 'unwelcome and threatening intrusion of commercial and propriety interests into the core of Internet administration' (Mueller 2002, p.181). To other key groups it was a major irritant (prospective entrants, trademark owners).

From a US government perspective, however, the expiration of the NSI contract (which allowed the NSI to control the 'root zone') raised fundamental questions for the future of Internet governance. The implication of NSI not participating in ICANN (it claimed intellectual property rights in the database of dot com, dot net and dot org registrants and potentially had 75 per cent control over the domain name market if the agreement was simply terminated) was that it could lead to the de facto privatisation of the root in its hands, fragmentation of the Internet and ultimately loss of control of the root zone for the US government.

With both the NSI and the US government having significant bargaining power, a compromise agreement was negotiated. According to Weinburg (2001, p.12) 'the US government...was able to use its negotiating leverage to cause NSI to recognize ICANN's policy authority', whilst at the same time, NSI was able to secure terms that reinforced rather than undermined its own market dominance of the NSI generic TLDs (dot com, dot net, and dot org). As a powerful company in its own right, with an established position in the existing TLDs and a close association with the US government, NSI was able to secure a lucrative material stake for itself in the governance pattern which evolved. In a final agreement with the US government, it acquiesced to facilitate competition in the TLD registrar market; to separate its registrar and registry business; and to recognise and sign a contract with ICANN (Mueller 2002: p.183). In return, NSI was aware that its dominant, well-established, presence in the domain name registration market would allow it to maintain a secure future commercial position. From a US government perspective, through its control of ICANN and agreement with the NSI,[16] it held on to the key levers of power for controlling the development of Internet governance.

ICANN was thus established as a self-governance structure in 1999, representing an institutionalisation of regulatory functions for the Internet, and in the same instance, new and experimental ground in global governance structures. Such structures had been developed over a short but intense period of negotiations in the latter half of the 1990s. ICANN was established as an international, not-for-profit organisation under Californian law with responsibility for the global management of IP address space allocation and protocol parameter assignment; Internet domain name system management; and Internet root server system management. This technical and managerial remit aside, it soon became clear that in performing its functions, ICANN would necessarily step into the controversial arena of global public policy.

THE EU AND THE FORMATION OF ICANN

The process leading to the emergence of ICANN as a new international organisation for Internet governance was one with which the EU had considerable involvement; which did not though necessarily translate to substantive influence. Whilst Europe had developed a relatively strong position in telecommunications historically, the early significance and emergence of the Internet went largely unnoticed (authors' interview, 2004). Through much of the 1980s and 1990s, EU Member States had undertaken a process of steady liberalisation and Europeanisation of their telecommunications sectors (see Chapter 3) and, as a consequence, the EU level assumed a position of some significance.

In terms of the broader leading-edge developments in ICT, the EU commenced a debate on the Information Society in 1994 with the release of the Bangemann Report, soon followed by the launch of the first phase of an Action Plan for the Information Society (European Commission, 1994). Neither of these developments showed any great recognition of the burgeoning presence of the Internet. In technological terms, Werle (2002, p.146) argues that around this time, the European Commission, Member State governments and the European computer industry were concentrating their efforts around the Open Systems Interconnect (OSI) standards suite for, in considerable part, industrial policy reasons and thereby neglected developments in the Internet's key technical protocols, TCP/IP. At the national level in the EU, around the mid-1990s, levels of Internet penetration were comparatively low, as was general awareness of the Internet's significance in policy-making circles.

Thus, it was with some concern, interest and even alarm, that European communications policy-makers learned of the significance of the events unfolding in US policy circles. In this respect the influence of the EU on the formative process of ICANN was in the first instance a reactive one, with the European Commission demonstrating its skills as a policy entrepreneur in order to carve out a role for the EU in this global policy area. As the Internet did not possess any historical technical, economic or institutional roots in Europe's national contexts, it was comparatively easy for the Commission to adopt a helmsmanship role. Equally, the global nature of the Internet suggested that the European Commission's designated function as a representative of its Member States in international negotiating fora could be deployed to fruitful effect. The EU, through the Commission, was possibly the best way of securing Europe's interests in this important scenario of globalisation, as well as acting as a shield against its most undesirable effects. However, the extent to which the EU would be able to participate as a primary mover in the development of ICANN was open to considerable doubt, given its limited knowledge of the policy area.

The European Commission reacted to the emergence of the IAHC with some trepidation and key members of its Information Society Directorate attempted to mobilise a EU response. As has happened many times in EU ICT policy-making, the Commission liaised closely with, and drew on, the expertise of business interests (Simpson 2000) – in this case, those involved in the European country code domain name industry and European Internet Service Providers (ISPs) primarily (authors' interview 2004). As a result, the Commission attempted to exert its influence and ideas through directly lobbying the US government in order to express opposition to the IAHC and to bemoan the lack of European involvement in the evolution of the process. The reaction to the Green Paper was equally negative, the Commission declaring it a clear attempt by the US to unilaterally impose policy authority over the Internet (European Commission 1998a).

Key differences between EU and US approaches to the regulation of ICT also became apparent at this time as the Commission worked to introduce its own framework into the evolving Internet governance process. Whilst the EU developed a broadly neo-liberal policy outlook and a series of practices in the ICT area, the EU neo-liberal policy model was distinctly different from other regions, including the US (see Venturelli 2002). The EU approach reflected its long established preference for a coordinated (regulated) self-regulation as opposed to the private self-regulatory model that underpinned ICANN's *modus operandi*, a difference that also resonated in other International Fora such as the Global Business Electronic Dialogue (GBDe) (see Green-Cowles 2001). In this case, the creation of ICANN, a new organisation for global Internet governance that would operate outside the influence of governments, went against the grain of EU thinking on the need to have regulation not only to protect, but also to promote, the public interest. However, the EU was to achieve only limited success in promulgating its preference in the post-Green Paper deliberations since the White Paper made it clear that governments would only be able to participate in ICANN's processes in an advisory capacity. This became manifest with the creation, in 1999, of the Governmental Advisory Committee (GAC).

Although the GAC's establishment, on the one hand, was a compromise for the EU in terms of its traditional governance style; on the other, it did give it a policy foothold in ICANN's affairs which it attempted to exploit, and thus could be seen as a partial success. Moreover there is evidence to suggest that the EU, through deliberative manipulation, was able to (working within ICANN's established governance framework) secure a significant change of emphasis in relation to the GAC's relationship with the ICANN board, and more importantly, a transformation in the regulatory rhetoric established at ICANN's inception. Moreover there was a clear shift from the primacy of private self-governance to that of the development of a public-private partnership,[17] something more in line with the EU's own public policy tradition (Christou and Simpson 2004). As part of ICANN-GAC reforms aimed at the creation of the public-private partnership, a series of ICANN-GAC liaisons were created to facilitate two-way communication between the relevant ICANN constituency on policy matters.[18] The GAC also created a series of working groups to engage with the appropriate ICANN Supporting Organisations and Committees (GAC 2003 p.3).[19] This created a closer and probably, de facto, influential role for government in the affairs of ICANN, an outcome that sat well with the EU's preference for what it termed co-regulation.[20]

The US White Paper provided other indications of how the EU was able to exert some leverage in the negotiations leading to the creation of ICANN. The decision of the US government to leave to further deliberation by the international community the details of ICANN's structure and functions (not least the creation of new TLDs) suggested something of a tactical withdrawal, on the surface at least. Similarly, the declaration that the new organisation's dispute settlement procedure would be overseen by the World Intellectual Property Organization (WIPO) reflected in part, a proposal promoted by the EU. Nonetheless, in a response to the White Paper, whilst the Commission acknowledged progress on the recognition by the US of the Internet as a global resource, it cautioned that more progress on this matter was necessary (European Commission 1998b).

As the previous section has indicated, the international deliberative nature of the final stage of the formation of ICANN, manifest in the IFWP, was undermined and superseded by the exertion of the material interests of the IANA-GIP policy axis. By this stage, Mueller (2002, p.180) argues that the EU had become part of a coalition that broadly accepted the IANA-GIP policy frame. However, as part of this, the European Commission was able to successfully exert its own material interests to gain three seats on the Interim Board of ICANN in return for its support (authors' interviews, 2004). Overall, nonetheless, the EU, whilst exerting some influence on the process of ICANN's conception, played a relatively minor role. In particular, ICANN was established on US territory in US law. The US government illustrated its ultimate control over the Internet's key resources and its power in shifting the course of policy events related to their governance terms.

CONCLUSION

This chapter has shown that the emergence of a framework for Internet governance has been reflective of a continuous process of negotiation and attempted reconciliation between key stakeholders with conflicting perspectives on the underlying approach to be taken. The academic and technical community, responsible for the basic architecture of the Internet in the 1980s, envisaged a decentralised, free and networked approach to its regulation with no involvement for governments (Barlow 1996) or the private sector: the Internet and the architecture that accompanied it, alongside its non-territorial nature, did not lend itself to the traditional methods of regulatory control within defined 'sovereign' geographical boundaries – in fact, it negated such control (Johnson and Post 1997, p.6).

The Internet's rapid commercialisation, however, and the increase in demand for domain names brought to the fore regulatory (trademark) issues and with this competing visions of Internet governance. Moreover the private sector and the wider Internet community fought for regulatory structures that would give them a greater voice in managing the domain name system, whilst also ensuring rules were in place that secured a competitive market in cyberspace. The consequent power struggle that ensued over control of the domain name space (and ultimately the 'A' root zone), essential to influence and shape the governance of the Internet, was resolved by the US government. Stepping out from the shadow of hierarchy that it had been operating under, the 'ruler of the root' (Mueller 2002), as the most powerful and authoritative claimant, imposed its own solution, which inevitably incorporated many of the principles demanded by key commercial actors, in which private self-governance and voluntary compliance were guiding premises.

The EU played a relatively minor role in the creation of ICANN, and ultimately, the governance principles that underpinned it. Its eventual interjection in the global deliberations that took place prior to ICANN's establishment, however, did serve to highlight key differences in the preferred governance approach for the Internet between the US and the EU, with the latter's perception of self-regulation clearly derived from embedded traditions of regulation based predominantly on the traditional Community method (and public authority involvement) (Héritier 2002). However, given the powerful position of the US and the EU's delayed intervention in discussions to establish ICANN, it had to accept self-regulation as the starting point for the governance of ICANN. In addition it also had to accept that its influence in the day-to-day affairs of ICANN through the GAC would be relegated to a mere advisory capacity. The GAC, however, was seen by the EU as a vehicle for persuasion within ICANN's structure, and was promptly utilised to manipulate a shift in discursive emphasis (if not embedded change) to governance and regulatory forms that the EU was more familiar with, namely public-private partnership (see Chapter 7).

NOTES

1. Using packet switching technology meant that computers within a network could operate independently of each other. For example, if you had a wide area network (WAN) with fifty sets of computers attached, if five of the networks malfunctioned, the other forty would not also crash, since they could send chunks of data to each other without the whole WAN malfunctioning.
2. The Advanced Research Projects Agency (ARPA) changed its name to Defense Advanced Research Projects Agency (DARPA) in 1971, then back to ARPA in 1993, and back to DARPA in 1996.
3. Bolt, Baranek, and Newman, a military contractor and a consulting firm.
4. The IETF itself remains a private, informal organisation with no legal form (Hofmann 2005, p.4).
5. Other actors at the Centre Européen pour la Recherche Nucléaire (CERN) Laboratories in Switzerland (where Lee developed the WWW) also played a major role in developing some of the major building blocks of the WWW including the Hypertext Transfer Protocol (http), Hypertext Markup Language (html), and the Universal Resource Locator (url) (Franda 2001, p.10)
6. Up until this privatisation the IETF was the only standards organisation for the Internet.
7. The name resolution side of the DNS is an interdependent, distributed, hierarchical database, at the top of which lies a single data file that contains the list of the machines that have the master lists of registrations in each TLD (Froomkin 2001 p.10). This is what is known as the 'root zone' or 'root' and the authority in charge of 'the root' assigns unique Top Level Domains (TLDs), with each TLD divided into Second Level Domains (SLDs). The registrant of the SLD in turn has the exclusive authority to assign unique third level domain names, and so on down the hierarchy. At the apex of the DNS pyramid is a set of *thirteen* 'root servers', each of which lists the IP addresses of the computers containing the zone files for each of the TLDs. At the next level are the computers holding those TLD zone files, each of which lists the IP addresses of the name servers for each SLD it controls, and so on.
8. The US government as controller of the root could add or take away domains names at will.
9. The Internet Society (ISOC) is a private organization chartered by members of the Internet Engineering Task Force (IETF) with the aim of representing the 'Internet Community' (the legal arm of the IETF). The IETF was a part of the Internet Architecture Board (IAB) (previously Internet Activities Board) and its function was to discuss issues concerning Internet governance. However its function eventually became more specialised after the IAB set up an open procedure for these discussions. The popularity of the resultant discussion forums meant that the IETF led protocol development and dealt with immediate technical concerns, with long-range planning being dealt with by another IAB body the Internet Research Task Force (IRST). ISOC's agenda was, however, to primarily represent the interests of the US computer and academic community, which did not sit well after the commercialisation of the Internet and the proliferation of new interest in

the Internet's development by business, commercial and governmental players in the US and globally (see Franda 2001, p.45–47).

10. See for example Froomkin (2001, p.11) on the issue of US ownership of the 'root' and establishing alternatives to the 'root'.

11. Ten of the thirteen root name servers (including the 'root') are located in the US, with the other three located in Stockholm, London and Tokyo.

12. Internet Architecture Board

13. See http://www.gtld-mou.org/docs/faq.html for details.

14. NSI would be required to separate its registry and registrar functions.

15. The GIP was made up of elites from 16 Internet, telecommunications and e-commerce firms.

16. See Mueller (2002, pp.194–196) for specifics of a series of agreements between the Commerce Department, NSI and ICANN which saw the NSI agree to enter into a registry contract and a registrar accreditation contract with ICANN.

17. This view was also put forward by the ICANN President in a review of ICANN's procedures in 2002, suggesting that ICANN's early deep scepticism of any government involvement had given way to a more realistic vision of how the Corporation should evolve, that of co-regulation.

18. There are nine such liaisons with parts of ICANN such as its ccTLD Names Supporting Organisation, its Generic Names Supporting Organisation; Root Server Advisory Committee and At Large Advisory Committee.

19. There are six working groups on issues such as internationalised domain names; gTLDs; ccTLDs and IP versions 6 (IPv6)

20. At a more practical level, however, doubt has been cast over governments' willingness to devote the necessary resources to the GAC which this would require (authors' interview 2004).

3. The European Union and the governance of the communications sector

Historically, the governance of the main elements of electronic network communications in Europe – principally telecommunications and audiovisual broadcasting – set their constituent industrial and commercial activities apart from other sectors of the economy. This reflected the perceived economic nature of production and service provision, as well as the political and social importance of broadcasting and telecommunications and has been well documented in the academic literature. Equally well documented has been the series of highly significant *changes* which have occurred, over approximately the last 20 years, in the governance of 'traditional' communications in Europe, amounting to nothing short of a transformation in the case of telecommunications (see for example: Humphreys 1996; Doyle 2002a, 2002b; Humphreys and Simpson 2005; Bartle 2005; Thatcher 1999; Natalicchi 2001).

The aim of this chapter is not to revisit and chart the original structure and subsequent changes to European network communications *per se*. Rather, its aim is to illustrate the, in some cases well-established, in others newly embedding, communications governance context within which EU and national Member State policy-makers considered the challenges of governing the Internet as it, somewhat belatedly, became an important part of European communications policy and regulation from the mid-1990s onwards. The chapter's core argument is that such an illustration is imperative in providing a basis for understanding the nature of recent EU policy for Internet governance, in particular Internet commerce. Specifically, it provides an explanatory context to appreciate the extent to which the EU would readily embrace – or by contrast baulk at and attempt to re-fashion – elements of the 'new', though contested, governance agenda of the Internet emerging principally from the US and suffusing global policy debates from the mid-1990s. It also provides the context for considering the significant extent to which the EU's governance of e-commerce is different from its approach to other aspects of electronic network communications.

The chapter commences with a brief overview of the main governance – specifically regulatory – parameters of European electronic communications. This illustrates, inter alia, the legacy and significance of state ownership and intervention in electronic communications. In complement, it also illustrates the 'public good' nature of communications services and the subsequent importance placed on the delivery of universal access and service and, by contrast, restrictions on certain kinds of communications content. It then proceeds to document briefly the set of major changes which have impacted, albeit unevenly, the regulation of the audiovisual and telecommunications sectors in Europe. Here, a complex, interrelated plethora of changes in the technologies and political economy of communications gradually altered its productive and commercial structure, the services it provided to consumers and the shape and detail of its governance. Regarding governance, the differing effects across the audiovisual and telecommunications fields of two major phenomena are highlighted: internationalising/globalising economic activity and the emergence of the EU as a new institutional locus for, and source of, communications governance and regulation. Here, it considers and illustrates the extent to which a regulatory state (Seidman and Gilmour 1986; Majone 1994, 1996), both at the national and EU level, has emerged in electronic network communications in Europe.

The final part of the chapter focuses on the policy debate which the EU undertook on Information and Communications Technologies (ICT) convergence in the latter half of the 1990s. Technological and, to some extent, market convergence in the communications sector put pressure on European communications policy-makers to consider the degree to which a common regulatory framework for different composite parts of communications could be created (European Commission 1997a). The debate also placed particular focus on new convergent techno-commercial platforms and networks, most notably the Internet. It shows how the EU's early treatment of Internet governance, as a result of the convergence debate, reflected the tensions between 'traditional' (corporate state) European approaches to communications governance, more recent neo-liberal (regulatory state) 'reformist' policies, notably those practised in telecommunications and, finally, the 'new' liberal and libertarian governance agendas prominent in international Internet policy-making circles. The chapter argues that consequent policy confusion and flux led, first, to the employment by the EU of a 'wait and see' policy on the Internet and, subsequently, to the development and deployment of a diverse, diffuse and tentative set of governance strategies, evident not least in Internet commerce policy. The political economic significance of these strategies and the governance forms within which they have been developed is the subject of subsequent chapters of this book.

THE STATE AND ELECTRONIC NETWORK COMMUNICATIONS IN EUROPE – TELECOMMUNICATIONS

Whilst it is no exaggeration to claim that the era of almost complete state dominance of electronic network communications is long-ended, it is not the case that the state (here taken to encompass both its national Member States and the EU itself) no longer plays a significant role in the governance of communications across Europe, including the emerging electronic economy of the Internet. To begin to understand the persistent prevalence of the state in the sector, despite wholesale changes in the technologies and markets of communications and their associated political economy, it is important to illustrate how deeply embedded, flexible and robust state influence has been in the development of European electronic communications.

Throughout most of the 20th century, telecommunications services in the vast majority of the 25 countries which now comprise the EU were delivered through a series of state-owned monopolies which were in many cases also responsible for the provision of postal services (and were thus known as Postal, Telegraph and Telephone companies [PTTs]). Secondary sector telecommunications activities were barely more competitive with oligopoly the pervading market structure aimed at supplying national PTTs for the most part, though a number of European telecommunications equipment firms did develop strong commercial presences in non-European international market contexts. In telecommunications service provision, international intermarket penetration was nonexistent, international telephone calling instead being facilitated through a series of commercial 'interface' agreements between national PTTs, whose accounting rates bore no relation to the actual cost of interconnection and carriage, thus making international calling prohibitive for many telecommunications users. This system of international call charging was developed within the cartel-like European Conference of Postal, Telegraph and Telephone companies (CEPT) and, at the global level, the International Telecommunications Union (ITU). Thus, there was no international foreign direct investment in the European telecommunications sector and only a very limited, highly particular, form of international 'trade' in services that was by no means free and open.

The above structure for telecommunications service provision was, to say the least, unusual and would, in normal circumstances, have raised the concern of economists on a number of grounds, notably market dominance, pricing of goods and services, and technological progress. However, the overriding influence and guiding hand of the state in the telecommunications sector was used to justify and perpetuate the existence of monopoly (or near monopoly) service provision. Underpinning such state influence was a connected two-dimensional economic and social rationale. First, on the economic side, it was argued that the tendency for a monopolist service provider to behave in economically inefficient ways could be thwarted by state ownership of the PTT which would thus act in the interest of telecommunications consumers. Second, and related to this, it was argued that the socially desirable goal of providing as much of the population (and eventually all) with a telephone service as quickly as possible could be achieved through utilising excessive 'profit' made from monopoly privileges in two ways. On the one hand, investment capital to construct costly fixed-link telecommunications networks could be readily deployed to extend network coverage to outlying areas. On the other hand, through a process of tariff re-balancing, each telecommunications user would pay more or less the same price for a telephone service, irrespective of the real economic cost of its provision. In this way, the state, through ownership of the telecommunications service provider, assumed ultimate responsibility for guaranteeing universal service and ensuring economic efficiency and longer–term technological progress. As a consequence, the state, until at least the middle of the 1980s across the EU, exercised a massively pervasive influence on the structure, functioning and evolution of its telecommunications sector. However, through the 1970s and into the 1980s, this system became increasingly questioned and was soon the subject of open contestation in forerunner telecommunications reform economies, most notably the UK. Nonetheless, the influence of the telecommunications 'corporate state', acting in a 'classic' service provider and strategic planner role, proved in many cases highly resistant to the new political economic pressures for change (see discussion later in this chapter).

THE STATE AND MASS ELECTRONIC NETWORK COMMUNICATIONS IN EUROPE – THE AUDIOVISUAL SECTOR

Arguably, the role and influence of the state in the European audiovisual sector was even more deeply pervasive than in telecommunications. The structure of the audiovisual markets of EU Member States (those of the former communist bloc excepted) and their underpinning rationale, bore several similarities to the traditional situation in telecommunications, though also two key interrelated differences. The first important difference concerns the nature of content transmitted as part of audiovisual service provision. The second concerns the fact that the audiovisual network communications system is one-to-many, as opposed to one-to-one in nature as in telecommunications. That audiovisual network communication potentially involved the 'open' transmission of voice (initially as part of radio broadcasting) and subsequently images (with the advent of terrestrial television) led government to consider closely the positive potential, but also the possible dangers, inherent in such a system. Rather like in telecommunications, however, the consequent social and political arguments for a strong state presence in audiovisual broadcasting were underpinned by an analysis of the nature of the broadcasting market, in particular the public good characteristics of its output. There were, for example, inherent difficulties in securing payment for television programmes at the point of consumption, since a programme might be viewed by any number of people (without the knowledge of the programme maker and/or broadcaster) other than the consumer who might notionally have paid for it in the first place. From a different perspective, that of economic efficiency, the marginal cost of supplying extra viewers with a programme already made and broadcast to at least one customer is usually zero (Doyle 2002a), assuming the broadcast network is in place, and thus to exclude these customers undermines economic welfare maximisation in the broadcasting economy. These two characteristics suggested to policy-makers that audiovisual output should not be paid for at the point of consumption and that some other means of financing might occur, such as a licence fee, commercial advertising, subscription or even direct funding through the public purse (Graham 2000).

A third important economic characteristic of audiovisual broadcast markets – the existence of externalities, both positive and negative – became intrinsically linked to the argument for close involvement of the state in the sector. Here, the messages and meanings which could be portrayed in the consumption of audiovisual products and services underpinned subjective concerns about unsuitable content, inappropriate viewing and moral decline in society. There was also concern about the power of broadcasting to persuade citizens in the course of their political and other (such as consumptive) decision-making. In a political context, this has the potential to erode and stifle democratic debate; in a commercial context, it could damage competition and, ultimately, innovation and technological progress. Thus, the pursuit of (state-secured) media pluralism became a goal in western European democracies. However, similar to the situation in telecommunications, there is a debate on the relationship between market structure and policy outcomes in the case of securing and maintaining pluralism (see Doyle 2002b).

In a positive vein, certain broadcast outputs were seen to be merit goods which would not be produced in sufficient quantities were their provision left entirely to market forces. Such outputs might be described broadly as informative and educative in nature whose consumption might help to enable fuller participation by the citizen in society. In addition, even if programmes of this kind were available in sufficient quantities, consumers might only realise their true utility after they were consumed and would eschew their purchase in a free market scenario (Graham 2000), thereby foregoing the opportunity of utility enhancement through 'discovery'. Related to both the merit good and pluralism arguments, the view that broadcasting, if left to market forces alone, would not cater for minority viewing interests – principally cultural, religious and sporting – was also put forward in the design of audiovisual broadcast networks across Europe. A final, and arguably the most important, factor in the creation of state-dominated audiovisual broadcasting systems across western Europe, was technology, or more specifically the limitations imposed by broadcasting spectrum scarcity. The limited capacity of terrestrial radio and television networks stood in stark contrast to the many possibilities for using them and called forth a socio-political solution, which came to be questioned increasingly through the last decades of the 20th century, though which still remains robustly defended across most of the EU's territories. Given the perceived vital social and political needs which broadcasting could address, allied to the requirement to ensure that its potential negative consequences were curtailed as much as possible, it was argued that these could be most effectively and appropriately delivered through a system which was, for the most, part state-owned, and in all cases, tightly controlled through independent public regulation. Though being the key determinative actor in the creation and maintenance of the general features of this system, importantly states remained 'at one remove' from day-to-day decision-making on the content of schedules, as well as the assessment of their performance against set public goals, due to the need to fulfil one of the cornerstones of the system, namely party political impartiality and freedom of speech.

Thus, in practice, broadcast schedules were carefully prescribed to offer a variety of programming which catered for pluralism as well as the promotion of common values and ideas and which informed, educated and entertained users of the system. This approach created a series of free to air public service broadcasting systems across western Europe, resourced through a combination of compulsory licence fees and commercial advertising within which a series of publicly owned broadcasters predominated along side a smaller number of commercial broadcasters, many of whom themselves were governed by tight public service remits (see Siune and Truetzschler 1993). Thus, as in the case of telecommunications, the state, through its role in defining and guaranteeing public service provision, justified on a series of economic, political and social arguments, came to occupy a vital, deeply embedded position in the development of mass audiovisual electronic network communication across the countries of the EU.

CHALLENGES TO STATE INFLUENCE IN EUROPEAN ELECTRONIC NETWORK COMMUNICATION

Since the beginning of the 1980s, the unique traditional structure of telecommunications across western Europe was gradually and irrevocably changed and with it the role and significance of the public sector in its governance. However, such fundamental developments merely altered, rather than diminished, the influence of states in this part of the communications sector. As a consequence, classic post-World War II interventionist behaviour has gradually given way to activity which has come to be associated with the 'competition state' (Cerny 1997) on the one hand and the regulatory state (Moran 2002, 2003) on the other. This has involved, *inter alia*, a gradual waning of governance through public ownership to be replaced by market liberalisation and (at least partial) privatisation and governance through the establishment of independent regulatory authorities. It is also exemplified in the growth of an 'international competitive consciousness' amongst states in telecommunications manifest in somewhat neo-mercantilistic strategies of competitive emulation through domestic sectoral reorganisation and re-regulation.

A number of important factors have played a complex and interrelated role in what has become widely accepted as a wholesale transformation in telecommunications, most notably, technological change, the impact internationally of domestic telecommunications reforms instigated in the US, international market and regulatory competition, economic globalisation, the growing acceptance of neo-liberal ideology promulgated in the first instance by the US and the UK and institutional reorganisation at the domestic (in the form of re-regulation) and EU levels (in the form of significant, though by no means wholesale, Europeanisation of policy and regulation) (see Humphreys and Simpson 2005).

TECHNOLOGICAL CHANGE AND COMMERCIAL OPPORTUNITY IN TELECOMMUNICATIONS

As noted above, a broadly similar structure characterised the telecommunications sectors of western European states despite the fact that their political systems and industrial policy traditions and practices were often markedly different (Webber and Holmes 1985). However, a wave of technological change impacted on the sector, radically altering the ways in which telecommunications traffic could be transmitted and received and leading to the emergence and growth of new industrial and commercial spheres most notably in satellite and mobile communications. Arguably even more transformational in its impact was the digitisation of telecommunications signals which facilitated the expansion of telecommunications terminal equipment to include computers. In this way, a whole new array of commercial end user services, known as Value Added Network Services (VANS), incorporating voice, numerical data and text largely, but with the potential to add video images to this gamut, became possible. With the emergence of multimedia communications technologies and associated services of this kind, epitomised eventually by those available through the Internet, the historical distinction between one-to-one and mass communications – the essential difference between telecommunications and broadcasting – has been eroded gradually (see discussion later in this chapter). This period of technological disruption in the once stable, even stagnant, telecommunications sector, called forth a fundamental questioning of the structure of telecommunications provision across western Europe, and with it the role of the public sector. Such a challenge emerged from a number of disparate quarters. A range of companies from, notably, both computing hardware and software production (particularly those of the US in the first instance) and cable television supply began to press to be allowed to become players in what was still a highly restrictive telecommunications service supply market (Humphreys and Simpson 1996). On the demand side, increasingly vocal multinational corporate business users – both individually and through national and EU peak level representative associations – expressed frustration at the lack of availability of reasonably priced, good quality, new VANS, the provision of which they were aware was technically feasible and, they considered, essential to facilitate their ambitions of international expansion in an era of growing economic globalisation.

Two other important sources of calls for change to the way European telecommunications was structured came from quarters that might be described as 'outside observers' of the sector. For business analysts and economists, it became increasingly clear that technological changes occurring in telecommunications and their (potential) consequences were altering the market structure parameters of the sector. Whilst there was some questioning of whether fixed link voice telecommunications was still the (near) 'natural monopoly' of old, a debate which is to a considerable extent still unresolved today, a much more convincing argument contended that the market for VANS was readily contestable and could sustain competition. This argument was reinforced by the knowledge that the PTT incumbents had little or no experience in providing services which utilised converging computing and telecommunications technologies, or indeed mobile and satellite communications services.

Finally, the telecommunications sector through most of the 1980s and 1990s became something of a 'cause celebre' for those parties promulgating economic policy underpinned by neo-liberal ideology. This had both a 'philosophical' and a highly practical dimension. The former extolled the benefits of domestic and global free market competition, withdrawal of the state from direct intervention in industry through privatisation and the creation of independent regulatory authorities to oversee free market competition in conjunction with the judicial system's enforcement of general competition law. As applied to telecommunications, which eventually became widely viewed as a tailor-made case for such reform, this first became manifest in the US in the 1980s when, in the time of the 'new Right' Reagan administration, the US Department of Justice made a decision which allowed IBM to enter the telecommunications market. In a second important ruling, it concluded a case which had been brought by MCI against the US telecommunications giant AT&T to the effect that the latter was permitted to diversify into data processing. In return, AT&T was divested in 1984 of its regional telephone companies. These companies were required to provide other long-distance carriers, competing alongside AT&T, with interconnection rights. The US government also opened to limited domestic and international competition the market for telecommunications equipment. This new, rapid infusion of competition into the US market affected operators and equipment manufacturers alike who now sought, with increased motivation, international market share to compensate for a tougher domestic competition climate (Hills 1986). They were aided in this goal by the US government, which robustly argued for open and reciprocal telecommunications market access to be granted to US firms, particular in those countries with which it ran a telecommunications trade deficit (Dyson and Humphreys 1990).

In Europe, the kinds of ideas and policies being promoted by the US unsurprisingly gained most enthusiasm from the neo-liberal Thatcher administration (1979-90) in the UK which, through the 1980s, developed and implemented a radical and controversial series of policy changes aimed at putting neo-liberal principles – such as injecting competition into markets and privatising state-owned concerns - into practice. The telecommunications sector had come under the light of scrutiny before the IBM and AT&T court decisions in the US, though these and other changes outlined above provided further support for, and impetus to, change in the UK. Though a very different sector from the US in history and structure, the UK government undertook a series of measures aimed at the same result, namely a liberalised re-regulated domestic telecommunications market. Nonetheless, the first steps in this direction were rather limited. The telecommunications arm of the UK PTT was hived off from that providing postal services and was renamed British Telecom. A second operator, Mercury Communications, ensured the less-than-radical replacement of monopoly by duopoly in the UK voice telephonic market. In 1984, a further move in the neo-liberal direction was taken with the privatisation of BT, though this was only a partial, albeit a majority, share offering. At the same time, and arguably more radically, competition was introduced into the market for VANS and mobile telephony and, very significantly, and independent national regulatory authority, the Office of Telecommunications (Oftel) was created to regulate the evolving competitive market. These changes taken together, particularly the latter, marked the beginning of a radical departure from the traditional state-led model of telecommunications governance developed across western Europe for most of the 20th century.

The changes wrought by the US–UK neo-liberal policy axis in telecommunications soon gained the attention of governments on the European continent (Morgan and Webber 1986). Whilst there were (in some cases deep) ideological misgivings about the adoption of neo-liberal practices and the relinquishment of a statist approach to the communications sector, the apparent practical benefits which were accruing to the UK sector – in terms of service   innovation   and   quality,   inward   investment   and   economic competitiveness – proved significant in leading to an opportunistically motivated consideration of policy change (see Humphreys 2002). Allied to this, a perception grew, heavily promulgated by advocates of change from political and business circles that, in the face of a globalising economy, states which did not engage with the perceived international market imperatives of globalisation – deregulation, state withdrawal and open competition – would be locked out of the benefits of late 20th century capitalism. As a consequence, in telecommunications at least, something of a process of competitive liberalising re-regulation (Humphreys and Simpson 1996) spread quite quickly across the economies of much of western Europe, in the process radically altering the role of the state in electronic network communications.

Many of the consequent changes were broadly in line with those being enacted by the US–UK policy 'vanguard'. However, the particular political and institutional characteristics of EU Member States had a determining effect on the exact nature of policy change in telecommunications, as well as its timing (see Hulsink 1999) illustrating the refractive role which states have been able to play in communications in an era of globalisation (see Thatcher 1999; Humphreys 1990, 1992) in which (and despite the fact that) the prevailing economic trends have been vaunted as inevitable and unstoppable. In France, for example, very little liberalisation of any real substance occurred in the 1980s, apart from in the provision of VANS. Though telecommunications equipment players, notably Alcatel, had begun to develop an international market orientation, the French PTT, the DGT, maintained a monopolistic grip on voice and (most) data services and practised a protectionist equipment procurement policy (Thatcher 1999). Whilst in Germany too there was, in the 1980s, considerable pressure for liberalising telecommunications reform, this was diluted in classic corporatist policy deliberations which ensued, resulting merely in liberalisation of telecommunications terminal equipment and VANS markets, with voice telephony services and control of the fixed link telecommunications infrastructure remaining in the hands of the German PTT (Humphreys 1992).

However, in the 1990s, telecommunications liberalisation and with it a mutation of the 'paternalistic' state into the 'competition state', proceeded remarkably swiftly across continental European EU states. A key reason for this was a gradual change of view of the incumbent telecommunications operators (PTTs), which were beginning to awake to the potential domestic and international revenue-generating possibilities to be pursued in a globally liberalised telecommunications market. There was also the distinct concern about possibly trailing in the wake of earlier liberalised and internationally oriented competitors from the US and the UK, which were already gaining experience of the rigours of market competition. However, three important quid pro quos lay in the strategic reorientation necessary to benefit from these opportunities. First, it would be necessary to become at least a partly privatised company fully engaged with the ethos and practices of market competition. Second, in the first instance at least, it would be necessary to set up international alliances with fellow competitors to deliver the kinds of ambitious global-reach services being demanded by multinational business telecommunications users. Finally, and most painfully, the ticket price for entry into the global telecommunications 'game' would be the abandonment of domestic market protectionism and foreclosure wherever it was perceived to exist by one's competitor countries.

It was highly significant that this *volte face* was evident in two of the EU's most important economic and political entities, France and Germany. As Humphreys and Simpson (2005, p.34) point out '[o]nce these two countries had swung their weight behind further liberalisation, the centre of gravity among the Member States shifted significantly, constraining others to follow suit, and allowing the [European] Commission to press on with its reform at the European level'. Thus, in other EU Member States, noted in the 1980s for the expression of distinct reluctance to structural alteration of telecommunications, there was evidence of change. In Italy, public telephone companies began to develop an international orientation (Natalicchi 2001), as did those of Spain and Portugal (Jordana et al. 2003). Furthermore, the accession to the EU in the mid-1990s of Sweden and Finland, countries with liberal telecommunications regimes, considerably bolstered the 'reformist contingent' of Member States. Aside from the sector-specific issues in telecommunications, these fundamental changes can be explained by a broader embrace of the idea that a globalising world economy necessitated domestic structural reforms broadly along the lines of partial or full privatisation of industries (and indeed other activities traditionally under the aegis of the state), re-regulation, and domestic and international market liberalisation. However, as Viven Schmidt (1996a, 1996b) has noted, the detailed implementation of this essentially neo-liberal orthodoxy evidences considerable variety, particularly across western Europe, explicable by domestic political-institutional factors. The robustness of domestic idiosyncrasies of this kind was evident even in the face of another powerful force for homogenisation – the Europeanisation of telecommunications governance.

EUROPEANISATION OF TELECOMMUNICATIONS GOVERNANCE

The early 1980s witnessed the emergence of telecommunications as a policy area of growing significance for the EU. For a sector which was so nationally rooted historically, the Europeanisation of telecommunications policy has become another remarkable dimension of the fundamental changes affecting this part of electronic network communications and acted as the spur to (attempted) change elsewhere within it (see below). From an academic perspective, the Europeanisation of any policy area is significant from two broad dimensions. First, the process, if extensive enough, can result in significant developments at the EU level itself. Here, it is important to consider the influence which Member States are able to exert to ensure that their policy preferences are incorporated into agreed EU policy, as opposed to those of other Member States, but also EU institutional actors, notably the European Commission, as well as, increasingly, an array of individual and 'collective' actors from business and civil society quarters. Second, the success of any EU policy is contingent on the extent to which it is implemented at the national Member State level. In this case, a vital consideration is the extent to which States feel it necessary, and are able, to adapt the prescriptions of EU legislative activity to suit their domestic institutional environments and practices.

In the case of EU telecommunications policy, both of these issues have been to a very considerable extent overshadowed by the vital structural techno-economic constituents of change in the sector, in particular economic globalisation. Indeed, a key issue in the literature on European telecommunications policy has been the extent to which the EU as a political-institutional construct has been a determining influence on the course of policy development. Some, such as Thatcher (2004), have downplayed the importance of the EU compared to other factors, especially national Member State preferences. It has been argued that the EU at most acted in partnership with states (Thatcher 2001a), carefully ensuring that its liberalising reform measures were not only in line with state preferences but were synchronised to the pace of change at the national level. By contrast, others such as Schneider and Werle (1990) and Sandholtz (1993, 1998) have argued that the EU institutional level, in particular through the role exerted by the European Commission, has been essential in driving the agenda of change forward in telecommunications.

Both these perspectives in their different ways highlight the importance of accounting for the role of the EU in situations of globalising or global techno-economic activity, something which is essential in examining the emerging governance of the Internet economy. In telecommunications, a sector which has developed an increasingly global 'consciousness' from its traditionally inward-looking national roots, a complex relationship has evolved between the national and the EU levels in which both contexts have been able to exert and sustain influence often – at various points of policy development, transposition and implementation – in tension with one another. On the one hand, the EU has been able to exert influence on the course of telecommunications at the supranational level. This has been evident in its use of coercive measures at key junctures, exercised through the strong powers of enforcement it possesses in the area of competition policy. This has been applied both to open markets deemed illegally uncompetitive and to make judgements on key proposed corporate reorganisations (in the shape of mergers and acquisitions) in the sector. In a different, though no less important manner, the EU through the European Commission, has aimed to move forward telecommunications reform by more subtle methods. Once telecommunications was targeted as a new area of policy development, the Commission employed a varied mix of strategies to bolster and cement a new regulatory framework across its Member States in which the EU institutional level would play an important role. It is important not to mistake elements of these actions by the Commission as it merely riding the crest of the liberalisation wave, since, as noted above, states at one and the same time were neither convinced of the need for broadly similar levels of liberalisation, let alone on a timetable for its EU-wide realisation. It is also important to note that, as early as the mid-1980s, for example, the Commission was taking great pains to point out the threat to the EU from its main trading competitors, the US and Japan (European Commission 1984), which were attempting to capitalise on techno-economic change in the sector, albeit in different ways, a proselytising role which has continued throughout the development of its telecommunications policy and is reflected in recent policy pronouncements on Internet commerce. The Commission has also acted as a key point of contact for governmental and other interested parties. It has launched, at strategically important junctures of policy development, reviews of existing agreements, in the process 'naming and shaming' states which were slow to comply with agreements made, as well as consultation exercises with the aim of promoting a subsequent step change in liberalisation.

Nonetheless, the significantly intergovernmental nature of the EU is such that it would have been impossible to make EU Member States agree on the creation of such an extensive liberalisation framework were it not deemed to be in their individual interests, on balance. Thus, the EU level in telecommunications proved attractive to Member States, albeit for a range of different reasons. For those in the vanguard of the liberalisation process, the EU was an institutional platform to promote the neo-liberal reform agenda and increase the chances of its acceptance in other Member States. For others, the EU level represented a way of taking advantage of the commercial possibilities of new telecommunications through gaining access to international markets, not just within, but also beyond, the EU, as well as securing the preservation of key public service goals which were strongly held and encapsulated in universal service. For smaller EU Member States, telecommunications liberalisation presented the opportunity of infrastructure modernisation, service enhancement and multiplier inward investment, notwithstanding the threat to their indigenous telecommunications suppliers.

Thus, as Humphreys and Simpson (2005, p. 64) argue, EU 'policy activity resulted in mostly deliberative, rarely coercive, transfers of ideas and practices in which resigned acceptance of the new realities of telecommunications mixed with proactive intentions to capitalise on its new commercial opportunities were evident'. This has occurred primarily since the

European Commission has aimed to secure agreement with, and consensus between, Member States on the various stages and associated timing of EU telecommunications policy development.

The practical consequence of the emergence and growth of EU telecommunications policy has been, by any comparable standards, remarkable. A steady growth of EU policy-making competence in the telecommunications arena has emerged from the late 1980s onwards. The early attempted liberalising moves to open up the market for telecommunications terminal equipment (European Commission 1988) and VANS (European Commission 1990) were the most controversial points in the history of EU telecommunications policy, reflective of the fact that a significant number of Member States (largely the 'southern' EU states plus Belgium) were contemplating the idea of reform of their role in telecommunications with reluctance, whilst a pro-liberalisation lobby (led by the UK and the Dutch but also containing more 'moderate' reformers such as Germany) wished to push the agenda forward swiftly and had, in the case of the UK, already gone further down the road of liberalisation than the mandate of either of these two measures. The 'political spice' in this mix was provided by the European Commission, which, aware of the loggerhead which existed and bolstered with tacit support from the 'reformist camp', aimed to issue the directives conveying the proposed liberalisation directly into force, bypassing the normal Council of Ministers route, and justifying its action through reference to article 86 (formerly article 90) of the Treaty of Rome, which, it argued, gave it the right to take appropriate action to remove instances of unfair competition in markets where public undertakings (in this case PTTs) had been granted special rights (see Schmidt, S. 1996; Thatcher 2001a).

The outcome of this period was a classic EU compromise negotiated through a period when the 'traditionalists' changed into 'reluctant liberalisers'. The constituents of the compromise (which became known as the Open Network Provision compromise) were the passage of the two directives with the concession that Member States could impose public service obligations on private service providers using leased lines from the public infrastructure (Woolcock et al. 1992, p.69) and the simultaneous agreement on a framework directive on Open Network Provision which laid the ground for a raft of further specific directives. Some of these (notably in the areas of licensing and interconnection) set out the rules for a uniformly functioning, liberalised EU market in the areas to which they pertained. Others, notably those related to universal service, established and protected at EU level the public service elements which had traditionally underpinned telecommunications nationally and which were still considered as much a priority as new liberalising measures by many Member States. Finally, this period in EU telecommunications witnessed a recognition of the importance of the European Commission in telecommunications policy with affirmation by the European Court of Justice of its right to use article 86 as a consequence of two separate legal challenges – to the terminal equipment and VANS directives respectively – from the 'Southern' camp[1] prior to the agreement of the ONP compromise.

In the 1990s, the further Europeanisation of telecommunications proceeded apace within a framework of liberalising re-regulation. Though there were occasional sticking points regarding the exact mechanics and timing of the process and the extent of the EU's regulatory role (see Humphreys and Simpson 2005), EU institutional involvement in telecommunications expanded significantly. What has emerged in governance terms is something of a (not necessarily equal) partnership in which an international, that is EU-wide, regulatory framework has been devised at the European level and implemented nationally, a process which is still very much ongoing and evolving. A key juncture occurred in the 1992–94 period when EU Member States, after a period of consultation and negotiation, decided to complete the EU-wide liberalisation of all telecommunications services, the most notable inclusion in this respect being voice telephony .

The following year, spurred on by the conclusions of the Bangemann Report (European Commission 1994) on the position of Europe in the emerging global Information Society (IS), Member States resolved to create EU-wide liberalisation of all telecommunications infrastructure in order to complement their 2003 Resolution, the date for both to occur set at 1 January 2008 (European Council of Ministers 1994). To enable the onset of a completely liberalised EU market in telecommunications a clutch of directives was passed in mid-1990s on voice telephony; mobile communications, satellite communications, cable television, authorisations and licences, interconnection and universal service (see Humphreys and Simpson 2005). This quite unprecedented and detailed package became known as the '1998 Framework'. Its transposition and early implementation, closely monitored and reviewed by the European Commission, gave a strong flavour of how telecommunications governance had been altered across the EU in a relatively short period of time. In particular, it highlighted the changing specifics of the role of the state in this part of electronic communications network governance as the 21st century began. Here it was clear that state influence, though exercised differently, remained very important in European telecommunications governance. Specifically, the old 'corporate state' interventionist patterns were being replaced by new regulatory state structures and practices, themselves of a very interventionist nature. EU telecommunications policy also provided evidence of the emergence of regulatory state activity at the European level; in other words, the growth of the European regulatory state (Majone 1996). Thus, whilst markets were liberalised (albeit to varying degrees depending on the type of the telecommunications market and the state in question) the number of rules necessary to nurture and ensure the mandated degree of competition was often high (Levi-Faur 1999) – (often tightly) managed competition had replaced state-controlled monopoly and oligopoly.

Similarly, the legal framework for telecommunications governance gave considerable implementation scope to Member States. The vital role played by National Regulatory Authorities illustrates the pains taken to deliver subsidiarity in this policy area. As a consequence, though EU Member States have reorganised their telecommunications sectors along broadly similar lines, the detailed mechanics of the EU-wide liberalised telecommunications market exhibited clear differences across Member States. Historic national political-institutional structures, cultures and practices have ensured the kind of path dependence that has contributed to an idiosyncratic implementation of EU legislation. This has been to some extent enabled by the predominant use of the directive at EU level, the spirit and substance of which must be transposed into national Member State law before implementation, thereby giving considerable scope for latitude in interpretation of meaning.

Examples of this pattern of behaviour are abundantly evident in EU Member State-'reformed' telecommunications policies. They relate to issues such as the ability of the Member State to transpose speedily and implement legislation which has been agreed, differing outcomes evident according to whether federal or more centrist political systems exist, as well as to the political hue of the dominant party at any particular time. Equally significant has been the relationship between government and the set of National Regulatory Authorities established for telecommunications where concerns have been expressed over the influence exercised by the former over the latter. Another example relates to the degree of privatisation of the incumbent (where national governments have often held significant minority stakes and have rarely followed the UK first-mover model of [eventual] complete sell-off); licensing strategies; and local loop unbundling (see Humphreys and Simpson 2005, Ch. 4). This is clearly reflective of the robustness and individuality of the national level regulatory state across the EU, even in a situation where a common governance perspective and commensurate set of regulations have been agreed.

MOVING BEYOND THE REGULATORY STATE – FURTHER REFORM OF TELECOMMUNICATIONS AT THE EU LEVEL

Nonetheless, as the 1998 framework 'bedded down' and European-wide competition became 'normalised', the key question arose regarding if, when and how the tight grip of the regulatory state might be loosened. This, essentially a telecommunications debate, became enmeshed in the second burning communications policy question of the late 20th and early 21st century, namely the often complex regulatory implications of the convergence between broadcasting, the Internet and telecommunications. The convergence debate and its ramifications for EU policy for broadcasting and the Internet are dealt with in the remaining parts of this chapter. In terms of telecommunications, the main upshot was a proposal, emanating from a European Commission review and consultation exercise (European Commission 1999) conducted in the light of the 1997 Green Paper on convergence (European Commission 1997a), to create a new regulatory framework for electronic communications. Though the name is suggestive of a comprehensively convergent regulatory approach to the whole of electronic network communications (and even beyond), the subsequently agreed Electronic Communications Regulatory Framework (ECRF) was very much telecommunications-focused in terms of services, albeit rather more 'across the board' in terms of communications infrastructures (that is, it covered networks and infrastructures used for broadcasting, the Internet and telecommunications).

Its first and main consequence was a legislative streamlining of the existing 1998 Framework, through a very significant reduction in the number of legislative measures from 20 to 6. In terms of communications infrastructures, the approach was to be technology-neutral across all fixed and mobile communications networks, even those utilised for terrestrial broadcasting. Second, and thought to be highly significant for the growth of Internet use in the EU, a new recommendation to unbundle the telecommunications local loop, a major impediment to competition and customer access, was put forward which subsequently became a regulation (European Parliament and Council 2000a), and by definition did not require transposition into Member State legislatures, reflecting the urgency with which the need to eradicate this perceived problem was viewed (see Chapter 5). Third, the ECRF proposals were underpinned by the quest to find areas of communications regulation in which the EU and its Member States' regulatory grip could be relaxed. Taken to its ultimate conclusion, this could mean the replacement of ex ante regulation, the classic embodiment of the regulatory state in an era of globalisation, by general EU competition law (Humphreys and Simpson 2005). This element of the ECRF could be seen as the first sign of EU and national policy-makers wishing to move beyond the regulatory state in electronic communications, a theme which, as we explore later in this book, resonates in the EU's treatment of Internet Commerce governance, expressed nevertheless in a different way. It is also significant to note that the 1999 Communications Review consultation mentioned the possible use of self-regulation, something which would have been considered heretical to refer to with regard to telecommunication only a decade previously.

The legislative highlights of the ECRF, which became operational across EU Member state in July 2003, were the creation of a competition directive (European Parliament and Council 2002a) to subsume all the existing telecommunications liberalisation measures of the 1998 Framework, partnered by the 2000 regulation on local loop unbundling (European Parliament and Council 2000a) as the liberalisation 'duo' of the ECRF. On the harmonisation side of the package, a general framework directive (European Parliament and Council 2002b) accompanied four others on, respectively, access and interconnection (European Parliament and Council 2002c), authorisation (European Parliament and Council 2002d), universal service (European Parliament and Council 2002e), and data protection and privacy (European Parliament and Council 2002f).

BROADCASTING, STRUCTURAL CHANGE AND THE ROLE OF THE ROLE OF THE STATE

Though different in the specifics of their operation, the predominance of public service broadcasting systems (PSB) across the vast majority of EU states – Luxembourg being the exception – underpinned by the features outlined earlier in this chapter and ensured that, even in situations where broadcasters with a PSB remit garnered their revenue from commercial advertising as well as licence fee payment, the system in which they operated did not develop into an overwhelmingly market oriented one (Humphreys 1996, p. 120). The relationship between public service broadcasters and the state has naturally been an important and often contradictory one. Whilst there is considerable evidence, in certain cases, of state intervention in the system, for example in the appointment of the membership of broadcasting regulatory bodies, it is important to note that the kind of 'direct' state intervention which characterised the organisation of western Europe's telecommunications systems was largely absent. Broadcasters themselves have had the delicate and often difficult task of trying to be at one and the same time as independent as possible from the political establishment and yet politically accountable in the content that they provide to viewers (Humphreys 1996, p. 121).

Thus, whilst qualitatively different to the historic situations in the telecommunications sector, until the 1980s terrestrial broadcasting systems across most of the EU tended to be dominated by public interest goals, detached (to varying degrees) state paternalism and heavily circumscribed competition in which the pursuit of excellence in programming was, for the most part, the driving force and where even most of the limited number of commercial broadcasters which existed were given clear public service remits. However, from around the 1980s onwards, the western European broadcasting system underwent a major upheaval which has contributed to its radical restructuring and with it a questioning of the significance of the role of the public interest considerations, if not the direct role of the state. In particular, as in telecommunications, the important structural pressures of technological change and economic internationalisation/globalisation called forth a thorough questioning of the structure and logic behind traditional systems.

Humphreys (1996, p. 160) suggests that the subsequent period of flux has exhibited six broad interrelated features. First, there has been pressure to liberalise the sector through the licensing of new privately owned commercial operators. Second, there has been pressure to delimit or even absent these new commercial broadcasters from having to take on public service obligations. Third, the emergence of new satellite technology in broadcasting called into question the efficacy of national systems of regulation which could increasingly be circumvented effectively through internationalised, that is cross-border, broadcasting taking advantage of 'regulatory arbitrage' opportunities between EU states. Fourth, the broadcasting viewer came to be considered more and more as a consumer, as opposed to a citizen with communications needs and rights. Fifth, broadcasting has come to be viewed by those with an interest in promoting commercialisation as a 'run of the mill' economic sector, as opposed to the special economic case outlined earlier in this chapter. Technological change has had an important facilitatory role in this argument since the emergence of fibre optic cable, satellite and then digital technology (which touches terrestrial, satellite and cable broadcasting systems) expanded hugely the number of television channels available. This considerable extra capacity undermined the traditional view of public service broadcasting as being the best solution available in a technologically constrained low bandwidth environment. The cross-border potential of broadcasting, in tandem with its liberalisation through commercialisation, led to the emergence of media companies with international commercial ambitions. These companies, such as those owned by Rupert Murdoch and Silvio Berlusconi, were keen to develop further their international cross-media interests raising both domestic and international competition concerns across Europe. Sixth, all these trends have inevitably called forth a fundamental re-evaluation of the role of traditional PSB in western European polities. A key related issue here is if not whether, then how, the PSB remit might be delivered in a multi-channel era of capacity abundance and potential system flexibility.

The effects of these pressures for change in broadcasting across western Europe in the 1980s and 1990s were dramatic. In their analysis of the structure and characteristics of national systems between 1980 and 1990, Brants and Siune (1993, p.104) illustrate clearly an infusion of commercialism in the sector. By 1990, the 41 predominantly public service television channels of the 17 western European countries studied had been joined by 36 new commercial stations, most of which were delivered through the newly deployed direct broadcasting by satellite systems. Perhaps even more significant, pure public monopoly broadcast systems (i.e. financed solely by licence fee levy) had disappeared by 1990 to be replaced by mixed revenue systems (where public broadcasters gain revenue from licence fees and commercial advertising) or, more in evidence, dual systems (made up of a combination of pure and mixed revenue public broadcasters and private commercial broadcasters).

THE EU AND BROADCASTING POLICY

To what extent did the structural pressures of technological change and globalisation create a fertile ground for the development of a broadcasting policy by the EU in the way that helped to transform the telecommunications part of the electronic communications sector in western Europe? Whilst the EU had begun to develop a broadcasting policy since the mid-1980s both its coverage and influence have been considerably more modest than in the telecommunications case. The area where the EU, and specifically the European Commission, have been most active in the audiovisual sphere is in competition policy. The considerable commercialisation and intra-European (more limited) internationalisation of broadcasting provided opportunity to, and arguably made it incumbent upon, the powerful Competition Directorate-General of the European Commission to intervene where deemed necessary.

The policy backdrop to this activity was the initiative, launched by the EU in the mid-1980s, to create a Single European Market (SEM), something which was deemed to require considerable legislative readjustment at national and EU levels in order to free up the markets for goods, services, labour and capital across the EU (European Commission 1985).

In broadcasting, this became manifest as the Television Without Frontiers directive (European Council of Ministers 1989). In the area of competition policy, Commission activity has had two noteworthy dimensions, reflective of the changing nature of broadcasting across its territories. On the one hand, it has targeted the (proposed) commercial activity of new service providers, notably, on two occasions, ruling against attempts by an alliance of German companies – Bertelsmann, Kirch and Deutsche Telekom – to establish a digital pay television consortium (Pauwels 1998). This proposed enterprise, with clear ICT convergence characteristics, was ruled out on the grounds of its potential effects on market share in the areas of television programme rights, conditional access and cable TV (Humphreys 1996). On the other hand, the Competition DG of the Commission has scrutinised closely the behaviour of public broadcasting companies, on occasion upholding the complaints of commercial broadcasters about the privileged access to programme rights that their public service broadcaster counterparts were afforded (see Collins 1994). In particular, it has been argued that these broadcasters gaining their revenue from a combination of licence fees and commercial activity might fall foul of EU Treaty rules on unfair state aid (European Commission 2001a). Very importantly, however, these attempted moves by the EU into regulation of PSB provoked a strong defensive reaction from Member States, which to a much greater extent than in telecommunications, continued to guard their right to regulate PSB at the national level. As a consequence, the Commission has had to tread more carefully, acknowledging the primacy of subsidiarity in this area whilst not conceding its right to comment on specific cases (European Commission 2001a).

The difficulty faced by the EU in establishing a strong policy presence in the domain of mass electronic communications regulation is further underlined by its failed attempts to develop a policy on media pluralism. This area proved too controversial for Member States to concede any policy leverage to the EU level. A 1996 draft directive on media pluralism provoked strong disagreement over its proposed way of measuring market concentration (see Harcourt 2005) and a subsequently remodelled 1997 draft directive under the label of media ownership was too broadly defined and (thus) potentially ineffectual to secure agreement, eventually being shelved (see Michalis 1999) and is unlikely, at the time of writing, to be reactivated as a policy initiative.

The experience of the EU in these core areas of broadcasting illustrate how significant the state, working at the national level, still remains in the regulation of broadcasting, despite experiencing quite similar kinds of structural pressures in terms of technological change and internationalisation as those affecting telecommunications. It is clear that the much exaggerated, potentially homogenising, effect of internationalisation/globalisation was to be resisted with considerably greater force by states in the broadcasting domain, blunting any appetite to transfer, even partially, control in the regulation of broadcasting content to the international level through the EU. This was illustrated to powerful effect in the late 1990s when, as noted in the previous section, the EU Commission proposed to Member States that they reconsider the regulation of electronic communications in the light of convergent trends in technology and markets.

CONVERGENCE IN THE COMMUNICATIONS SECTOR AND EU POLICY RESPONSES

As noted above, the late 1990s witnessed a debate at EU level on the governance and, specifically, the regulatory implications, of the apparently inexorable convergence of ICT. Deliberations on the impact of technological convergence on the communications sector were nothing new, since one of the major structural and commercial opportunity-creating changes in telecommunications was the convergence between computing and communications technologies, heralding the growth of new VANS, but also vastly improving the speed and efficiency of traffic routing through the development of fully electronic switching. Indeed, the French even referred to this convergence through coining a new term, 'telematique' (telematics). In the early 1990s, breakthroughs in the ability to digitise broadcast signals created further potential scope for convergence and led to a consideration of the extent to which broadcasting and telecommunications services might be delivered simultaneously across a range of fixed-link and airwave-based infrastructures. That digitisation now cast its 'cloak' across the spectrum of electronic network communications meant that IT products and services – for example, computer games – could be delivered across broadcasting and telecommunications networks thus calling into question traditional boundaries between the sectors (Beat Graber 2004). These technological and commercial developments emerged around the same time as, and significantly influenced, deliberations on the IS which reflected the increasing pervasiveness of ICT in the social and economic of life of the EU and beyond. The growth of, and expectations around, the Internet, which epitomised many of the convergent trends in technologies and services, added to the sense that a burgeoning series of techno-economic developments necessitated, at the very least, a review of the current regulatory arrangements – specifically the regulatory barriers – between broadcasting, the Internet, IT and telecommunications. A core aspect of this, from the perspective of the European Commission, was the possibility of creating an EU regulatory framework 'à la telecommunications', to cater for convergence (Simpson 1999).

However, the 1997 consultation Green Paper on convergence launched by the Commission (European Commission 1997a) illustrated the very considerable differences of opinion which existed among a range of interests with a stake in converging ICT environments on whether, let alone how, convergence should be dealt with at the EU level. In an effort to move the agenda forward in a way that it had done successfully in its 1992 Telecommunications Review (European Commission 1992), the Commission presented Member States with three possible ways in which to deal with convergence. These options ranged from inaction through to a comprehensive overhaul of existing arrangements to create a new common regulatory framework for all communications networks and services (European Commission 1997a). As in the 1992 review, the Commission did markedly more than present a series of possibilities to its policy constituencies, expressing as it did a discernibly clear preference for the most radical of the three options (Humphreys 1999).

The controversy surrounding the Green Paper in essence centred around the potential regulatory treatment of communications content which, in broadcasting – where it originated overwhelmingly – as noted above, was covered by highly specific regulation in order to pursue and maintain the key public interest goals around pluralism and universality of access (Humphreys 1996). Broadcasting also has developed important characteristics associated with nation states and often regions within them, notably of a cultural and linguistic kind.

It soon became clear to those wishing to push forward the creation of a convergence regulatory framework within the European Commission (principally policy architects within the (then) IS and Competition Directorates-General) that the impediments to the inclusion of content issues were two-fold and substantial – and in this case insurmountable – in nature. First, despite the impact of the structural factors of technological change and globalisation, at the end of the 1990s there were still very strong pressures to maintain broadcasting regulation separate from that applied to other parts of the communications sector, notwithstanding the fact that broadcasting had, as shown above, become much more commercialised since the beginning of the 1980s. Second, it also became clear, even in those Member States which had shown some penchant for re-regulating in a more convergent way at the national level – notably the UK but also Italy – that there was little or no willingness to see issues related to the regulation of communications content within a more convergent ICT governance paradigm dealt with at the EU level (see Levy 1997, 1999; Simpson 2000).

By contrast, there was considerably more enthusiasm for creating a common regulatory framework for communications infrastructures. Since it was now perfectly feasible for content to be carried across the array of communications network infrastructures, the chosen approach was to modify the application of the 1998 telecommunications framework to extend its application to broadcast networks, even those used primarily for the carriage of public service content. As noted above, this approach eventually yielded the 2002 Electronic Communications Regulatory Framework. The logic of the policy decision was that all communications services outside of voice telephony and VANS – both considered to be private communications in the traditional telecommunications sense – were to be excluded from the ECRF. Nonetheless, the apparently straightforward separation of content issues from carriage issues either ignored – for reasons of political expediency-or was ignorant of, the complexities of the relationship between public interest issues in broadcasting and network access in the digital multimedia era. It further underestimated developments in telecommunications VANS (in the broadest sense) which, though delivered direct to the private user, could be argued to have content concerns akin to those historically covered by broadcasting.

The idea of delivering a suite of content-laden electronic services to the end-user is a classic embodiment of the richness and flexibility pursued and demanded in new multimedia information and communications environments. However, it creates the clear possibility of blurring the distinction between private and 'public interest' communications services. For example, it is now technically and commercially possible to receive television broadcasts on mobile phones, something likely to become more and more popular and (thus) pervasive in the future. But will such provision be classified as broadcasting, VANS or advanced mobile 'video telephony'?

THE CONVERGENCE DEBATE AND THE EU'S REGULATORY TREATMENT OF THE INTERNET

Whilst the debate over broadcasting within a possible convergent regulatory model of electronic communications at EU level took centre stage in the late 1990s, the convergence policy deliberations were also highly significant for their consideration of the possibilities for including the Internet in any new framework. Indeed, there was no little irony in the fact that the rather modest ECRF merely covered Internet infrastructural (principally access) issues, for in the convergence Green Paper the Commission highlighted the Internet as the blazon of convergent trends in ICT (European Commission 1997a). What then explains the exclusion of Internet-related matters from the agreed package? The obvious 'surface' explanation is that the ECRF deals with communications infrastructure (and infrastructural services) and thus this automatically excludes the burgeoning array of Internet services, termed 'Information Society' services by the EU, since these are content-rich.

   A deeper examination yields a two-fold explanation related, first and primarily, to the nature of the Internet and its governance and, second, to the institutional fabric of the European Commission. The Internet, though having emerged and developed within the socio-technical culture of the US computing and academic communities, clearly has global reach characteristics and potential. This, allied to the growing awareness of ability of the Internet to facilitate the development of an international e-marketplace and e-economy, meant that around the time of the EU's debate on convergence, an important series of deliberations were also occurring at the international level on how the Internet's key technical resources might be managed, as well as how the delivery of a mushrooming series of services to an increasingly enthusiastic cadre of online consumers might be governed. Though dominated, for obvious reasons, by the US governmental, technical and commercial constituencies, the EU, through the European Commission, did attempt, but with only moderate success, to play a part in the key policy decisions made around this time. These principally concerned the management of the Internet's key technical resources which deliver its system of naming and addressing, known as the Domain Name System (DNS) (see Chapter 4), for which the Internet Corporation of Assigned Names and Numbers (ICANN) was created in 1999 (see Mueller 2002).

   Within the institutional confines of the EU, the challenge for those Internet policy pioneers in Directorate General Information Society of the European Commission was that there was not wide enough appreciation, either within the rest of the Commission or across the EU as a whole, in the mid-1990s, of the commercial significance of the Internet (interview, European Commission, 2004). Most Member State governments and policy makers in the Commission itself had been concentrating their policy energies on other aspects of the communications sector, not least the radical re-regulation of telecommunications outlined above. It is important to note that they had, however, since the mid-1980s, been acutely aware of the need to build advanced electronic communications networks and provide new services across them on an interoperable EU-wide basis. However, research and development initiatives such as the RACE programme (see Sharp and Peterson 1998) provide evidence that this quantum leap into a new techno economic context was to be delivered through upgrading and replacement of the existing fixed-link telecommunications networks (Werle 2002). The debate on the IS conducted at EU level in the 1990s similarly stressed the need to deliver across the board telecommunications liberalisation as the key to the realisation of a flourishing IS and made only passing reference to the Internet (Bangemann Report 1994). It was only in the very late 1990s that the EU began to appreciate fully the relationship between telecommunications and Internet infrastructure with the Commission's rather urgent policy initiative on unbundling the local loop, by then recognised as a serious impediment to growth in Internet take up in the EU (European Parliament and Council 2000a). From this point on, the Internet occupied a central position in the minds of communications policy-makers at both the national and EU level as evidenced in the EU's eEurope initiative which had the Internet at the core of many of its policy goals (European Commission 2002) (see Chapter 5).

Thus the global gravitational pull of Internet governance (Humphreys and Simpson 2005) and the current unresolved uncertainties about how it should evolve (see Chapter 7), alongside the relatively poor understanding of the potential importance of the Internet for the EU in the mid to late 1990s, contributed very much to issues related to the regulation of Internet content remaining outside the ECRF agreed by EU Member States in 2002. The EU, has, however, aimed to deal with pressing issues of Internet governance outside of the ECRF's confines. In 2000, it attempted to address the issue of electronic commerce regulation through the enactment of a directive (European Parliament and Council 2000b), as well as other policy initiatives of an 'ancillary' nature (see Chapter 5). It has also launched and developed a system of governance for the first ever international TLD dot eu (European Parliament and Council 2002g) (see Chapter 4). The remainder of this book provides a detailed analysis of the EU's attempts to govern these important elements of the European electronic communications network economy. Finally, the EU has also aimed to deal with the regulation of illegal and harmful content on the Internet through prescribing a mixture of self-regulation by commercial providers and end-users underpinned, where necessary, by the legal system (Halpin and Simpson 2002).

CONCLUSION

This chapter has illustrated the changing role that the state has played in communications governance in the EU. The experiences of national Member States, and more recently those of the EU itself, in the traditional 'staples' of the communications sector, namely broadcasting and telecommunications, have played an important part in emerging governance approaches to newer policy areas in the electronic network domain, notably the Internet. As shown in this chapter, the role of the state has been vital in the evolution of communications governance across the EU. Original interventionist or 'positive' monopoly state ownership and provision of telecommunications has given way to regulatory state behaviour governing, at one remove at both the national Member State and the EU levels, a liberalised and globalising sector. Due to sensitive issues around the social and political power of mass communications media, juxtaposed with the avowed need to provide audiovisual content of various kinds as a right of citizenship, the state's role in broadcasting in Europe was equally distinct. Positive state interventionist tendencies were evident in the use of both state ownership and public funds in the provision of public service broadcasting. However, elements of the regulatory state arguably existed in traditional broadcasting through the provision of independent (from government) regulatory authorities (sometimes part of the public service broadcaster as in the case of the BBC's Board of Governors) to oversee the performance of broadcasters. As shown, unlike in telecommunications, despite extensive commercialisation and some internationalisation pressures, the traditional governance structures for broadcasting content – protective of national cultural, linguistic and political pluralism evident across the EU – have proved resistant to change on the whole, with the EU coming to play only a relatively minor role, occasional forays into competition policy issues notwithstanding.

The Internet and services delivered and consumed across it has provided a unique policy challenge for the EU and its Member States, not least because the Internet is an embodiment of convergence between the above two core elements of electronic communications. The creation of a governance framework within the EU for the Internet reflects, first, the challenges of resolving issues related to the regulation of content posted and hosted on, and exchanged across, electronic communications networks within the EU for commercial and social purposes. Second, it reflects the need to resolve a raft of often thorny global governance issues, many of which require (or could benefit from) having a united EU perspective to put forward in existing and newly emerging fora designed to deal with them. The unsatisfactory and temporary solution to these policy challenges has been to employ the EU as a policy negotiator in evolving deliberations on Internet governance, whilst, for the time being, as part of a 'wait and see' strategy, to keep Internet content regulation issues outside the ECRF agreed in 2002. This 'solution' has resulted in a number of EU Internet policy strands, some of the most important of which relate to issues of Internet commerce. It is to the nature of these, and their implications for the governance of the communications sector in Europe as a whole, to which the remainder of this book turns.

NOTES

1. The most vociferous members of which were France, Italy and Spain.

4. The dot eu Top Level Domain

The creation of the dot eu Top Level Domain (TLD) was seen as a facilitator for accelerating the growth of e-commerce in Europe within the wider e-Europe initiative agreed by the European Council in Lisbon in March 2000. The origins of the idea, however, were rooted in developments on Internet governance at the global level and the increasing importance of TLDs following the commercialisation of the Internet in the 1990s. The EU, although not a primary mover in the initial development of governance arrangements for the Internet, soon realised its economic and strategic significance and developed several policies to influence its direction, included as part of its broader Information and Communications Technologies (ICT) policy priorities.

One such policy in terms of the Internet Domain Name System (DNS) was the dot eu TLD initiative, a primary aim of which was to create greater visibility for the EU's internal market in the 'virtual' marketplace, and alongside this, a clear identity for the EU on the Internet. At a practical level the dot eu TLD would allow public organisations and private interests to register a specific domain name, thereby allowing their identification as 'Europeans', linking them unambiguously to the EU geographically and commercially. The EU also hoped that the dot eu TLD would enable the acceleration of the benefits of the information society within Europe and even contribute to combating 'the risk of digital divide in neighbouring countries' (European Parliament and Council 2002).

This chapter analyses the extent to which the system of governance emerging for dot eu is representative of the governance forms and regulatory modes outlined in Chapter 1 and in particular how far the EU has been able to reconcile the general principles of Internet management with its own regulated self-regulation style characterised by a strong public authority presence. It considers and evaluates the central characteristics of the dot eu regulatory framework, how it has developed structurally and what this means for the governance of the European e-economy.

The chapter's main contention is that the governance emerging for dot eu corresponds to a model of European transnational networked governance, with an EU-ised twist. Here, dot eu is developing in the form of a public-private regulatory network, whereby a European TLD Registry, Eurid, sits at the core with other key functions dispersed to a range of actors, namely private registrant companies, Alternative Dispute Resolution (ADR) providers and validation agents,[1] responsible for day-to-day regulatory activities around the functioning of dot eu. The hierarchical shadow of the European Commission is a vital public element of this network, ensuring compliance with, and implementation of, public policy rules (PPR) formulated to provide a precise framework for governing dot eu.

Dot eu represents the application of two potentially contradictory forms of regulation – on the one hand, those embedded within the EU as regulatory state and, on the other, those of the Internet community. This governance structure is novel in the EU in communications policy and has important implications for future regulation of the Internet and other aspects of electronic network communications, should it prove efficacious.

This chapter proceeds with a brief contextual history of the idea of the dot eu TLD and its emergence. Thereafter, an assessment of the perspectives and influences of key actors in the formation of the dot eu governance framework is undertaken. Following this, the mechanics of the dot eu TLD governance network are described and analysed, in particular the PPR and the nature of the shadow of the state in emergent governance arrangements. Alongside this, the key self-regulatory features of the dot eu transnational network of governance are considered. In conclusion an assessment is made of the governance forms and regulatory modes observable in the development of the dot eu TLD.

THE BACKGROUND TO THE DOT EU TLD

The dot eu TLD emerged as an idea when the Internet was becoming increasingly important as an economic asset in an era of global commercialisation in the mid to late 1990s. The strategic and political economic significance of the management of the Internet's technical and organisational resources grew as activity around the Internet became ever more expansive. A vital element of the Internet's technical infrastructure was the DNS, a hierarchically ordered system, wherein TLDs played a crucial role at the 'root' of Internet addressing (see Chapter 2).

Historically, domain names developed either as generic (dot com, dot net and dot org etc...) or country code entities (dot de, dot uk, dot fr etc...) allowing in particular business users to exploit the opportunity to develop strategic positions in the global electronic marketplace (see Froomkin 2001; Weinburg 2001; Froomkin and Lemley 2001). It was no surprise then that the increased interest in and significance of domain names led to efforts to design and implement a governance framework and system for these important Internet resources, leading to the creation of the Internet Corporation for Assigned Names and Numbers (ICANN) in 1999 (see Chapter 2). The creation of ICANN brought with it concern amongst EU officials, as the self-regulatory principles that underpinned the institution were contrary to embedded regulatory norms within the European governance space. The EU was very critical of the way in which ICANN was organised structurally (see Chapter 7).

Notwithstanding this, the idea for dot eu, put forward in the late 1990s, was driven primarily by the healthy and at that time expanding market in Internet-based companies, famously heralded as the (short-lived) 'dot com boom'. Global political and economic considerations and EU institutional process ultimately determined the emergence of dot eu as an initiative, and importantly, its progress operationally. The European Commission's involvement in developing policy towards Internet governance emerged in the mid to late 1990s. It was, however, by no means a coordinated or coherent approach but rather somewhat compartmentalised, with little horizontal linkage between the Directorate General Internal Market (DGMarkt) and the Directorate General Information Society (DGIS) of the European Commission. As Chapter 5 illustrates, although the EU launched a debate on the Information Society (IS) in 1994, producing the Bangemann Report and a subsequent Action Plan for the IS (European Commission 1994), the Internet was not an issue prioritised on its agenda. Telecommunications reform was seen as a more urgent project and the Internet received peripheral recognition and attention.

European policy-makers did begin to take a keener interest in the development of Internet from the mid-1990s when its growing commercialisation pointed to new and pressing opportunities and challenges. The European Commission's DGIS was the key protagonist from which Christopher Wilkinson emerged as something of a 'product champion' for dot eu. His remit was to monitor progress on the evolving governance arrangements for the Internet, of which, an important prerogative for him, was to ensure that it developed in a truly global nature. Leading the negotiations for the EU in ICANN's formative stage, he was pivotal to the EU's request for the creation of the Governmental Advisory Council (GAC) in ICANN, allowing states to participate, though only on a consultative basis. Inside the EU, the lack of expertise and interest within the Council of Ministers on Internet policy led to the formation of the Internet Informal Group (IIG). The IIG, chaired by Christopher Wilkinson, was responsible for the preparation of policy positions on the Internet for deliberation in the GAC (authors' interview 2004).

The creation of such an 'ad hoc' quasi-formal group within the Council of Ministers was again reflective of EU telecommunications policy priorities at the time. The Council working group responsible for the Internet was telecommunications-oriented, and 'too busy' to deal with the range of new governance issues relevant to a burgeoning Internet. In addition to this, the complexity of these issues, juxtaposed starkly with an only moderate though rising level of knowledge, meant that the Presidency of the Council did not have the competence to deal adequately with questions raised and the IIG thus became the collective voice of the EU in matters of Internet governance (authors' interview 2004).

The recommendation to create a dot eu TLD came directly from Christopher Wilkinson[2] in a period following the European Commission's (late) interjection on deliberations to create ICANN. There were several underlying objectives for creating dot eu from a European perspective, based on the political economy of the global digital environment. The EU hoped to exploit the dot com boom and the business interest it created, whilst also taking full advantage of the limited choice available within the generic TLD industry (dot com, dot net and dot org). Furthermore, dot eu would imbue European 'virtual' business with a distinct EU trademark to operate in cyberspace, carving out an identity in the global political economy for Internet commerce. Within the Regulation which the EU produced for dot eu, the Commission saw a complement to existing country code Top Level Domains (ccTLDs), and argued that the profile of the Single Market would benefit substantially from this policy initiative.

Once the idea for a dot eu was born, its advocates foresaw an early launch, precisely because of the prevailing positive economic climate. This however proved, in hindsight, to be very ambitious, as both global procrastination (in ICANN) and, to a much greater extent, EU internal process, served to erect obstacles and constrain the development and operationalisation of dot eu. At a global level, the EU recommendation for dot eu to the ICANN Board was initially met with some hesitancy. As noted in Chapter 2, ICANN was an organisation that had purposefully been established with minimum government involvement in its policy procedures in order to enhance policy efficiency. The EU, by contrast, had governmental interests at its core, and with this, a tradition of inflexible policy deliberation and lowest common denominator solutions: these were organisational concepts that did not sit well with ICANN at the time.

The EU solution was both innovative and straightforward. Since ICANN was set up as 'a private entity for the benefit of the Internet Community as whole' (US Department of Commerce 1998a), the European Commission consulted widely amongst this community in Europe, mainly through the European Community Panel of Participants in Internet Organisation and Management (EC-POP), in order to secure their support for the development of the dot eu TLD. This shrewd political manoeuvring from the Commission helped to limit the ICANN Board's ability to reject the dot eu proposal, as to do so would be to effectively dismiss one of its core founding principles.

Once accepted, the more practical problem of accreditation of an unprecedented international regional domain name remained to be solved. The International Standards Organisation table (ISO-3166-1) was the reference template for the existing national and organisational domain naming system.

Dot eu did not fit, however, within the standard ISO table's conceptualisations, and thus needed an additional resolution to be passed by the ICANN Board, based on a reserved code (alpha-2 code 'EU') that did not appear in the standard ISO table, but was set aside for use, if and when required. The EU's special status meant that it could utilise the alpha-2 code as a regional domain name following a decision taken by the ISO Maintenance Agency to allow it for 'all uses, including Internet uses'. In a response to the European Commission in May 1999, the ISO Maintenance Agency decided, 'to extend the scope of the reservation of the code element EU to cover any application of ISO 3166-1 that need[ed] a coded representation of the name European Union', with 'no objections against the exceptionally reserved alpha-2 code element being used as a ccTLD identifier' (Letter of Correspondence September 1999)[3]. Therefore, a potentially difficult situation was remedied through an existing provision within the domain naming system, and the ICANN Board was content to accommodate the EU in its request (author's e-mail)[4].

Within the EU, deliberations on which regulatory form dot eu should be based commenced. Perhaps predictably, EU policy process and legal requirement determined its shape and progress. A certain cleavage within the Commission (and actors in the domain names business) argued for the dot eu to be launched as a technical project, thus avoiding the bureaucracy that accompanies a legally based approach requiring the passage of EU legislation usually in the form of a directive or a regulation, and thus ensuring quicker implementation. However, on the opinion of the Commission's legal services, any such notion was soon rebuffed. It was argued that dot eu needed to be underpinned by an appropriate legal process and framework, with the underlying rationale that there were fundamental public policy issues at stake. Dot eu therefore required a legal Community text to establish through a viable framework the functions, responsibilities and obligations of the EU and the private actors that would be involved in its regulation, in particular the dot eu Registry. This view prevailed and resulted in a process leading to the proposal of a dot eu TLD Regulation (European Parliament and Council 2002). The Regulation provided a policy framework embedded within the EU legal process, and outlined the administrative and regulatory roles of the actors involved in managing dot eu.

THE DOT EU TLD REGULATION: CONSULTATION AND STAKEHOLDERS

Following a public consultation on the possible creation of a dot eu TLD in February 2000[5] the European Commission, in a working paper published around the same time, considered several options in relation to the possible kinds of regulatory model for dot eu TLD. There was, however, a certain inevitability that any governance framework for dot eu, to be acceptable, would have to be compatible with the wider institutional requirements of the EU and incorporate regulatory traditions with which the EU was familiar. Whilst an entirely private, commercial solution was considered as an option, it was theoretically a 'lame duck', as according to the Commission it might have given rise to issues under competition policy. Similarly, an option to delegate responsibility for management of dot eu internally to the Commission was seen as highly problematic, in particular since 'Member States which had reorganised the their ccTLD Registry [had]...put in place structures based on the not-for-profit, cooperative model' (European Commission 2000d, p.8). The most appropriate framework, it was concluded eventually, was a public-private hybrid, not-for-profit, cooperative model, with the EU as ultimate controllee. Such a framework, it was argued, would meet key legal requirements and provide protection from anti-competitive behaviour. It would also, in governance terms, guarantee a neutral administration and ensure that the views of the private sector on the matter were accommodated.

In July 2000, the European Commission affirmed these broad conclusions.[6] However, it also emphasised that 'consultations with the interested private and public sector participants and the users associations in Europe to define a suitable structure for the Registry operation and registration policy for the .EU Domain Name' (EC-POP 2000a, p.2) would continue. This issue was then also discussed at substantial length with a variety of industry interests in a workshop convened under the auspices of EC-POP, where agreement was reached to constitute an interim steering group (ISG) for the purpose (EC-POP 2000b). The vision of the ISG, with three prominent officials from DG IS as members, including Christopher Wilkinson, was for a new TLD Registry that would combine 'reliability, economy and competitiveness with a high level of credibility, trust, creativity and transparency for Internet users'. The ISG saw the urgent need for a dot eu TLD to expand the DNS name space, but more importantly, to 'offer Internet users an alternative registration policy in order to foster a trusted electronic marketplace which would give a new visibility to European business and consequently support the development of electronic commerce' (EC-POP 2000a, p. 2).

In putting forth a framework for governing dot eu the ISG recognised that, although the Registry model should reflect the basis of best practice, and the commercial and competitive objectives of a Registry operating in an international electronic commerce environment (including relevant global technical rules), it carried with it at the same time a clear implication for the EU, in an institutional and territorial sense. There was from the outset therefore, an indication that within any model for dot eu the fundamentals of EU policy and law would have to be incorporated (ibid. p.4). The Report of the ISG effectively mirrored the conclusions of both the public consultation

(February 2000) and the Commission Communication (European Commission 2000c) on dot eu, simply covering the relevant issues in greater detail. Of central importance was the recognition that there would be a policy role for both the European Commission and the Internet community. More pertinently, both the Commission and the Member States expressed a clear preference for a model that included an oversight function for the EU to protect its public policy traditions once the Registry for dot eu was operationalised (ibid. p.5). They also acknowledged the importance in creating a governance framework for dot eu of already existing liberal models for ccTLD governance at the national level across the EU, as well as global rules and practices.

The manipulation of a global protocol established within the Governmental Advisory Committee (GAC) of ICANN also provided an opportunity for the EU to reinforce its own regulated self-regulatory tradition within the framework for governing dot eu. Such a protocol considered that the laws of the relevant public authority or government would be binding on ccTLD registries. In addition, it confirmed that, 'where the delegate of the ccTLD does not have the support of the relevant community...and of the relevant public authority and community...ICANN [can] exercise its authority with the utmost promptness to reassign the delegation' (cited in European Commission 2000d, p. 5). In this instance, the dot eu TLD Registry would thus be bound by EU jurisdiction given that the EU was, by definition, the competent authority. Nonetheless, there was also recognition that the EU's governance responsibility should be kept to a necessary minimum, given the highly decentralised nature and structure of the Internet, and the private statute of ICANN. Setting a familiar tone of equivocation, however, the European Commission still reserved the right for the EU as the relevant public authority to exercise ultimate oversight and supervision of the dot eu domain, 'should the need arise' (European Commission 2000d, p.5).

A direct oversight role for the Commission was evident in the governance framework agreed in the dot eu Regulation (European Parliament and Council 2002g), with a key role also for the Council's Communications Committee (which replaced the Telecommunications Committee), not least in the formative stages of the policy initiative. Although the finalised framework reflected elements of post-regulatory thinking in the operational management of dot eu visible in self-regulatory provisions, the EU regulatory state was still a strong presence and in defining the parameters of any such self-regulatory activity through contractually based agreement with the designated dot eu Registry, Eurid. Characteristic of a model of self-regulation in the shadow of the state, or the mixed (public-private) mode 'concerted action' (see Chapter 1), the EU ensured the compliance of Eurid through setting substantive conditions within clearly delineated public policy rules (see below). Furthermore, within the regulation there was a clear stipulation of the fundamental rights that would be retained by the EU, relating in particular to intellectual property, the Registry database, and, importantly in governance terms, the right to re-designate the Registry should Eurid not fulfil its tasks in compliance with the regulatory framework (European Parliament and Council 2002).

Thus, although the Commission and EU Member States recognised within the regulation the principles of 'non-interference, self-management and self-regulation', clearly, in the case of dot eu, this was not possible without prejudice to community law and regulatory practice. The dot eu Regulation provided for the possibility of post-regulatory solutions for the implementation of dot eu in the form of voluntary guidelines, contracts between the Registry and private actors within a regulatory network, and the development of codes of conduct. However, the EU also ensured that should this experiment in regulated self-regulation prove less than optimal or in the worst case scenario unworkable and democratically unaccountable, then it had the power to delegate responsibility for its governance elsewhere and according to a different system, if necessary. So although the regulatory framework provided for a public-private hybrid model, the power relationship within it was not equal. The approval of the Commission was required at every stage of policy development to the extent that an informant from the organisation which was eventually chosen to operate the dot eu Registry, noted the extent to which the registry was 'tied up to the Commission' (authors' interview 2004).

REGULATING DOT EU: THE PUBLIC POLICY RULES AND THE SHADOW OF THE STATE

In response to a competitive tendering process, the European Registry for Internet Domains (Eurid) – a consortium of the Belgian, Italian and Swedish country code TLD registries[7] – was awarded the contract to operate the dot eu registry on the 22 May 2003. The PPR and a 'Service Concession Contract' were subsequently agreed between the European Commission and Eurid, effectively framing the operational backdrop and rules for the dot eu TLD. Following a dual-phased sunrise period dot eu was effectively opened up to general public registration on the 7 April 2006, and has thus far attracted over one million registrants (see http://www.eurid.org).

The PPR have provided the most fundamental source of Commission influence over the dot eu governance arrangements – the 'public' element of the public-private model. Public policy issues include: extra-judicial settlement of conflicts policy; public policy on speculative and abusive registration of domain names; policy on possible revocation of domain names, including the question of *bona vacantia*;[8] issues of language and geographical concepts; and treatment of intellectual property and other rights. From the formative stages of the PPR in 2003, Commission officials and the Member

States determined their substance through discussion in the EU Communications Committee. Eurid representatives, however, did not have the opportunity to influence initial deliberations, as the EU insisted that they 'could not input into the process until a contract had been signed with the Commission' (authors' interview, August 2004).

Eurid expressed concern that without its participation, the PPR could become unnecessarily restrictive since the majority of Member States[9] lacked expertise in running Registries and were thus open to Commission influence. A secondary concern was that if the PPR rules were particularly hands-on, then this might lead to a higher expectation amongst Member States on the efficaciousness of regulation in managing the dot eu TLD Registry. It was argued on the contrary, that evidence suggested that as 'simple a model as possible...worked for successful Registries' (authors' interview, August 2004). When Eurid eventually did contribute to the discussions, it emphasised the need for a light touch self-regulatory model based on contractual agreements and rules, rather than that based on traditional EU regulatory forms. This input reflected the model which it proposed to the EU in its bid to become the dot eu registry.

Eurid was also critical of the fragmented nature of the interinstitutional deliberations on dot eu in formulating the PPR, which caused unnecessary delay and confusion in agreeing the final form of the text. It instead favoured a 'joined up approach'[10] in order to increase the knowledge base and practical efficiency. This outlook was akin to that used regularly amongst the private not-for-profit concerns in Europe that managed ccTLDs. Despite the interinstitutional constraint Eurid gradually increased its influence in the PPR deliberation, and its more liberal views on a model for dot eu were clearly reflected in the final draft of the PPR. However, a greater level of intervention than it would have preferred was incorporated, reflecting the EU's penchant for regulatory state practice.

The interventionist elements were attributable more to the legal services within the Commission rather than any Member State position on the issue (Member States had resolved most of their issues in phase one of the deliberations on the Regulation). As one Eurid representative recalled, 'the PPR took a long time but my memory of it is that this was more down to the legal services than the Member States' (authors' interview 2004). Where issues arose for the Member States, it was related more to gaps in the Regulation and certain Member States' misunderstanding of the technical side of domain name reservation and allocation. In this sense, the policy process was also a socialisation process where there was a significant amount of learning on the part of Member States (in particular those that still operated a less neo-liberal system of ccTLD governance) to understand fully registration issues, and the dot eu governance model (authors' interview 2004).

Although no controversial issues arose for Member States,[11] Eurid did indicate a concern with the broad interpretation of the 'sunrise period'.

Historic precedent suggested that such a period only ever catered for established trademarks. With dot eu, however, the legal services of the Commission were determined to cover all aspects of registration and abuse, 'public' as well as 'private', which made the sunrise issue more complex. For the Commission's legal services, any issue with a public policy implication had to be wrapped up in the watertight and legalistic norms of the EU framework. The registration and languages issue was another which the EU customised. A legal ruling during the period of negotiation of the PPR highlighted the issue of EU citizens' rights to be able to register their domain name under any community language. Although the original business model proposed by Eurid in its bid to run the dot eu Registry included a provision to this effect, this only intended to be voluntary in nature and determined by available resources once dot eu was operationalised.

The Commission legal services, however, insisted during the deliberations that, 'everything should be in every language' and that Eurid could not begin to operationalise, administer or manage dot eu until this was the case. The issue then quickly escalated from voluntary inclusion in the original Eurid proposal to 'thick' excess in the PPR. Here, for example, even though within Malta there was no facility for registering a domain name in Maltese, the dot eu Registry had to ensure such a service was offered. This episode was a clear indication of the difference in regulatory approach between the Internet community and the EU regulatory state, which no doubt contributed to the delay in the creation and operationalisation of dot eu and its system of governance (authors' interview 2004).

The level of detail laid out in the PPR was then very far from archetypal private self-regulation and reflected the significant level of authority that the Commission held over the regulation of dot eu. Ultimately, the Commission had exclusive and irrevocable rights to the data on the dot eu database[12] and the authority to re-designate the registry (to an alternative company) should Eurid not comply fully with any aspect of its contract (European Commission 2004, article 15). Overall, the shape of the PPR for dot eu differed significantly from the one Eurid had in mind when bidding to be awarded the contract to operate the dot eu registry. The original model proposed by Eurid had been fundamentally altered during deliberations and negotiations to agree and adopt the PPR. The outcome was a model that was imbued with a higher degree of EU regulatory state practice than envisaged by Eurid.

An indication of what would have been excluded by Eurid from the PPR provides further interesting evidence of the 'cultural' schism between its private self-regulatory approach and the EU's regulated self-regulation. An important issue concerned geographical restriction, namely the requirement that EU citizenship was necessary to register a name under dot eu. This, Eurid argued, was excess bureaucracy that would be difficult to monitor and implement, an impractical addition to the PPR that reflected the primacy of regulatory legalism over self-regulatory market practice. Another issue concerned the perceived excessive complexity of the sunrise period. Here the PPR provided explicit instruction for a phased registration period that would be managed and organised by Eurid. In its first phase, public bodies with prior rights to domain names would have a two-month period in which they could apply to secure them. Thereafter, a second stage would occur in which, for two more months, both public and private interests could apply to assert prior legal rights to a domain name to be registered under dot eu (European Commission 2004).

Such stipulations by the Commission indicated the EU's 'dual' approach to the regulation of dot eu, and from a Eurid perspective, reflected a move to a more complex, over-bureaucratic model, ironically more akin to the proposal 'that came second [in the selection process]' rather than the more liberal model that Eurid had proposed (authors' interview 2004). The EU incorporated but was able to adapt at the same time practices of Internet governance developed at the global level, notably within ICANN. This resulted in the prioritisation of trademark owners established in the 'real' economy which wished to expand and protect their interests and reinforce their identity in the virtual world of Internet commerce. In addition, however, the EU privileged the rights of public bodies (at the behest of Member States) to register their domain names under dot eu, an indication that its public policy traditions would underpin its approach to the operational aspects of dot eu. Consistent with the regulatory state approach to dot eu, validation agents selected by Eurid in an 'objective, transparent and non-discriminatory manner, ensuring the widest possible geographical diversity' (European Commission 2004, article 13) would form a temporary, but important, part of the trans-European regulatory network for dot eu, with the responsibility to investigate the validity or otherwise of the claims to prior rights asserted by interested parties.

The Eurid proposal for dot eu was based on the Belgian model of TLD management, which was highly regarded by its peer group and based on industry self-regulation, characterised by voluntary codes of conduct, self-produced quality of service labels and a representative panel of stakeholders within the Registry. Moreover, the Belgian model was a hybrid of the US and UK systems, which took a regulatory 'hands-off' approach to registration and the operational of aspects of managing domain names. The PPR rules, however, made the dot eu model much more complex through specifying in procedural detail the relationships to be developed by Eurid in relation to the day-to-day process of registering names under dot eu. A key example of this is the arguably excessively detailed procedure outlined regarding how registrar companies should be appointed by Eurid, and on the requirements of applicants to domain name registrant companies (see European Commission 2004, article 5).

The EU's hands-on approach was reflective of the regulatory activity which characterised European regulatory state intervention in the communications sector and suggests that the shadow of public policy may cast long over the governance of dot eu. Although Eurid understood and accepted the implications of the Commission's need to be accountable as a public body in terms of the control and auditing dimensions of dot eu, it also indicated that 'there was a little more than expected on the operational side of things' (authors' interview, August 2004). This perceived tendency to over-regulate operationally was also visible in the establishment of the post-regulatory elements of governance for dot eu notably, codes of conduct for registrars and Alternative Dispute Resolution (ADR). Regarding the former, whilst Eurid was given responsibility for creating the codes of conduct, at the request of its legal services, the Commission had to approve them in order to ensure compliance within its 'sphere of competence'. Regarding the latter, the PPR outlined a series of specifications to be employed in the regulation of dot eu. Although the ADR procedure outlined in the PPR was reflective of core ADR practice developed in the global policy environment, notably within the World Intellectual Property Organization (WIPO) it also, in contrast, provided the scope for the EU to manipulate the ADR procedure to suit its own regulated self-regulatory governance preference. For example, in order for ADR to take place, participants needed to comply with a detailed set of specified procedures outlined in the PPR, even though Eurid was in charge of the appointment of ADR providers and the delegation of responsibility for conducting the ADR procedure would be devolved to it. Framing the core elements of this procedure was an over-elaborate attention to detail, reflective of classis regulatory state behaviour with an emphasis on defining clear process and practice for governing dot eu.

The EU's regulated self-regulatory approach, providing a legal framework and defined procedures within which dot eu can be governed, in theory could resolve the potential problems of private self-regulation: accountability and transparency. The fact that the PPR were drafted by an Expert Group of the EU's Communications Committee which was also charged with reviewing the development of the EU's Electronic Communications Regulatory Framework – a predominantly tele-communications policy-focused set of measures – suggests that the more detailed regulatory *modus operandi* of this part of the e-communications sector exerted influence on the nature of the PPR. The role played by Eurid in the PPR proceedings, by contrast, emphasised the merits of self-regulation and aimed to act as a counterweight to such tendencies. Despite this, however, the EU was able to inject into the dot eu model 'a lot more regulation than expected' (authors' interview August 2004).

REGULATING DOT EU: SELF-REGULATORY FEATURES

When designated as the dot eu Registry, Eurid's remit was to 'organise, administer and manage the .eu TLD in the general interest and on the basis of principles of quality, efficiency, reliability and accessibility' (European Parliament and Council 2002, article 4). It is such principles, as well as an attempt to separate the politics from the process, that underpin agency delegation within the regulatory state. In the dot eu Regulation, there was a clear effort to separate the functional and institutional aspects of the Registry from the oversight responsibilities of the European Commission. The draft concessions contract attached to the dot eu Regulation asserted that, 'Under no circumstances may the contractor [that is, the registry] or his staff be integrated into the Commission's administrative organisation...The contractor shall not represent the Commission...[and] shall inform third parties that he does not belong to the European public service, but that he is exercising tasks on behalf of the European Community' (European Parliament and Council 2002, Annex 4, article 2).

Nevertheless, despite the intent indicated in such a statement, EU institutional procedure clearly impinged on the efficaciousness of the process of operationalising dot eu. The differences in approach between the European Commission and Eurid were clearly visible once again in developing the form of the final concession contract. Circumstance also conspired against a swift completion of the process since a change of personnel occurred within the Commission at a crucial period, which meant that Eurid, although twice approving a contract, had to await amendments and certification from newly appointed personnel, before eventually signing the contract in October 2004 at the third time of asking (authors' interview 2004).

Whilst elements of the regulatory state model have clearly pervaded the EU's approach to governing dot eu, with the shadow of the Commission clearly visible, self-regulatory elements have also been developed on the operational side.[13] Here, Eurid's structural make-up is reflective of existing global (those in ICANN) and ccTLD Registry forms (in particular the Belgian model) which have developed in a self-regulatory context. Thus, whilst, on the one hand having to ensure compliance with EU norms through its contract and the established public policy framework, on the other hand, Eurid must also manage the dot eu Registry according to self-regulatory business practice characteristic of the ccTLD industry (see Eurid – Articles of Association).

First, the responsibilities delegated by Eurid to the actors (validation agents, the ADR provider(s) and registrants) in the transnational governance network for dot eu by Eurid must be in line with established rules formulated within ICANN's GAC for the administration and delegation of ccTLDs. Second, the configuration of the Eurid Board, with a diverse mix of members, is reflective of the more liberal ccTLD models of regulation in EU Member States, underpinned by a belief in inclusive, representative governance, at least in theory. A third important self-regulatory element in Eurid's make-up is its Policy Council. With the potential to have as many as 25 representatives from the Internet community in Europe, it must be consulted by the Eurid Board regarding any decision taken on registration policy. Eurid can only ignore the opinion of the Policy Council if it can demonstrate that to comply with it would be detrimental to its welfare[14] and remit. Eurid's relationship with ICANN will also be of critical importance in relation to the way in which governance of dot eu evolves in the future. Most significantly, its affinity with the private self-regulatory model operating globally within the Internet community, in contrast to the EU's regulated self-regulatory approach to dot eu, has implications for how the public and the private elements of the trans-European network for dot eu will play out in practice.

Although codes of conduct developed by Eurid for Registrars must be approved by the European Commission's legal services, there are nevertheless classic elements of private self-regulation emerging for the governance of dot eu here. Notably, Eurid was given the task of developing a voluntary code of practice for the network of registrar companies, which will include elections from the body of dot eu registrants to form a panel to hear complaints against registrars which have allegedly breached this code[15]. However, as the latter are accustomed to a much more out-and-out self-regulatory commercial environment the shadow of the Commission might very well act as a deterrent to Internet companies wanting to sign up to such codes, and more broadly from becoming registrars for dot eu (authors' interview 2004). The extent to which the public agencification of responsibility in this trans-European regulatory network for dot eu translates into practical influence in its private component remains to be seen. A lot is likely to hinge on the performance of Eurid, which will play the central position in the trans-European regulatory network for the governance of dot eu. It is likely to be required to achieve a balance between its European regulatory state responsibilities on the one hand, and its out and out self-regulatory instincts, on the other.

CONCLUSION

As an experiment in governance, the dot eu model illustrates beyond conceptual inference the mechanics of a public-private mixed model of regulation within a European governance constellation. Within such a model there are contradictory modes of regulation, with private self-regulatory and post-regulatory elements sitting, somewhat uncomfortably, alongside EU regulatory state practice. The result is a system of regulated self-regulation structured in the shape of a trans-European public-private regulatory network. The developing dynamic within the dot eu governance system provides an interesting, albeit tentative, picture of how responsibilities and actor relationships are unfolding within the regulation of the EU e-economy. It also gives some insight into whether more efficient, accountable and responsive regulatory forms in the European electronic network economy can occur.

The long-term success of the dot eu TLD is dependent on the performance of the regulatory modes instilled within its governance framework. This is likely to hinge on the extent to which two contrasting regulatory cultures instilled within the dot eu governance model can be reconciled. So far, there has been more of an interface between, rather than a synthesis of, the EU regulatory state model for communications with the Internet Community governance model of private self-regulation for TLDs, but it is not until the network has been established more firmly that anything other than tentative conclusions can be drawn regarding its efficacy. Nonetheless, some concluding observations can be made at this juncture.

First, the EU's chosen policy instrument to launch dot eu – a legally based Regulation – had an adverse impact on the pace at which the initiative developed. The EU's interinstitutional decision-making procedures delayed the operationalisation of dot eu considerably and fundamentally challenged the political economic rationale for its creation in the first instance. The excessive bureaucratic and segmented approach to policy formulation inside the EU, alongside the rotating staff responsibilities and competences delayed the establishment of the governance system for dot eu. The main consequence of this time delay was that the Internet community's existing suspicions of state intervention in Internet-based commercial activities was reinforced.

Second, although the public-private model contains elements of private self-regulatory practice, the overarching nature of the public shadow embedded within the PPR could have several consequences for the functioning of the dot eu governance system. The European Commission's reluctance to relinquish too much control in what it considers, traditionally, to be its area of competence, does not reconcile well with private actors within the network that have a preference for self-managed, self-regulatory forms of governance, defined by the Internet Community. The fear of overbureaucratisation may prove a deterrent to those actors wishing to enter the network or participate in voluntary codes of practice.

Third, and interrelated, self-regulatory modes of governance are much more flexible than legally binding regulations, which require a lengthy process of consultation and which are usually fairly cumbersome. In the face of rapid technological developments in the e-communications sector, private self-regulation is much easier, as it eliminates the need to negotiate with the complexities of the EU policy-making process. This might well be the case with the public-private hybrid of dot eu, since there is considerable private actor flexibility and discretion in adapting to changes in context without recourse to the Commission. However, there is also potential for delays in reformulating structures and processes, and reacting to private interests and public demands because of the overarching presence of the European Commission, which could cause many problems in the future and ultimately determine the success or failure of the experimental dot eu governance model. Private self-regulation does hold a number of potential disadvantages which, as noted in Chapter 1, mean that it is rarely evident in its purest form and is usually shadowed by the public sector to some degree or other. The opportunities for firms to act as free-riders in a market governed by pure self-regulation and the fact that market players are unlikely to consider the broad, longer-term interests of consumers and users in their market means that governments have tended to assume that 'backstop' interventionist powers are essential to stimulate optimal self-regulatory behaviour (Christou and Simpson 2006).

Fourth, the way in which the shadow of hierarchy translates itself in practice within the developing trans-European network for dot eu has clear implications in terms of decisional autonomy and the exercise of coercive power. With thick public policy rules providing a strong operational visibility for the European Commission, any necessary responsive action by Eurid will necessarily be bound by bureaucratic process, thus giving it a relatively weak coercive power base. Conversely, on a day-to-day basis, if a critical mass of private actors is 'locked in' to the self-regulatory features of the dot eu governance model, Eurid could, de facto, become a powerful actor in the network, despite its otherwise apparently weak position.

Finally, although too early to make any substantive comment, issues such as mutual trust and cooperation, professionalisation of actors in the network and ultimately a common regulatory philosophy, will all have an impact on the performance of the dot eu governance model system. It will take time for such characteristics to develop since, although much learning has occurred in the policy formulation phase, operationally, considerable socialisation and familiarisation needs to occur. Eurid's role in the network will be to ensure that private actors comply with the public policy framework agreed with the European Commission and formalised through the service concession contract. It will also include the facilitation of coordination, cooperation and exchange of views between private actors in the network (private network communication) working under a common framework (i.e. in establishing and implementing a common code of practice). How successful Eurid will be in this is very much dependent on the trust that private actors have in the mechanisms within the network to resolve problems and disputes. Here, the role of the European Commission as an experienced and skilful political actor, in terms of balancing different interests and resolving disputes, might prove a useful asset within the dot eu network. It could also, however, if perceived negatively, be seen as an unnecessary constraint in resolving disputes efficiently and effectively, through self-management and established private network practice.

On a broader level, the dot eu experiment is demonstrative of the 'EU-isation' of global policy developments. The Internet, which developed and became commercialised in an era of neo-liberalism, was imbued with a global logic from the outset and is a prime example of where private modes of regulation can develop. Dot eu can be seen as a symbol of EU resistance to such pure private modes, facilitating policy development on its own customised regulated self-regulatory path, reflective of embedded European governance approaches. The EU in responding to the challenge of global Internet commerce developments has demonstrated that the shadow of hierarchy is very much integral to any interjection in key economic issues within the global political economy.

NOTES

1. See http://www.eurid.eu/ for details.
2. Verified in several interviews with leading officials in DG IS and the Internet Community.
3. Letter from the ISO 3166 Maintenance Agency to the Commission of September 1999.
4. Email exchange with a former ICANN director (29.1.04) and a former ICANN CEO (29.1.04).
5. Which confirmed strong support for the proposal to create a new Internet TLD for the EU. http://europa.eu.int/ISPO/eif/ InternetPoli ciesSite/Dot EU/Work Doc EN.html; http://europa .eu.int/ISPO/eif/ InternetPoliciesSite/Dot EU/Work DocEN .html
6. See http://europa.eu.int/ISPO/eif/InternetPoliciesSite/DotEUMay2000/EN.html; http://europa.eu.int/ISPO/eif/InternetPoliciesSite/DotEUMay2000/EN.html
7. The Belgian partner in Eurid is DNS BE; the Italian partner IIT-CNR and the Swedish partner is NIC-SE.
8. That is, domain names whose registrations are not renewed or whose holders cease to exist.
9. Even the more experienced Member State representatives, in particular those from countries which operated a light-touch approach for regulation of the Internet, were concerned that the PPR would be 'a little on the heavy side' (authors' interview 2004).
10. An informant explained that this inferred a process whereby all participants 'sat down together' to achieve a more efficacious outcome; in this instance the EU Member States, European Commission legal services, and other relevant parts of the European Commission and Eurid.
11. The only thing that the Member States did insist upon was that all public bodies had prior rights. One Member State representative wanted PPR to embed a rule within it that allowed the reservation of the names of all the municipalities in the country. There was no collective support for such an option, however, and so the original mechanism was agreed whereby the rights of public organisation could be registered in Phase One of the sunrise period (authors' interview 2004).
12. See http://www.denic.de/media/pdf/net/part_2-5-b-iv.pdf for the difference between a thick and thin model.

13. http://www.eurid.eu/en/euDomainNames/timetableLaunch (September 2005)
14. The Policy Council can also issue opinions on any issue of its own volition, though these are non-binding on Eurid's Board of Directors. The Chair of the Policy Council sits on the Eurid Board.
15. http://www.eurid.eu/en/euDomainNames/codeofconduct.html

5. The EU and Internet commerce regulation

One of the most significant incentives to broaden and eventually to universalise the reach of the Internet is its ability to act as a forum for commercial activity. Though inevitably hyperbolised in the mid to late 1990s – the years of the short-lived dot com boom – Internet-based e-commerce has come to occupy a small but noteworthy and still expanding part of the European economy. For the EU, the emergence of e-commerce presented opportunities as well as quite daunting policy challenges in a number of areas. Though it had realised the importance of technologically advancing electronic communications networks for conducting business activity since the late 1980s, the emergence of the Internet held the potential for a quantum leap forward in developing a European electronic marketplace. Its architecturally decentred and open nature stood in stark contrast to the 'closed' electronic environments delivered by the then 'state of the art' available in business-to-business scenarios, such as Electronic Data Interchange (EDI), into the development of which the EU had invested significant time and resources.

Since the middle of the 1980s, with the launch of its SEM (SEM) initiative (European Commission 1985), the EU had embarked on a series of regulatory measures to create 'across the board' free(r) and liberalised, that is competitive, European markets in goods services, labour and capital. By the mid-1990s, with the task to a considerable extent accomplished, the EU's role in the governance and neo-liberal strategic development of European markets was an embedded part of the European political economy. It was unsurprising, therefore, that newly emerging Internet commerce soon became a policy priority, particularly for the European Commission, an important part of whose role is to act as a policy pioneer in new areas of the European economy. A central aspect of the EU's consideration of Internet commerce was the governance strategies which should be devised to ensure its rapid take up by EU consumers and, in the process, to secure a prominent position for EU firms in what was, in the late 1990s, considered to be a highly lucrative area into which extending commercial presence was *de rigeur*.

The purpose of this chapter is two-fold. First, it provides an account of the main features of the EU's efforts to develop a regulatory framework for Internet-based e-commerce. It illustrates how the Internet as a commercial phenomenon became a central part of the EU's policy portfolio aimed at creating the so-called Information Society (IS). It proceeds to describe and analyse in detail the regulatory core of the EU's Internet e-commerce policy, which we argue has three dimensions: the *'sui generis'* framework directive on e-commerce; a number of legal measures which complement the key stipulations of the directive on e-commerce in relation to the mechanics of e-commercial transactions but also apply more widely; and finally a series of 'backdrop' supportive legal measures which have relevance to the commercial environment within which electronic transactions take place. From this core has emerged two contrasting governance modes: regulation through the well established EU legislative process and, by contrast, self-regulation involving the emergence of codes of conduct and Alternative Dispute Resolution (ADR).

The chapter's second purpose stemming from this is to provide a conceptual explanation for the form of governance activity witnessed in this area. In its treatment of the regulation of e-commerce, the EU provides an example of what Vesting (2004, p.286) describes and advocates as public law-making looking 'for a connection with the processes of self-organization and self-regulation that spring up along the technological paths of modern society'. Here, the chapter contends that a quite complex, differentiated governance form is emerging epitomised by the novel conjunction of 'hard' legal measures which, ironically, stipulate, though do not make mandatory, a series of voluntary, 'soft' self-regulatory modes whose 'default' alternative is the use of the legal system. This model shows evidence of, on the one hand, the European regulatory state and, on the other, the post-regulatory state (Scott 2004), which, paradoxically, did not evolve from the regulatory state itself in the case of Internet commerce. This state of affairs can be explained by the nature and uncertainties of the Internet and e-commerce. Thus, EU Internet commerce policy is influenced at one level by the delegated, legalistic neo-liberal character of the EU and, by contrast, the private self-regulatory origins of the Internet at the global level. At another level, practical issues such as the extent to which e-commerce is a public or private activity, legal precedent, and developments in technologies facilitating e-commerce add to the challenge of providing a coherent governance package, which to date the EU has not succeeded in doing.

THE EU, THE IS AND INTERNET COMMERCE

Internet-based e-commerce is a still relatively small though nevertheless important and growing part of commercial activity conducted across the EU. In a business-to-business context, in 2001, 24 per cent of all enterprises across the then 15 EU countries made purchases using the Internet and EU companies generated €95.6 billion of sales. Around 81 per cent of EU enterprises used the Internet, of which 68 per cent had a webpage mostly used to market products and give information on prices. However, only 13 per cent of all enterprises made any sales via the Internet and, of these, a modest 38 per cent generated 5 per cent or more of their total sales through this route (Eurostat 2004). In 2003, it was calculated that across the EU as a whole merely 27 per cent of EU enterprises undertook online purchases, though this rose to nearly 50 per cent for large businesses compared to 33 per cent for medium-sized businesses and only 25 per cent for small businesses (Eurostat 2005a, p.6). Regarding business-to-consumer e-commerce, in 2004, an average of approximately 17 per cent of EU citizens were claimed to partake in online shopping, with variations evident between the leading-edge Internet economies whose participation rate went as high as over 30 per cent and, by contrast the new EU Member States where the participation figure did not rise above 7 per cent (Eurostat 2005a, p.4). Focusing specifically on Internet users, a separate study calculated that almost 44 per cent across the EU-25 had ordered goods or services over the Internet, a figure which rose to 48 per cent for the 15 Member States making up the EU until the May 2005 accessions (Eurostat 2005b, p.5).

The EU's involvement in e-commerce originated prior to the popularisation of the Internet. This involved primarily research and development initiatives, such as the Trade in Electronic Data Interchange (TEDIS) programme, related to improving the potential of closed network business-to-business e-commerce to flourish. In regulatory terms, EDI relied on changes which were occurring to the competitive structure of fixed-link telecommunications network markets. Here, gradual market liberalisation which was occurring through the 1980s and 1990s across the EU (see Chapter 3) began, albeit slowly, to make leased lines – the capacity essential to facilitate EDI – more readily available and also cheaper to obtain. Like much of the liberalisation which took place across telecommunications, the EU played an important role, not least in this case through the passage of an important harmonisation directive on the matter within the framework of Open Network Provision (ONP).

In a broader policy context, by the early 1990s, the EU was developing a much greater awareness of the potential economic significance of e-commerce. The increasing pervasiveness of ICT in economic and social life as well as their potential to be harnessed for future economic and social development led the pursuit of the IS to become both a political cause celebre and strategic policy goal for the EU. The IS was by no means a novel concept, having its roots in academic work on the post-industrial society (Bell 1974) which argued that the technologies upon which 20th Century Fordist economic growth was based were now outmoded and being replaced by new forms of economic activity based on the technologies of information. Like all periods of techno-economic change, the emergence and growth of information technologies were associated with futuristic (and unrealistic) predictions about their transformative capabilities, often underpinned by technologically determinist assumptions (c.f. Toffler's 'third-wave' theory). Nonetheless, the idea of creating a European IS, based primarily on new economic activity harnessing emerging ICTs, would prove both politically alluring and practically useful for EU policy-makers in the mid-1990s.

That this was to be the case became evident in 1994 with the publication of a cornerstone policy document entitled *Europe and the Global Information Society*, more popularly known as the Bangemann Report, named after the Chair of the High Level Group on the IS, assembled by EU Heads of State to consider the matter (European Commission 1994). The Report epitomised a conjunction between the hyperbolic expectations of enthusiasts of the IS and the urgency which the European Commission had become accustomed to injecting into policy documents which it hoped would stimulate Member States to develop policy further at the EU level. Thus the Report exhorted '[t]ide waits for no man, and this is a revolutionary tide, sweeping through economic and social life. We must press on...action is needed now so that we can start out on the market-led passage to the new age' (European Commission 1994, p. 1).

The major theme of this Report was the ability of a liberalised and Europe-wide market to deliver the benefits of the IS in terms of economic growth, new services and employment opportunities, though the rife economic determinism pervading its arguments was undisguised, since it was contended that '[t]he market will drive, it will decide winners and losers...the prime task of government is to safeguard competitive forces' (European Commission 1994, p.7). The Report highlighted the potential of commercial activity over electronic communications networks, though its emphasis was very much on developing higher speed, larger capacity versions of Europe's traditional fixed-link telecommunications networks. In fact, what turned out to be the rather limited French videotext system, known as Minitel, was given as an example of successful e-commerce.

Aside from focusing on the opportunities which might be realised from capitalising on the potential of new ICT, the report also placed considerable emphasis on the impediments to their attainment. Here, a key issue was the need to 'identify and establish the minimum of regulation needed, at the European level, to ensure the rapid emergence of efficient European information infrastructures and services' (European Commission 1994, p.11) in a competitive market. The solution advocated was a significant acceleration in the pace of liberalisation of EU Member States' telecommunications networks which, as Chapter 3 has shown, had begun with the passage of a number of, at the time, controversial directives. However, the resolution by Member States in July 2003 to liberalise the market for voice telephonic services on an EU-wide basis – a direct consequence of the 1992 Telecommunications Review (European Commission 1992) – marked a significant step towards complete liberalisation of the telecommunications market. Nonetheless, whilst telecommunications services were to be liberalised by 1998 (European Council of Ministers 1993), the market for infrastructures across which they are delivered was still highly uncompetitive. As a consequence, the Bangemann Report urged Member States to move towards complete liberalisation of telecommunications infrastructures, something which provided a significant spur to the agreement to do so made by Member States towards the end of 1994 (European Council of Ministers 1994).

The emphasis in the Bangemann Report on the development of a European electronic marketplace through liberalisation and upgrading of telecommunications reflects the extent to which the Internet was off the EU communications policy 'radar' in the early 1990s. In fact, the Report did provide some reference to the emergence of the Internet but this served merely to highlight the lack of knowledge among Europe's communications policy elite about its nature and, more importantly, its significance for e-commerce in the EU. For example, it was argued that 'INTERNET is based on a world-wide network of networks that is not centrally planned. In fact, nobody owns INTERNET...INTERNET is so big, and growing so fast, that it cannot be ignored' (European Commission 1994, p.21). However, within merely three years, the Internet was to become the underpinning technological basis for the EU's strategy to develop e-commerce within the context of a broadening set of policy measures on the IS. These were set in motion in the immediate aftermath of the Bangemann Report with the launch by the EU of an Action Plan for the Information Society (European Commission 1994), based on a series of very loosely defined targets which concluded the Report in areas such as teleworking, distance learning, telematics services for small-to-medium sized enterprises and road traffic management.

SPECIFIC POLICY MEASURES DIRECTED AT THE REGULATION OF INTERNET COMMERCE – THE EU'S 'EUROPEAN INITIATIVE IN ELECTRONIC COMMERCE'

The extent to which the Internet soon came to dominate the EU's thinking on the development of e-commerce is no more clearly illustrated than in a European Commission 1997 communication on a proposed *European Initiative in Electronic Commerce*. In contrast to the earlier largely Euro-centric focus on closed network European e-commerce, this report declared at the outset that '"Born global" electronic commerce encompasses a wide spectrum of activities, some well established, most of them new. Driven by the Internet revolution, electronic commerce is dramatically expanding and undergoing radical changes' (European Commission 1997b, p.4).

The positions laid out in this document can be regarded as a landmark indicator of the approach subsequently adopted to Internet commerce by the EU. The European Commission employed its classic tactic of noting how the opportunities of e-commerce were being grasped most firmly by Europe's main global trading competitors, though only the US was mentioned in this instance. Drawing on developments in the European 'offline' commercial sphere, the report noted the symbiotic relationship between the SEM and commercial activity that might be developed in the online sphere. This line of thought led eventually, in 2002, to the establishment of a largely technical initiative whose aim is to create the Single European Electronic Market (SEEM) (Bonfatti and Borras 2005), though arguably the EU's e-commerce policy developed since the late 1990s had this broad goal in mind *per se*. If any parallels with the creation of the SEM agenda are appropriate, then the most obvious one is that to create a uniform EU-wide market for online commerce is a task of enormous complexity involving a plethora of often cross-cutting regulatory issues. The European Commission, in acknowledgement of this, argued that the EU should create a policy, to be implemented by 2000, with four strategic dimensions: technological and infrastructural; regulatory; promotional, training and demonstration; and securing European interests in global governance fora for e-commerce (European Commission 1997b, p.2).

The Commission argued that the development of an appropriate regulatory framework for e-commerce should be underpinned by four principles: no regulation unless absolutely necessary; all regulation to be informed by the goal of creating liberalised market activity across-the-board in goods, services, labour and capital; regulation with a particular goal must ensure that it addresses all relevant elements of the business value chain relevant to the particular activity; and regulation should be developed to cater for clearly defined general interest goals (European Commission 1997b, p.15; see Figure 5.1).

The first objective gave an early indication of the Commission's desire to promote innovative, flexible, regulatory approaches in order to make the governance of e-commerce as light-touch as possible. Whilst mutual recognition was a key tactical tool adopted by Member States to speed the realisation of the SEM in the latter half of the 1980s, here the Commission also argued for the development of 'appropriate self-regulatory codes' (European Commission 1997b, p.14). It also stated clearly its preference for the country of origin principle to govern legal matters arising from international cross-border e-commerce within the EU, something that underpins the SEM. The second stated objective provided further strong early evidence of the extent to which electronic communication, occurring as part of a typical e-commerce transaction, would be dealt with within the most liberal market context possible. The stated objectives under this principle were the creation of coherence, predictability and operational simplicity clearly targeted to meet the interests of producers and service providers.

Ongoing identification of market barriers and legal impediments
Consideration of measures in 'horizontal' areas,
the regulated professions, commercial communications, contract law,
accountancy, e-crime and security, data protection, intellectual property,
taxation and public procurement
Contribution to policy deliberations on e-commerce in global governance
fora
Development of policy communication on the consumer dimension of the IS
Creation of an action plan on e-procurement
Creation of learning and training initiatives in e-commerce

Source: Adapted from European Commission (1997b).

Figure 5.1 Main Proposed Elements of the EU's Regulatory Framework for E-Commerce

By contrast, the fourth principle of the Commission's suggested regulatory framework for e-commerce was underpinned by public policy concerns directed at protecting consumer welfare and promoting citizen interests, in the main. The key issues identified were accessibility and privacy as well as other undefined public interests. A policy challenge for the EU in developing a governance framework for e-commerce was to produce a regulatory framework which would maximise as much as possible the interests of both producers and consumers, though as argued below it is the former group which has been catered for, to a greater extent, in the policy measures which have emanated from the EU from the late 1990s onwards. A potentially thorny area in this regard concerns the nature of electronic contracts between parties to an e-commerce transaction. Aside from the legal status of the contract itself, the Commission highlighted a series of ancillary issues such as advertising, marketing and other promotional activity related to a particular product or service. Here, it was noted that legislation of a 'generic' nature, which it was argued directly applied to the field of e-commerce was in place in areas such as distance selling, the terms of consumer contracts, and misleading advertising. However, the Commission claimed that the law prevailing in Member States at the time was problematic in terms of recognition of electronic contracts since, in certain cases, there were stipulations that a contract needed to be backed by handwritten documentation. Work was also needed, according to the Commission, on the development of electronic payment systems (European Commission 1997b, pp.16–17).

Aside from the above policy areas, the Commission defined a series of what it termed 'horizontal' policy areas. These would make an essential contribution to the development of e-commerce across the EU, though they could arguably be viewed as equally 'assistive' or ancillary in nature as electronic payment systems and commercial communications. In particular, work was needed in the areas of data security and privacy, where the development of a system of digital signatures became a stated imperative. In the area of consumer privacy, the Commission noted the significance of the EU's framework directive on the protection of personal data. Another area considered vital was the establishment (where necessary) and protection of the intellectual property rights of producers partaking in e-commerce, where the Commission acknowledged the importance of developments taking place within the World Intellectual Property Organization (WIPO). Finally, the Commission focused on the need to create an appropriate environment for indirect taxation of e-commerce, particular concern being given to the possibility of extending the Value Added Tax (VAT) and customs duties regimes (European Commission 1997b, pp.18–19).

EU STRATEGIES FOR THE IS – THE INCREASING IMPORTANCE OF THE INTERNET

Sector-specific measures, such as those contained in the Commission's e-commerce initiative, were not, as the 1990s progressed, the only broad policy context within which economic activity conducted through the Internet was championed. Though at the margins of the EU's consideration of the IS in the mid-1990s, by the end of the decade the Internet had moved centre stage in its strategic plans. This is no more clearly illustrated than in the eEurope initiative launched in conjunction with the very ambitious declaration, made by EU Heads of State at the Lisbon summit in 2000, to take action which would make the EU the most 'competitive and dynamic knowledge-based economy in the world' (European Council of Ministers 2003a, p.2). Two of the ten policy goals contained in the initial eEurope Action Plan made direct reference to the Internet and e-commerce: cheaper Internet access and accelerating e-commerce. The European Commission in proposing the initiative underlined three key impediments which the EU faced in its efforts to maximise the benefits of new digital technologies: for both business and consumer users, expensive, slow and insecure access to Internet and e-commerce environments; a lack of digital literacy among EU citizens; and an underdeveloped entrepreneurial culture, particularly in relation to the tertiary sector of the economy which was either made up of, or reliant on, ICT services (European Commission 2000a, p.5).

Regarding the first impediment, the Commission became acutely aware of the relationship between what it saw as a slower than acceptable liberalisation of the telecommunications sector across the EU and a related take up of the Internet by private users. The key issue was that, in order to access the Internet, users needed to be connected from their terminals, to the main telecommunications trunk networks across what is termed the 'last mile' or 'local loop'. Despite EU Member States having agreed to complete liberalisation of their telecommunications markets by 1998, two years later, it became clear to the Commission that certain parts of the telecommunications markets were proving stubbornly resistant to the implementation of liberalisation. The 'local loop', historically the highly lucrative preserve (in terms of revenue) of national incumbent telecommunications operators, was in the Commission's view a prime example, a situation imbued with even more urgency because of its knock-on implications for the uptake of the Internet and the growth of business-to-consumer commercial activity across it. In its eEurope proposals, the Commission advocated the immediate mobilisation of a three-pronged strategy, all directly related to speeding up and/or refining the liberalisation of telecommunications, namely: unbundling, that is creating some kind of competition within, the 'local loop'; a reduction in the price charged for both domestic and intra-EU cross-border leased lines; and a significant easing of licensing requirements to become a telecommunications service provider to the effect that licences (for the provision of specific services) should be replaced by general authorisations (covering a range of related services).

So urgent was the situation, in the view of the Commission, that it took the unusual step of issuing in July 2000, shortly after the aforementioned Lisbon European Council meeting, a proposal for a regulation which would mandate Local Loop Unbundling (LLU) across the EU by the beginning of 2001 (European Commission 2000b). This meant that telecommunications incumbents would be required to provide access to their local loop facilities in a commercially fair and non-discriminatory way. The Commission's urgency regarding LLU was shared by Member States and the European Parliament, so much so that the regulation was adopted hastily and entered into force according to the terms of the Commission's proposal (European Parliament and Council 2000a). The use of a regulation ensured that it would not be necessary for Member States to transpose the legislation's spirit and substance into national law, a process which can often result in well-catalogued time delays and 'on the ground' ambiguities.

Nonetheless, within a year of the Regulation coming into force, concerns were expressed, from both the European Commission and new entrant telecommunications operators, about the nature of LLU which was unfolding in Member States. One important regulatory innovation, emanating from the UK around the same time as the LLU Regulation, provided an alternative way of ensuring cheaper access to the Internet provided on a competitive basis. It arose as a result of the UK incumbent, BT, launching a system of flat rate, unmetered Internet services to consumers. The UK regulator at the time, Oftel, soon mandated BT to provide its competitors with non-discriminatory interconnection arrangements which would allow them also to offer such services to customers (Roy 2002, p.111), a move soon followed by other regulatory authorities across the EU (*Telecom Markets*, 31.07.2001, pp.4–6). By 2004, the European Commission was able to report that the number of unbundled local loops across EU telecommunications markets had risen from 1.8 million in July 2003 to 3.8 million in July 2004 (European Commission 2004b, p.6).

Regarding the eEurope initiative's goal of 'accelerating e-commerce', the Commission's focus was placed firmly on the establishment of a suitable governance framework which would deliver a single European electronic marketplace. The avowed approach contained three key elements. First, the Commission urged that the emerging range of directives related, both directly and in an auxilliary way, to e-commerce should be agreed, transposed and implemented effectively as soon as possible. Central to this was the directive on e-commerce, which was passed shortly after the release of the Commission's eEurope communication, as well as legislation in areas such as data protection and privacy, and distance selling (see below). Second, the Commission advocated the adoption by the EU of the informal governance methods of self-regulation and what it referred to as co-regulation, though no attempt was made to distinguish between the two or to highlight the circumstances in which they might be deployed. These new (for the EU) regulatory approaches, such as alternative dispute resolution (ADR), were seen to be particularly important given the rapidly innovating nature of e-commerce and its inherent global logic. Third, the European Commission declared strong support for the creation of the dot eu TLD which, it was argued, would provide companies with a European trading identity in the e-marketplace (European Commission 2000a, p9). The dot eu policy initiative is covered in detail in Chapter 4.

The launch of eEurope, agreed to by its Member States in 2000, marked a new phase of the EU's IS policy that placed the uptake and usage of the Internet as one of its core features. Initially a two-year programme, eEurope, was extended for a further three years in 2002, with a modified series of goals, within which the use of the Internet for economic and commercial purposes continued to feature prominently. Here, emphasis was placed on the development of high-speed broadband communications delivered through a variety of interconnected platforms, such as the Internet, the airwaves and digital television. Alongside this, the second phase of eEurope continued to stress the importance of affordable access to the Internet, the uptake and use of sophisticated ICT by EU firms, and the further development of e-business activity (European Council of Ministers, 2003a).

THE DIRECTIVE ON ELECTRONIC COMMERCE

Though not specifically mentioned in the EU's 1997 Initiative on E-Commerce, the European Commission the following year put forward what has become its centrepiece legal measure aimed at delivering an appropriate regulatory framework for e-commerce. The proposed legislation was given an open and quite ambiguous title, reflecting the complexity, but also the uncertainty surrounding the nature and development of thinking on a governance framework for the new e-economy in Europe. Formally titled the *Directive on Certain Legal Aspects of Information Society Services, in Particular Electronic Commerce in the Internal Market (Directive on Electronic Commerce)* (European Commission 1998a), it has come to be known simply as the *Directive on E-Commerce* (DEC). In this respect, the directive is misleading since it only covers a relatively small, but still crucial, number of matters essential to the regulation of e-commerce. The use of the term 'information society services' by the EU was deliberately broad and gave scope for future definitional expansion in the light of technological and commercial innovations. Nonetheless, the directive took significant pains to highlight what was an IS service; broadly speaking any commercial (or related) service activity carried out electronically across distance. Covered here are services related to online contracting, online information services supporting economic activity; commercial communications; services allowing search, access and retrieval of data for commercial purposes; information transmission services for commercial purposes; provision of access to a communications network; and hosting information provided by the recipient of a service. The directive excluded point to multi-point services, notably radio and television broadcasting but included point-to-point video on demand services (European Parliament and Council 2000b, paragraph 18) largely as a result of the conclusions of the debate on ICT convergence regulation which occurred in the late 1990s (see Chapter 3).

The key aim of the directive was to mandate a series of legal provisions to ensure that the conditions are in place to allow a single EU-wide market in e-commerce to function. Due to its intended concentration on the mechanics of competition in the electronic marketplace, the proposed directive was designed chiefly by the EU Commission's Internal Market Directorate-General (DG). That the Commission's IS DG, which at the time specialised in Information Technology (IT) and telecommunications matters (and now also deals with media policy matters), did not play a lead role in formulating the proposed directive clearly indicated a desire within the Commission to govern e-commerce outside the more hands-on regulatory frameworks which had existed across the EU for other types of electronic network communications and which had, since the 1980s, particularly in the case of telecommunications but also to a lesser extent in broadcasting, begun to become important at the EU level (see Chapter 3). It is possible to argue that transactions which occur as part of e-commerce do involve the delivery and exchange of content across electronic communications networks and could, therefore, be regulated through modification of existing regulatory provision in this area. However, this was a policy option studiously avoided by the EU. In any event, by the late 1990s, the EU's regulatory framework for telecommunications, a classic embodiment of the European regulatory state in electronic communications, was viewed increasingly as a necessary 'staging post' on the road to the kind of liberalised sector which eventually might only require general competition rules for its governance, for the most part. The aim of EU policy on e-commerce, in distinct contrast, was to create this kind of free market scenario, as much as possible, from the outset.

The European Commission's approach to e-commerce regulation was certainly tentative. This was due in no small part to the potentially global nature of e-commerce – the aim was to avoid creating the kind of hands-on regulatory framework which might be acceptable for an intra-EU context but which might, for EU firms in particular, serve as a regulatory straightjacket in the global electronic marketplace. Equally, the Commission did not wish to encounter the political embarrassment of having to unpick and re-fashion, several years 'down the line', regulation which by that stage had become outmoded or inappropriate due to the kind of rapid advancements in technology and commercial practices which, around the time of the directive's emergence, were occurring as part of the heady dot com boom. As Chapter 3 notes, one of the main policy conclusions of the EU's examination of a possible new convergent regulatory framework for ICT was that content issues would, for the time being, be considered separately from issues of infrastructure regulation which are now convergently regulated as part of the EU's Electronic Communications Regulatory Framework (ECRF) (see Humphreys and Simpson 2005). This immediately removed Internet and e-commerce policy from the convergence agenda. Constructing the e-commerce directive in the Commission's Internal Market DG served to remove yet further e-commerce from the complex 'clutches' of communications governance.

The content of the DEC reflected the intention to create an e-commerce marketplace functioning for the most part through the 'soft' legal measure of self-regulation, though framed, nonetheless, by a series of 'hard' legal rules which would govern the behaviour of parties involved in the online commercial world, principally buyers and sellers but also companies undertaking intermediary roles such as Internet service provision and web hosting. The DEC, by definition, needed to be transposed into national law and, thereafter, implemented at the national level and, like all directives, provided scope for national legal and regulatory governance traditions to accommodate its prescriptions (see Chapter 6). It was also designed as a framework piece of legislation, whose general parameters deliberately avoid detailed prescriptions regarding how they must be implemented in practice. This afforded the opportunity to operationalise more informal regulatory methods, notably mandated industry self-regulation and alternative dispute settlement.

In line with its core goal, the DEC's internal market clause declares the right of those parties offering e-commerce services to do so without restriction or impediment across the whole of the EU. However, the directive allows

Member States to act counter to the single market clause where it is considered necessary to protect the public interest, that is, to prevent crime and to protect public health, security and consumer welfare. Very conscious of the possibility that this might be used in the directive's implementation as a 'get out' to restrict electronic trade, it was agreed that the European Commission must scrutinise any instances where the derogation is employed, of which it must be quickly informed by the Member State in question. If necessary, the Commission was granted the authority to take a Member State to the European Court of Justice if the circumstances of the derogation were considered non-justifiable (European Parliament and Council 2000b).

The legal principle underpinning the internal market clause in the DEC (derived from its use in creating the non electronic SEM) contained a crucial and controversial implication regarding the settlement of disputes between buyers, sellers and intermediaries in the electronic marketplace. Very conscious of the agreed policy goal to accelerate the take up of e-commerce throughout the EU, Member States aimed to create as favourable a regulatory climate as possible for e-commerce pioneers already providing cross-EU international services. A second goal here was to minimise any legal disincentives which might exist for companies, operating in the 'real' commercial world, to move into the cross-EU online virtual marketplace. Despite the directive's assertion that it did not 'deal with the jurisdiction of the Courts' (European Parliament and Council 2000b, paragraph 23), the internal market clause inferred that the 'country of origin' principle – namely that disputes arising from e-commerce services and transactions were designated to be dealt with in the legal jurisdiction of the service provider – would be applied in the case of any legal disputes which might arise in the context of e-commercial activity covered by the directive's remit (authors' interview, European Commission 2004). Specifically, the internal market clause forbade Member States from restricting the ability to provide information services from another EU Member country. Following from this was the expectation that any service provider could expect to encounter the same legal environment in situations arising from cross-border economic activity as would be encountered domestically.

Whilst undoubtedly providing the kind of legal incentive to enter the online business world that EU firms would find attractive, the 'country of origin' principle was problematic on two fronts. First, it brought clearly into focus the relative treatment of producer and service provider interests, on the one hand, and consumer interests, on the other. Since the Bangemann Report and even before, concern had been expressed that EU IS policy was skewed too much towards catering for the requirements of European multinational capital and that, by contrast, statements about striving to cater for the more social aspects of the IS were even merely tokenistic in nature. Whilst the SEM project of the late 1980s and early 1990s was undoubtedly a business-oriented initiative, the transposition of its internal market clause into the realm of e-commerce had a direct effect on consumers given that most of the potential for e-commerce is seen to lie in the development of its business-to-consumer variety. In an earlier communication, the European Commission, in respect of the country of origin principle, argued that it 'guarantees effective redress against fraudulent or misleading IS services by ensuring that complaints are dealt with by regulatory authorities and courts with the most effective power to sanction offenders i.e. the ones under whose jurisdiction the offending supplier falls' (European Commission 1998a, p.2). However, contrary to this Dickie (2005, p.38) argues that the principle of 'home country control imposes geographical, political, cultural and linguistic distances between regulators and the individuals affected by the regulation which is greater than that which would exist if the "targeted" country was the controller'.

A second and closely related problem with the country of origin principal was less normative and much more 'pragmatic' in nature. It relates to stipulations existing (or in the process of being developed) elsewhere in EU law relating to the right of the consumer, deemed to be the weaker party *per se*, in general contractual matters. Here, the Brussels Regulation (European Council of Ministers 2000a) concerning the law applicable to jurisdiction and the recognition and enforcement of judgements in civil and commercial matters affords the consumer, in respect of disputes arising from consumer contracts, the right to decide the legal jurisdiction in which a typical dispute is heard.   Equally, in 2003, the EU produced a draft proposal for convention on non-contractual obligations in civil and commercial matters known as the Rome II convention, in which it was stated that '[t]he law applicable to a non-contractual obligation shall be the law of the country in which the damage arises or is likely to arise, irrespective of the country in which the event giving rise to the damage occurred' (European Commission 2003c, p.34). Third, in a not specifically EU context, private international law employs the 'country of destination' principle in determining the jurisdiction in which disputes arising from commercial activity are heard. Despite this, very importantly, the DEC states that 'provisions of the applicable law designated by rules of private international law must not restrict the freedom to provide IS services as established in this directive' (European Parliament and Council 2000b, paragraph 23). Even more confusingly, the directive goes on to state that that it 'does not affect the law applicable to contractual obligations relating to consumer contracts...this directive cannot have the result of depriving the consumer of the protection afforded to him by the mandatory rules relating to contractual obligations of the law of the Member State in which he has habitual residence' (European Parliament and Council 2000b, paragraph 55).

Since the Brussels Regulation, the Rome II convention and private international law could conceivably apply to matters related to e-commerce, it is important to note that they conflict with the 'country of origin' principle. Whilst tipping the normative balance back in the direction of the consumer, these measures point to inconsistencies in the EU's development of a regulatory framework for e-commerce. That those parties working on the Rome II convention did not take account of the country of origin principle in the DEC is particularly noteworthy and is arguably reflective of the low profile which e-commerce had across the commercial panorama of the EU, since the days of the dot com boom are by now some time in the past. More generally, conflictual states of affairs such as these highlight the fact that governing e-commerce in general legal fora may not necessarily ease the regulatory burden in practice.

Aside from the controversial and unclear issue of its internal market clause, the DEC was at times very detailed, and yet at others rather vague and generalised, in its coverage of the remaining elements of e-commerce to which it referred. Regarding the information which service providers are required to make available to customers, the directive laid out a set of detailed minimum criteria, even getting down to a fine detail such as the name and geographic address of the service provider in question, as well as other issues related to the registration of the service provider, any professional associations to which they might be affiliated, and VAT and pricing information. However, despite its detail, the directive is arguably weakened through not specifying sanctions which will be levied for failure to provide all required information to a consumer (Dickie 2005).

The directive also addressed the burgeoning problem in the online world of unsolicited commercial communications, or 'spam'. Member States were instructed to ensure that service providers who send unsolicited commercial communications consult and comply with optout registers which consumers could at that stage join in order not to receive such communication. In fact, the growing problem of spam motivated the EU to pass a subject specific directive in 2004 which required commercial providers wishing to send unsolicited information to secure the agreement of consumers in advance of the information being sent (European Parliament and Council 2002f). However, the fact that the majority of spam received by EU consumers emanates outside the EU served only to highlight both the ineffective nature of the directive and the need for efficacious global regulation of Internet communication in this respect.

In a similar way to its references to information requirements, the DEC was both detailed and contrastingly obscure in its treatment of the nature of contracts concluded online. A set of specifications were laid out regarding the minimum information which service providers had to give to online purchasers as well as the procedure for placing orders. In contrast to these rather detailed specifications, the directive was much looser in its call to Member States merely to encourage professional bodies to develop EU level self-regulatory codes of conduct regarding the nature and quality of information that should be provided to online consumers.

The directive laid out some important specifications regarding the liability, or more accurately the absolution from liability, of what are termed intermediary service providers. Broadly speaking, these companies are involved in tasks related to the transmission and storage of information between parties to an e-commerce transaction. The DEC declared that as long as they complied with conditions of access to the information stored, were not involved in the modification of information either stored or transmitted and had no actual knowledge of any illegal activity occurring around the transmission or storage of information, then these intermediaries would not be liable for prosecution by courts in the event of infringements of the directive or other illegal activity having been proven. Member States were forbidden to impose any obligation on them to monitor or investigate information which they transmit or store, though could establish requirements to take action in the light of allegations of illegal activities made by any party. It was also stipulated that Member States or their courts could require an intermediary service provider to take necessary action to terminate or even prevent an infringement (European Parliament and Council 2000b, articles 12–15). The latter measure, in particular, appears to undermine part of the reason for the non-liability clause in the first place – namely to make as light as possible the resource burden which accrues from having to adopt a monitoring role, which it was feared would deter these vital companies in the e-commerce market from providing their services.

The third chapter of the DEC dealt with issues of implementation. It is in this area that the extent to which the EU attempted to complement the hard legal specifications of the previous parts of the directive with stipulations which relate to softer, more informal governance methods becomes apparent. However, the prescriptions of the directive here are arguably too loose to be effective. Member States and the European Commission were merely asked to encourage the drawing up of codes of conduct at EU level regarding information requirements, the specifications of e-contracts and intermediary service provider liability, as well as the participation of consumer organisations in these processes. Regarding alternative dispute resolution, a classic embodiment of Internet self-regulatory governance, Member States were instructed merely to ensure that their legislation did not 'hamper' the creation of such arrangements. Equally, Member States were only instructed again to encourage bodies in charge of alternative dispute resolution to let the Commission know of activities in this area.

Developing a body of knowledge on current regulatory practice within the Commission would provide a good basis for the wider refinement and development of self-regulatory activity. It would certainly have provided the Commission with a stronger policy handle in the area and it is thus surprising that the Commission did not push for a stronger mandatory element to this provision. Importantly, earlier versions of the DEC stipulated significantly greater powers for the EU in deciding whether any national derogations were compatible with EC law; to create rules regarding cooperation between Member States' nominated authorities in the monitoring of IS service providers; and to amend the list of IS services which were to be excluded from the directive's scope. However, these were removed from the final version (Dickie 2005, p.135). However, the act of mandating – as opposed merely to guaranteeing protection for – activity of this kind could be argued to run counter to the principles of self-regulation itself. More practically, it is also reflective of the tentativeness with which the EU approached the governance of e-commerce at the time given uncertainties which prevailed over the nature and speed of its future development and the role of regulation therein.

Finally, Member States were required to develop cooperation with each other in the implementation of the directive's requirements, not least through the establishment of at least one contact point, giving the potential for a much needed trans-European governance network for e-commerce to emerge, though as Chapter 6 shows, there is little evidence of this having done so as yet. The very weakly developed stipulations regarding the utilisation of the European Commission as a repository for the development of knowledge at EU level in the relatively new area of electronic economic activity were evident, once again, in the instruction to Member States merely to encourage the communication of information on 'significant administrative or judicial decisions....regarding IS services and practices, usages and customs relating to electronic commerce' (European Parliament and Council 2000b, article 19, paragraph 5).

POLICY AREAS RELATED TO INTERNET COMMERCE IN EU

Whilst the DEC is arguably the central and most important legislative element of the EU's evolving governance system for Internet based e-commerce, it is far from the only one. Naturally, commercial activity conducted in the online world bears many similarities to its much more established counterpart which takes place offline in the 'real' as opposed to the 'virtual' world. Consequently, much of the legislation which the EU has developed to cover commercial activity *per se* is often directly applicable to the online e-economy. Aside from 'bespoke' legislation covering e-commerce, the EU has also, in certain instances, extended the provisions of existing legislation to cover online commercial activity within its IS policy. The result is that the present state of the legislative framework for e-commerce in the EU is expansive, detailed and complex. A European Commission official has commented that 'the legal framework on e-commerce in the EU...is big building blocks being put together, sometimes addressing one issue [and] preserving others'.

Whilst a considerable body of legislation deals with the activities directly related to commercial acts undertaken in the electronic sphere, the EU has also developed a series of policy lines which can be considered, in part, as a 'promotive backdrop' to the growth of Internet-based commerce among its territories. Whilst the policy details of these initiatives stretch beyond the scope of this chapter and the book as a whole, it is important to note that they refer to such areas as: projects to improve the security of electronic communications networks (European Council of Ministers 2003b; European Parliament and Council 2003); action against illegal and harmful content on electronic networks (European Parliament and Council 1999, 2003); copyright protection (European Parliament and Council 2001); and data protection and privacy (European Parliament and Council 1995; European Data Protection Working Party 2003a, 2003b; European Commission 2003a). In the latter case, the EU has also passed a specific directive on privacy in the electronic communications sector (European Parliament and Council 2002f), which replaced an earlier directive concerning the processing of personal data and the protection of privacy in the telecommunications sector (European Parliament and Council 1997).

In 1997, the EU passed a directive on distance selling (European Parliament and Council 1997) which provided some important early provision for e-commercial transactions prior to the DEC. In many ways, the directive could be seen as something of a safety net provision since it would 'apply insofar as there [were] no particular provisions in rules of Community law governing certain types of distance contracts in their entirety' (article 13). The directive was focused on securing the interests of consumers in:

> any contract concerning goods or services concluded between a supplier and a consumer under an organized distance sales or service-provision scheme run by the supplier, who, for the purpose of the contract, makes exclusive use of one or more means of distance communication up to and including the moment at which the contract is concluded (European Parliament and Council 1997, article 2)

In a number of key ways, the directive was a precursor to the DEC. It imposed a set of detailed specifications on goods and service providers regarding a minimum information set that they are required to give customers in contractual relations conducted at distance. It mandated a right of withdrawal period for the customer from the contract in respect of both goods and services, though the specific conditions differed in each case. The directive also included provisions regarding the performance of the supplier (in terms of fulfilling the contract), credit card payment protection, what was termed 'inertia selling', and unsolicited communication. In a separate related policy initiative, the EU has aimed to develop a system of electronic signatures to be used in e-commerce transactions (European Parliament and Council 1999).

Two further aspects of the distance selling directive are worthy of note regarding its implementation. First, it afforded the opportunity to Member

States to create voluntary self-regulation both in terms of compliance with the directive's stipulations and the setting up of what came to be known as alternative dispute resolution procedures, though they were not termed such in the directive. Second, in the extra-EU context, the directive instructed Member States to take necessary measures to ensure that the level of consumer protection in the directive was not denuded 'by virtue of the choice of law of a non-member country as the law applicable to the contract if the latter has close connection with the territory of one or more Member States' (article 12). This arguably rather vague specification was indicative of the EU's growing awareness of the importance of international business-to-consumer contractual relations in globalising markets, though the Internet was not specifically mentioned here and its salience may well have been inadvertent.

Another very important piece of legislation that, again, predated the passage of the DEC was the Transparency directive (European Parliament and Council 1998). This legislation was an extension of an earlier 1983 directive on the free movement of goods within the EU market. The 1998 directive referred specifically to IS services and required Member States to notify the European Commission of the detail of any new rules which were being developed nationally in relation to such services. On notification, a three-month period (extendable by one month if deemed necessary) was triggered in which both the Commission and other EU Member States would have the opportunity to comment on the proposal and, if necessary, propose changes to it. Importantly and unusually for the EU, this process would be open in the sense that service providers would be welcome to contribute comments on any new draft legislation (European Commission 1998b). The directive's core aim was to ensure that no impediments to the free movement of electronic services across the EU's Single Market would be created and that the country of origin principle would be respected, and like the distance selling directive, it too was something of a precursor to the DEC, though by 1998, the European Commission had presented an initial proposal for the latter.

The Commission even went as far as to suggest that, according to EU case law, any failure by a Member State to make the necessary notification would nullify the measure's effect on EU firms (European Commission 1998b). By 2002, the Commission noted that it had received a total of 70 such notifications from Member States though none of these proved a source of controversy. The lack of detailed knowledge in EU Member States on issues of e-commerce governance was reflected in the Commission's claim that 'there have been practically no reactions from the Member States [from notifications from other Member States], which have submitted observations in only nine cases. But above all, no Member State has submitted a detailed opinion' (European Commission, 2003b, p.15). The Commission was also highly critical of Member States noting they had 'adopted a considerable number of texts on IS services without prior notification'. Tellingly, the

Commission has noted that it has not 'received any objections [regarding Member States' failure here] from economic operators, probably because of ignorance of the extension of the scope of Directive 98/34/EC to include Information Society services' (European Commission, 2003b, p. 26).

A third area considered by the EU to be important in securing the mechanics of Europe-wide Internet commerce was the creation of a system of alternative dispute resolution. Like the cases of distance selling and transparency, policy work in the area predated the passage of the DEC. It was also 'generalist' in outlook and did not prioritise commercial activity in the online world. In 1998, the European Commission produced a *Recommendation on the principles applicable to the bodies responsible for out-of-court settlement of consumer disputes* (European Commission 1998c). Here, it noted the fact that many consumer disputes relate to transactions whose value is much less than the costs which would be incurred were a dispute to be pursued through the courts. Second, the length and complexity of the judicial process was seen as a further disincentive for consumers. Third, the Commission addressed the cross-border dimension of alternative dispute resolution, noting the value in setting up a recognised and trusted EU-wide system. The Recommendation addressed a number of the core features of out-of-court dispute settlement. It argued that such systems needed to demonstrate independence; transparency in terms of providing the parties to the settlement procedure with key information on its core features; and effectiveness through being, in particular, economical and expeditious. It was made clear that such settlement mechanisms should not preclude the parties from having recourse to the formal legal system, should the outcome of the dispute be deemed unsatisfactory, unless an agreement to the contrary was secured prior to the commencement of the process.

Many of the themes of the Commission's recommendation were revisited two years later by the European Council of Ministers in a resolution which focused on the cross-national dimensions to extra-judicial dispute settlement, calling for the creation of an EU network of bodies to be created for the purpose (European Council of Ministers 2000b). One of the most striking things about this statement was its recognition of alternative dispute resolution for the electronic network economy. The resolution began with a reference to 'the rapid development of new forms of marketing of goods and services, in particular through e-commerce' (European Council of Ministers 2000b, p.1). It also emphasised on several occasions, with consumer interests in mind, how the resolution of disputes (not necessarily arising from e-commerce transactions) could be more readily facilitated using online methods. Another important feature of the Resolution was its focus on less formal kinds of alternative dispute resolution bodies and systems, highlighting the emergence of a consciousness among EU Member States of a variety in forms of self-regulation. It was noted that the European Commission's 1998 recommendation did not cover those out-of-court bodies which 'do not formally propose and/or impose a solution, but merely attempt to find a solution by common consent' (paragraph 7). Finally, the Council of Ministers endorsed a recent initiative by the European Commission to create a European Extra-judicial Network (EEJ-Net) and asked Member States to take steps to set up an information point to enable consumers to obtain the necessary knowledge to gain access to, and participate in, out-of-court dispute settlement mechanisms (paragraphs 8–10).

In response to the lacuna noted by the European Council of Ministers in the European Commission's 1998 recommendation on out-of-court dispute settlement, in 2001 a further recommendation was produced addressed to those bodies involved in securing a consensual resolution of consumer disputes through out-of-court methods (European Commission 2001b). This document based the rationale for the extension of recommendations on these less formal, consensual means of self-regulation firmly on the emergence of new forms of commercial activity, particularly of a cross-border nature as epitomised in e-commerce. It also noted that the value of typical business-to-consumer e-commerce transactions was frequently low calling forth the need for inexpensive, electronically based dispute settlement mechanisms (European Commission 2001b, recital 8). Like its earlier counterpart, the resolution addressed a set of core areas whose principles should underpin the activities of the ADR bodies to whom they were addressed. Thus issues of impartiality; transparency through the provision of appropriate information about the nature of the procedure; effectiveness, including cost and periodic performance review; and fairness within the procedure and legal redress after it, if so wished, made up the essential parts of the recommendation (European Commission 2001b, principles A–D).

The EU's policy for Internet commerce is also noteworthy for its specific regulatory treatment of financial services bought and sold online. The area is one of the most well developed across the span of electronic commercial activities taking place across the EU – between 60–70per cent of Internet users of ages 25–54 undertook online banking activity in 2004 (Eurostat 2005b, p.5) – and is also highly sensitive. The EU's policy on e-commerce financial services is reminiscent of the leading-edge role which the sector played in spurring liberalisation of former public monopoly telecommunications networks in the 1980s. Based on the desire to see an EU-wide market in online financial services developing, the European Commission became aware of several EU Member States' desire to employ derogations to the internal market principle, based on the argument that this was in the best interest of investors (European Commission 2002). In an effort to stimulate the e-market for financial services and remove the legitimacy of arguments of this kind, the Commission put forward a position paper on how existing EU law (and its precedents) might be usefully applied to the area (European Commission 2003b).

The EU has developed two other key policy lines aimed at, first, promoting the market for e-financial services to consumers and, second, stimulating cooperation between Member States (European Commission 2001c). The overall policy package developed to date is largely archetypical of the general approach to e-commerce. Here, there is evidence of a combination of the use of the EU's 'hard' legal system combined with the 'softer' self-regulatory approach of alternative dispute resolution through advocacy of out-of-court dispute settlement. Third, the EU is aiming to create a trans-European networked system of governance in which the European Commission, designated national Member State bodies and private self-regulatory agencies are involved (Christou and Simpson 2004).

CONCLUSION

The EU's development of a policy for e-commerce in the electronic network economy is illustrative of the complexities of Internet governance and the increasing importance of the Union as a source of governance for the European political economy as a whole. The cross-border potential of transactions that could be conducted across the Internet ensured that e-commerce soon became associated with earlier moves by the EU to create a SEM. It was this policy history and trajectory, rather than that which had been developing at EU level for the governance of the electronic communications sector, which has shaped the policy initiatives which have emerged from the EU in the area of e-commerce over approximately the last decade. The fact that there were no strong traditions of governance for e-commerce at the national level, allied to the global policy challenges of dealing with Internet governance issues, added further weight to the argument that e-commerce should be readily and quickly developed as part of the EU's *acquis* and laid a fertile ground for this to occur.

This chapter has illustrated that the regulatory package for e-commerce developed by the EU is both wide-ranging and complex and, like the Internet itself, is still in the process being constructed fully. That said, it is possible to discern a governance model within which several 'traditional' and new regulatory modes are developing. In outline, despite the 'newness' of the Internet, the EU's approach to the governance of electronic commercial activity conducted across it has been far from radical. For the most part, the form of e-commerce governance reflects the 'hard' legalism (Eyre and Sitter 1999) of the European regulatory state, responsibility for which has been delegated gradually by Member States not least in response to trends of economic globalisation. Here, the EU's strategy can be usefully differentiated into the single, *'sui generis'*, bespoke measure of the DEC, other generalist directives dealing with the mechanics of the single electronic market, and third, a raft of 'backdrop' supportive measures in areas such as privacy and data protection. However, whilst the governance framework for e-commerce at EU level is somewhat 'standard-bearing', the kind of market regulation created within it is often commensurate with the self-regulatory governance agenda associated with institutions which have recently emerged to regulate various aspects of the Internet at the global level.

Thus, whilst the legislative framework constructed through directives is transposed into national government legislatures and will be policed by the European Commission, national governments and, if necessary, the European Court of Justice, the operationalisation of it through implementation will, in considerable part, take place through what are for the EU more novel mechanisms, such as alternative dispute resolution and industry codes of conduct. Overall, therefore, the current state of the EU's governance of e-commerce is an unusual conjunction between European regulatory state-like hard legislation and by contrast, 'soft' private-sector self-management. The latter's informal regulatory modes stipulated, encouraged and protected – though not *mandated* – in various EU policy measures are reminiscent of post-regulatory state activity and a governance approach to the Internet which emerged outside the EU. It is the EU and its relations with the global governance context for Internet commerce which Chapter 7 addresses.

6. The Directive on E-Commerce and the national dimension

The EU's approach to regulating e-commerce within Europe, as detailed in the previous chapter, involved governance characterised by the quite novel conjunction of 'hard' legal measures that make provision for – whilst not going so far as to make mandatory – voluntary, 'soft' self-regulatory modes whose 'default' alternative is the use of the general legal system. In theoretical terms, the Directive on E-Commerce (DEC) provides an important example of the European regulatory state in action in the European e-economy alongside, however, post-regulatory state elements, which, ironically, due to the nature of the development of the Internet, did not evolve from the regulatory state itself. Given this conclusion, an important question arises as to how such an (albeit less than radically) extended form of European regulatory state governance has been viewed within the national dimension across the EU. A key finding of research on the regulatory state in a context of economic globalisation has been that variety exists in its manifestation at the national level (see Schmidt 2002; Bartle 2002). This general conclusion has been evidenced specifically in the electronic communications sector, notably in telecommunications where there have been significant consequences for the transposition and implementation of EU legislation (Thatcher 2004; Humphreys and Simpson 2005).

This chapter explores the extent to which the transposition and implementation of the DEC evidences the ability of 'different national traditions regarding institutions, ideas and actors…[to] induce…important variations between different national regulatory practices' (Eliassen and Sjøvaag 1999, p.4). It is particularly concerned with an examination of the treatment by EU Member States of those elements of the DEC which are 'post-regulatory state-like' in nature. The findings of the chapter in the light of this enquiry are three-fold. First, there is strong evidence in the DEC's transposition of acceptance by Member States of the usefulness of legally provided and protected self-regulation (and by implication post-regulatory state practices) in the European e-economy. Second, there is also evidence of varying interpretations of how self-regulation should be created and governed in different Member States – the national intervening variable remains strong in governance which exhibit extensions of the well-established regulatory state. Third, there is evidence in the early implementation of the Directive of regulatory problems of a domestic and European transnational nature in the regulation of e-commercial activity. These relate both to the definitional ambiguities around issues such as the country of origin principle and liability of e-commerce service providers highlighted in Chapter 5, but also to institutional inertia and uncertainty, as well as variety at the national level.

The chapter draws on empirical data gathered in three EU Member States: Finland, the UK and Germany. This provides a limited, though important, cross-section of the DEC's transposition and implementation across the EU. Each State has not only its own distinctive political economy but is also a leading-edge player in the European e-economy. The chapter is structured as follows. The next section provides a brief overview of the general transposition and implementation of the DEC across the EU based on the European Commission's first (and at the time of writing only) evaluation exercise. The next three sections of the chapter provide an assessment of the governance models for e-commerce in Finland, the UK and Germany respectively. Finally, the chapter explores the conceptual and policy implications for the national and European dimensions of the transposition and brief implementation history of the DEC across the EU.

THE TRANSPOSITION AND IMPLEMENTATION OF THE DIRECTIVE ON E-COMMERCE

The Commission's first report on the transposition and implementation of the DEC (European Commission 2003) was positive, concluding that its core objective to create a legal framework for the development of the EU electronic single marketplace had been met in the main. The Commission reported that 12 of the then 15 EU Member States had transposed the Directive by the formal deadline of 17 January 2002[1] (European Commission, 2003, pp.6–19). Through the notification procedure which stipulated that Member States had to give prior notification to the European Commission of any draft regulation governing online services,[2] strong efforts were made to ensure the adoption of national measures compatible with the DEC. The Commission's Internal Market Commissioner, Fritz Bolkenstein, claimed that the DEC was 'helping e-commerce to take off in the Internal Market by ensuring that Europe's entrepreneurs...take full advantage of a domestic market of more than 370 million consumers' (http://europa.eu.int/rapid). There were, nonetheless, some delays in transposition 'due mainly to the horizontal nature of the Directive' (European Commission 2003, p.6). Those Member States which had fully transposed the Directive did so almost verbatim from the original. The initial stage of transposition focused on the internal market clause and the provisions concerning liability of intermediary service providers. Member States were, according to article 9 of the Directive, required to screen and modify existing national laws to remove any existing impediments to electronic contracting. For some Member States, it appears that the DEC prompted governments to formulate additional measures beyond the Directive's scope. The issue of online gambling, for instance, was included in national transposition measures in Spain, Austria and Luxembourg.

Beyond the initial transposition phase one of the most problematic aspects of the Directive concerned the application of the internal market clause in financial services, a market considered by some states still too diverse for this to occur successfully. On the other hand, the Commission and the European Parliament urged the 'full application of the internal market clause to the area of financial services, given that area's suitability for cross-border delivery' (European Commission 2003, footnote 41, p.9). A classic EU compromise solution was produced eventually in which provision for a Commission-granted derogation on a case-by-case basis was made, though no Member State has served any notifications to the Commission in this area to date.

The area of electronic contracting provided a complex regulatory scenario in its transposition. The relevant provision in the DEC (article 9(1)) was the obligation on Member States to ensure legal protection for e-contracting, accompanied by ancillary legislation in the form of the Electronic Signatures Directive (1999/93 EC) giving, effectively, equal status to electronic signatures. The Commission complained that a sample survey it conducted of websites in Member States between October 2002 and February 2003 showed deficiencies in the information provided thereon. On the other hand, there was evidence that service providers were able to adapt quickly to the legal requirements once errors were indicated. The main impact of this electronic contract provision on Member States was to bring about changes in the national interpretation of 'in writing' requirements. For example, in Germany, this could be seen in relation to insurance contracts and the obligation that prior information is given in writing. In addition, three Member States, France, Luxembourg and Portugal also included in their transposed legislation rules on dealing with the precise moment of the conclusion of the contract (European Commission 2003, p.12).

The Commission made important reference to the development of self-regulation through the emergence of professional codes of conduct for online commercial communications as a consequence of the DEC. The main purpose of these codes has been to preserve the independence, honour and dignity of such professions and to ensure that information provided is accurate (European Commission 2003, pp.10–11). However, whilst the Commission noted an increase in things such as trustmarks and labels in the initial period following the adoption of the Directive, there was a noticeable slowdown thereafter, which motivated it to establish an expert group to promote the elaboration of such codes in B2B internet trading platforms.[3] In its first report, the expert group report argued that, 'self-regulation depends on the willingness to respect the agreed rules and principles in reality' noting also that 'the credibility of voluntary agreed codes of conduct would...benefit from further enhancement of certification services and trust seals' (Report of the Expert Group on B2B Internet Trading Platforms, Final Report, p. 30). The development of codes of conduct, certification services and trustmarks are arguably important 'post-regulatory state' complements to the other soft forms of regulation – such as the out-of-court dispute resolution – outlined within the Directive.

The DEC's stipulations on the liability of Internet intermediaries and notice and take down procedures also proved controversial in transposition. Even though the former (articles 12–14) were transposed quasi-literally by Member States, in several cases the Commission complained that there has not been proper implementation, though it did not specify any detail in its report. It also noted instances whereby national governments provided limitations on the liability of providers of hyperlinks and search engines, which were not covered by articles 12–14. The argument here was that this was imperative for giving additional legal clarity to service providers, though the issue has proved controversial for the UK and Germany most prominently (see below). The Commission also argued that whilst the DEC had stimulated the establishment of clear notice and take down criteria and procedures[4] within Member States. Others, however, have argued that equivalent provision for 'putting back up' – specifically the circumstances in which this should occur – was absent from the Directive creating the potential for ambiguous interpretation (ERIC Brussels Symposium, 14.10.2004).

Finally, an important ambition of the DEC was the establishment of a series of contact points at the national level to monitor issues of transposition and implementation. Though these contact points were created in the DEC's transposition,[5] the expectation that they would provide a focus for greater transnational cooperation and coordination between Member States has not transpired to date. The development of the European regulatory state in the related telecommunications policy area has been characterised by the emergence of a trans-European network of regulators working at the national and EU levels (Humphreys and Simpson 2005). The complex arena of EU-wide e-commerce regulation could benefit from the creation of a similar arrangement. However, whilst the regulatory framework for e-commerce through Directives – not least of which the DEC – is classic European regulatory state activity, the self-regulatory measures provided for in the detail of the legislation, which by definition are looser and more informal, may militate against the rapid establishment of such a network. The regulation of e-commercial activity across the EU through the model chosen by its Member States appears to hold within it the innate problem of securing adequate, let alone comprehensive, cross-national policy coordination. This is further evidenced in the history of transposition and early implementation of the DEC detailed in three case study countries in the remainder of the chapter.

THE DIRECTIVE ON E-COMMERCE: GOVERNANCE AND IMPLEMENTATION IN FINLAND

Finland is one of the most technologically advanced capitalist economies holding a leading position in the Information and Communications Technologies (ICT) sector in terms of the number of Internet hosts and users (see International Data Corporation's Information Society Index). The Internet has been most commonly used in wholesale trade, business services and post and telecommunications, with 98–99 per cent of enterprises possessing Internet access. The overall values of Internet sales amounted to €3.4 billion in 2002, 85 per cent of which came from B2B e-commerce. Importantly, intra-Finish e-commercial sales accounted for approximately 80 per cent of all Internet sales (Statistics Finland 2003). In 2004, the total annual value of consumers' online shopping amounted to €2,100 million.[6]

The Finnish state has played an important role in the ICT sector in recent years principally by reforming the Finnish regulatory environment through deregulation, liberalisation and privatisation, as well as through support of innovation by direct funding and through ICT-based higher education. The state has also contributed to a stable system of industrial relations 'creating the conditions under which social partners representing capital and labour could agree on a strategy of competitiveness that would integrate workers' concerns and workers' rights (Castells and Himanen 2002, pp.140–45). Finland's Information Society (IS) strategy has co-regulatory objectives where the state has attempted to adopt a classic mediatory role between business and civil society. Here, networks involving businesses, private and public organizations and citizens have been created. In the mid-1990s, a high-level National Committee for Information Society Issues was formed, as well as a more broadly based National Information Society Forum. Finland has been pro-active in promoting the IS at EU level, declaring that 'it is essential…to make a full contribution in line with national interests to implementing the action programme on the information society drawn up within the European Union' (Council of State 1995, p.11, cited at http://www.uta.fi/~ttanka/finland.htm#).

Finnish e-communications policy is underpinned by the objective of creating a minimally regulated, competitively ordered, market. New communications market legislation covering fixed telephone networks, mobile networks and television and radio networks entered into force in 2003 due to the EU's Electronic Communications Regulatory Framework (see Chapter 3). As a consequence, Finland has aimed to govern communications through general competition and consumer regulations wherever possible with an emphasis on corporate self-regulation.

Finland's approach to the governance of e-commerce activity is underpinned by the view that 'it should not be treated any differently to [offline] commerce' (authors' interview 2004).[7] The Finnish model of ICT governance has informed the implementation of the DEC where an official in the Ministry of Transport and Communications noted that:

> I think our structure is also a bit different...our public sector is very active on building up our electronic services for instance...on the consumer side...so I think the idea is that we try to build it up...we like to speed it up from the government side so that we offer services and show the model perhaps...because business to consumer trade is not something that really interests businesses...I think B2B already happens quite a lot electronically...but not B2C... (authors' interview 2004).

Finland had a strongly embedded existing consumer protection framework that legislated beyond the provisions stipulated in the DEC. Combined with the view that no special regulation was needed for B2B e-commerce, there was no great enthusiasm for new legislation in relation to e-commerce amongst business, consumers or governmental authorities (authors' interview 2004). The Ministry of Justice was in the main responsible for the transposition of the DEC as it contained matters that fell under its remit relating in particular to private international law, electronic contracts and liability rules. There was also close liaison with other ministries involved in the negotiation and transposition, principally the Ministry of Transport and Communications[8] illustrating the cross-cutting nature of e-commerce.

The Finnish regulatory state contains a Consumer Agency and Ombudsman as well as a Consumer Complaints Board, both independent from government, to address consumer issues, including those related to e-commerce. For B2B matters, FICORA, the telecommunications regulator, was given a supervisory role in ensuring that those trading online fulfil the information requirements set out in Finnish law. The involvement of FICORA as an independent public agency, albeit in terms of a minimal oversight role, is unique among EU Member States where Internet commerce issues have been excluded from the remit of the telecommunications regulators because of their treatment under existing commercial, consumer and competition policy frameworks.

The Finnish approach to e-commerce is best characterised as light-touch (Finnish Telecoms Policy Report 2003, p.31) regulated self-regulation. Liberalism predominates with an emphasis on public-private coordination and cooperation. The DEC was transposed in Finland through, in the main, a new *Act on the Provision of Information Society Services*, as well as through minor amendments to three existing Acts: the *Act on the Protection of Privacy in Telecommunications and on Information Security in*

Telecommunications Activities, the *Consumer Protection Act* (78/1978) and the *Act on Unfair Business Practices*.

Whilst, like most Member States, there was confusion over the interpretation of the country of origin principle underpinning the DEC's internal market clause (authors' interview 2004), by far the greatest controversy centred on the issue of intermediate service provider liability. A clear conflict of interest emerged between existing constitutional arrangements in Finland and how the national government should transpose the liability requirements of the Directive. The Constitutional Law Committee of the Finnish Parliament argued that the notice and take down procedure that was proposed by the Finnish Government, through its E-commerce Working Party, endangered the freedom of expression guaranteed by section 12 of Finland's Constitution.[9] As a consequence, it was contended that 'an amendment should be considered to the government proposal according to which a court order would be required before the service provider would be obligated to prevent the access to information which infringes a copyright' (Kummoinen 2002, p.5).

In light of this conflict, the Finnish Government aimed to reformulate its original proposal to safeguard the freedom of expression provided for in its Constitution. A particular concern was the obligation placed on host service providers to remove illegal material to avoid liability (article 14). So significant was this issue, that it took up as much as half the Act formulated by the Finnish government in order to transpose the DEC. Finland used the possibility provided by article 14 (3) to establish procedures governing the removal of or disabling access to information. During the process, a difference of opinion emerged between telecommunications service providers on the one hand, and copyright holders, on the other. The former held the view that taking down information or disabling access to it should always be based on a court order or injunction by some other regulatory authority, which in governance terms required formal legal measures and process. The latter, however, in line with the view of the European Commission on notice and take down procedures, favoured the inclusion of the self-regulatory measure of self-initiative in taking down information and disabling access to it, particularly in respect of information received outside any formal notification or court orders.

The European Commission's view on the matter was that the Finnish Government's proposal and specifically, that related to exemption to liability of the host provider, went beyond article 14 of the DEC for cases other than infringements concerning sexual decency and incitement to hatred. The Commission argued that it did not take into account other possibilities for the service provider to obtain actual knowledge or awareness of unlawful information besides court orders or notification from copyright holders. In a similar vein, copyright holders argued that the proposal should be amended to take account of the ability to obtain actual knowledge through not only a 'fixed-format' notification but also through any other information that the service provider acquires of the existence of information infringing copyright on its server (Kummoinen 2002, p.6).

In the end, the final Act reflected a compromise where elements of both perspectives were incorporated. Here, it was established that 'it is not for the service provider to decide whether or not to take down material, but rather it is for the court to decide' (authors' interview, Finnish Ministry of Justice, 2004). At the same time, however, the Act also incorporated an alternative procedure for copyright infringements to allow the possibility of quick intervention when an unlawful activity was discovered. In the establishment of such a law there was clear evidence of policy-learning from the global Internet community, specifically the US Digital Millennium Copyright Act which deemed that 'the holder of the copyright had the right to demand that the information infringing his right be taken down and that the host service provider could rely on the notification and act according to it' (Kummoinen 2002, p. 7). Importantly, such an approach also meant that the Finnish transposition of the DEC with regards to hosting services would be unique amongst the Member States of the EU, since it incorporated a self-regulatory element buttressed by a firm formal legal backdrop. No other EU Member State interpreted article 14 (3) of the DEC in this way so as to establish national legal procedures – as opposed to codes of conduct – to govern the removal or disabling of access to unlawful information.

THE DIRECTIVE ON E-COMMERCE: GOVERNANCE AND IMPLEMENTATION IN THE UK

Since 1979, the UK has been a forerunner in regulatory innovation in the electronic communications sector. The replacement of the Conservative administration by New Labour in 1997 continued the penchant for creating a 'light regulatory environment',[10] in which UK business might develop competitive strength to meet the rigours of the global marketplace. The 1998 Competitiveness White Paper set the goal of making the UK 'the best environment in the world for e-commerce'. The UK's 2003 Communications Act, which transposed the EU's Electronic Commerce Regulatory Framework (ECRF), in line with EU policy, excluded matters of Internet regulation. The expressed aim of UK policy on e-commerce is to develop sufficient cooperation between industry and government to create a legal and regulatory framework ensuring clarity for businesses operating online and engendering trust amongst both consumers and business (UK Government Performance and Innovation Unit on E-Commerce 1999). This has been termed co-regulation (e-commerce@its.best.uk, 1999) within which context there is an emphasis on industry self-regulation. The UK government considered that 'existing legal and administrative frameworks for consumer protection and fair trading were in place that were in the whole adequate and applied equally well online as they did offline' (authors interview 2004).

In 2002, the UK was ranked third behind the Netherlands in terms of preparedness for e-commerce amongst European states (Economist Intelligence Unit 2002). The value of Internet sales increased by 81 per cent between 2003 and 2004, from £39.3 billion to £71.1 billion The proportion of businesses selling online rose by 24 per cent and the value of Internet sales to households rose by 68 per cent from £10.8 billion in 2003 to £18.1 billion in 2004. Nonetheless, sales across ICT networks other than the Internet still amounted to nearly three times the value of those over the Internet.[11]

The UK Department of Trade and Industry (DTI) was given the main responsibility for the transposition and implementation of the DEC alongside the UK Treasury, which dealt with aspects related to the burgeoning area of e-financial services.[12] The UK government aimed to retain much of the governance 'flexibility' inherent in the DEC in its own transposition to national law (authors' interview 2004).

In the UK, e-commerce regulation has been incorporated into the existing governance framework for commerce under the auspices of Office of Fair Trading (OFT) and Trading Standards. The majority of the DEC was transposed in the UK through the Electronic Commerce (EC Directive) Regulations 2002 (SI 2002 No.2013), and came into force between August and October 2002. In the transposition process, the interpretation of the country of origin principle and the limitation on liability of Internet intermediaries proved most controversial. Though the UK's initial interpretation of the Directive's provision regarding the internal market clause emphasised a country of destination approach, a consultation exercise conducted by the UK government yielded strong support from industry for the adoption of the country of origin principle. A later draft shifted emphasis towards mandating the country of origin approach, whilst recognising that it might be open to legal challenge in practice. Nonetheless, reflecting the ambiguity which pervaded the issue at EU level and elsewhere nationally, the final draft of the UK's legislation was seen as being 'rather silent on the issue' (authors' interview 2004) by a UK official.

The by now well-established ambiguity in interpretation of the internal market clause aside, an even more contentious issue concerned the implementation of the DEC's provisions on limiting the liability of intermediary service providers. The UK has emphasised voluntary provision and self-regulation of core aspects of the DEC related to notice and take down procedures, where the DTI adopts a discretionary oversight role. Particular difficulties arose regarding the definition of terms such as actual knowledge as well as activities which might be excluded from the application of this clause, the outstanding example being the liability of providers of hyperlinks and location tool services. A difference of opinion arose between communication industry representatives that advocated that these firms be covered by the provision and the UK government, which did not transpose the DEC to this effect. One prominent industry association (Yahoo Europe) argued that this would instil such caution in these companies as to be detrimental to innovation in an area vital to the development of business to consumer e-commerce.[13] There is also evidence that Member States that have included in their transposition of the DEC liability limitations for hyperlinkers and location tool providers have seen a growth in e-commercial activity due to the reduced likelihood of legal uncertainty arising (Yahoo Europe response to DTI, September 2005), unlike in recent German legal judgements on the matter (see below).[14]

A related issue of controversy in the implementation of the DEC in the UK concerned whether the regulation of notice and take down procedures should be undertaken through industry self-regulation, statutory regulation or some combination of both.[15] Consistent with its preference for self-regulatory proceduralism, the UK government did not embed any form of notice and take down procedure in its transposition. Instead, it encouraged the creation of voluntary codes of conduct – monitored by the DTI – for the removal of illegal material, a line taken recommended by the EU in the DEC. However, it was indicated that if the voluntary approach was seen to fail then a backstop statutory legal approach would be adopted. The effectiveness of this strategy has been called into question by the communications industry, which has criticised the system of the notice and take down procedures for its perceived lack of clarity. In particular, it has been suggested that the rules governing when a company is deemed to have received notice to remove material and the form that such a notice should take need to be strengthened. There has also been criticism of the process, deemed too complicated, by which claims that require action by service providers are identified and adjudicated upon. In addition calls were made for a counter-notice procedure to be made formal as part of an extension of the transposed UK version of the DEC. This would provide users with the ability to appeal against any decision to remove online content which they have posted. Here, the counter-notice procedure provisions in the US Digital Millennium Copyright Act of 1998 was cited as a model of good practice for clarifying issues of both 'take down' and 'put back' (Yahoo Europe response to DTI, September 2005).

The implementation of the DEC in the UK also provided some early evidence of the problem of imposing regulatory sanctions and remedies in cross border e-commerce. Soon after its transposition, the UK became the first Member State to exercise its right of derogation regarding the internal market clause (and country of origin principle) of the DEC. The specific circumstances involved the UK (industry-funded) self-regulatory body, the Independent Committee for the Supervision of Telephone Information Services (ICSTIS)[16] and the fraudulent use of premium rate numbers in the UK. Here, the UK made as many as five formal notifications to the

Commission, two of which made use of the emergency procedure provided for by article 3 (5) of the DEC.

In 2003, ICSTIS took action against Spanish and German-based companies, both of which were fined £75,000 and £50,000 respectively. ICSTIS highlighted the excessive connection charge of £1.50 per minute to the web sites run by the two companies which users incurred automatically without users' knowledge. Under ICSTIS Code of Practice, unless permission to do otherwise is specifically granted, online services must not cost more than £20 in total per transaction. On this basis, the web sites in question should have disconnected automatically after £20 of call spend. However, it was found that connection continued even when users tried to terminate the transaction by clicking on the close icon on the window menu bar. ICSTIS concluded that this automatic connection to the premium-rate service without the consent of users was a breach of the Computer Misuse Act 1990. ICSTIS furthermore highlighted other breaches of its code of practice. There was deemed to be failure to give pricing information in a 'price-per-minute' format, difficult to locate contact information, failure of the on-screen clock to display cumulative call costs and, finally, failure to require confirmation that users were over the age of 18 and that they were the bill payer. Access to the services provided by these companies to UK users was barred for a period of two years and both companies were also instructed to offer redress to complainants.

The situation was complicated by Regulation 4(3) of the DEC which provides that requirements, such as those of the ICSTIS Code, shall not be applied to the provision of an information society service by a service provider established in a Member State outside the UK where the code's application would restrict the freedom to provide IS services to a person in the UK from the Member State in question. On that basis, ICSTIS would not have been able to take action against non-UK companies. However, Regulation 5 of the DEC set out a number of exceptions to the provisions of Regulation 4. For example, under Regulation 5(1) enforcement authorities, such as ICSTIS, may take measures – which would otherwise not apply by virtue of Regulation 4(3), in respect of an information society service – deemed necessary for reasons of public policy, such as the protection of minors. However, Regulation 5(4) required ICSTIS, before taking any such action, to ask the Member States in which the service providers were established to take rectifying action. If this request was refused or ignored, then ICSTIS held the right to intervene provided it informed the European Commission and the Member State in question of its intention to do so. In this case, however, ICSTIS did not notify either the Spanish or German authorities before it took action against the companies because it chose to rely on a further exception, set out in Regulation 5(6), which allowed it to take measures against a service provider without first asking the local

Member State of the service provider to do so, if the matter was considered urgent enough.[17]

The ICSTIS case exposed some of the problems with the creation of a common legal framework to deal with abuses of cross-border e-commerce. Whilst it demonstrated that the provisions of the DEC were flexible in allowing independent agencies such as ICSTIS to tackle perceived abuses within the UK by non-UK companies, it also raised questions over the potential for restriction of e-commerce trade, as well as the operability of the country of origin principle. The decision by ICSTIS to impose regulatory sanctions aside, the case also shed light on the ability of regulatory bodies of whatever hue from different Member States to work together in the implementation of the Directive's provisions. As discussed below, the domestic political-administrative context in Germany militated against quick and effective liaison between UK and German authorities and triggered the unilateral action on ICSTIS's behalf. Not for the first time, it also pointed to the need to create a trans-European regulatory learning and enforcement network capable of providing comprehensive regulatory oversight across the European governance space in issues relating to electronic transactions.

THE DIRECTIVE ON E-COMMERCE: GOVERNANCE AND IMPLEMENTATION IN GERMANY

Germany's federally ordered political economy in which the regional Laender governments play key roles is reflected in ICT policy and regulation. The German approach to the development of e-commerce has aimed to create an environment that 'nurtures competition in order to step up development and use of innovative services in the public and private spheres and to the shape the transition to a mobile information society' (Federal Government of Germany 2006, p.3). Here, the pursuit of deregulation where possible, alongside the provision of a legal framework to ensure growth of its e-economy, mirrors Germany's famous social market economy model of capitalism and is ensconced in the 1997 Information and Communications Services Act. According to the World Economic Global Information Technology Forum 2002–2003, Germany improved its ranking significantly in the networked readiness index jumping from 17th to 10th between 2002 and 2003. Germany was recorded as possessing most websites per capita of any country in the world with around 85 per 1000 inhabitants as compared with 60 per 1000 in the US economy. In 2005, total online sales in Germany were estimated at around €6.1 billion.[18]

Policy deliberations on e-commerce emerged as part of the Federal Council for Technology set up by Chancellor Kohl in the mid-1990s to provide recommendations on the development of the Information Society

(IS). One key resolution was the need to create a regulatory framework for new ICT services, notably those related to the Internet, to promote economic growth. However, these policy deliberations served also to highlight conflicting perspectives held by Federal and Laender governments on how to regulate new IS services. The latter expressed a preference for regulating new Internet services in much the same tightly controlled way in which broadcasting was governed. The Federal government, by contrast, feared that such an approach could stifle the development of the Internet e-economy and instead advocated a minimalist, liberal approach, with nevertheless a strong legal framework to regulate core aspects of e-commercial activity such as liability, transparency and the protection of consumers. Subsequent deliberations led to an assessment of the relative competencies of the Federal and Laender governments in the context of moves to create a new more convergent regulatory framework for multimedia services. This culminated in 1997, after protracted and often difficult negotiations with the Laender, in Germany's first 'multimedia law', the Federal Teleservices Law (authors' interview 2004). The Federal level is responsible for telecommunications (through the Teleservices Act and the German National Regulatory Authority, RegTP) and commercial governance whilst the Laender level maintains responsibility for broadcasting (through the Media Services Act).

This dichotomy has produced a complex and at times problematic system. On the one hand, e-commerce is treated as a commercial policy issue and thereby is the responsibility of Federal government. However, this treatment has meant that no regulatory responsibility has been assigned to RegTP. Nonetheless, and by way of something of a contradiction, because e-commercial transactions involve the transmission of content across electronic communications networks, the Laender have assumed regulatory responsibility for specific regulatory issues arising from this activity.

The emerging governance system for the Internet-based e-economy in Germany was reflective of the core features of the EU's DEC (see Chapter 5) by no coincidence. Through developing a leading-edge position on the Internet economy the German Federal government was able to upload successfully many of its preferences for e-commerce to the EU level. A German government official asserted that 'there was a big influence of our multimedia law on the ECD [e-commerce Directive] because the direction is almost the same...but the ECD is going a little bit further because there is regulation with regard to electronic contracts' (author's interview 2004). Germany was the only Member State within the EU, prior to the DEC, to have existing legislation on e-commerce through the Teleservices Act and the Laender equivalent Media Services Interstate Agreement. The DEC included a number of aspects already legislated for in Germany such as provisions on liability of service providers, transparency and freedom of access. Nonetheless, the DEC extended German national provision on information and transparency requirements and introduced provisions such as those for electronic contracting (Teleservices Act 1997, see http://www.iukdg.de). The existing legislation on teleservices allowed German businesses more time than their European counterparts to acclimatise to provisions of the kind included in the DEC though lack of clarity in certain of the latter's provisions, most notably those on information requirements caused some concern (authors' interview, 2004).[19]

Like most EU Member States, interpretation of the internal market clause proved problematic, a particular refraction of this issue being evident due to the domestic political-institutional context. Here, the German Ministry of Justice was concerned with the question of competence within Member States in dealing with specific issues arising from adoption of the country of origin principle. This presented a particular challenge because of the dual system for ICT governance in Germany.[20] A clear example emerged in the case of ICSTIS highlighted earlier in the chapter, illustrating more than simply a problem of cross-national e-commerce regulation, something which the DEC proved incapable of solving. Although UK authorities complained to the German national contact point for the DEC at the Federal level, no power existed here to take direct rectifying action. The Federal government passed on the complaints to the relevant competent authorities at the Laender level, though here equally no responsibility was assumed, since Laender officials argued that the matter in question was essentially telecommunications regulation and was thus outside of their own sphere of competence At the same time, however, the German telecommunications regulator RegTP, argued that it too was unable to take action, though for a different reason in that the numbers in question were not German in origin (authors' interview 2004).

Whilst the DEC asserted the aim of creating EU-wide legal clarity for e-commerce producers and consumers, in Germany the issue of liability of hyperlinkers and web location tool providers proved a controversial issue highlighting another deficiency in the Directive. In the 'Heise'[21] case, where a German court found an online newspaper liable for the provision of a surface link in one of its articles which led to another web site offering illegal material. This ruling directly contradicted an earlier decision of the German Supreme Court in the 'Die Welt'[22] case, where the publisher of the newspaper, Die Welt, was held to have acted within the law despite the fact that a hyperlink located next to one of its newspaper articles led users to a web site offering illegal gambling. Such confusion appeared to illustrate an important regulatory gap which the DEC failed to address and highlights the importance of reviewing and updating the provision of the DEC in a complex and still evolving area of commercial activity. Overall, the early history of the implementation of the DEC in Germany points to the significance of domestic politics as well as providing a very clear illustration of situations in which cross-national regulatory contexts in e-commerce are poorly developed and in need of reconciliation.

CONCLUSION

The transposition and early stage implementation of the DEC across the EU provides evidence of the state of governance of the European Internet-based e-economy. Whilst it is essential to reiterate that e-commercial activity still amounts to a relatively small proportion of business conducted across the EU's Single Market, as Chapter 5 has noted, Internet commerce has expanded to levels where its governance is becoming an increasingly important issue for firms, consumers and governments.

The use of EU legislation by its Member States to govern in a more uniform fashion economic activity of transnational importance is a well-established strategic choice exercised by the regulatory state and has created, in turn, a regulatory state apparatus within the EU at the European level. As a consequence, the relationship between the national and European regulatory state has become a vital ingredient of the European political economy.

The chapter has illustrated that the transposition and implementation of the DEC, whilst exhibiting its own particular case-specific circumstances, bears several hallmarks of the regulatory state. Here, the national political-institutional context – the national intervening variable – has played a determinative role in the way the regulation of e-commercial activities is developing as illustrated by the examples of Finland, the UK and Germany in this chapter. However, the DEC, whilst being in certain respects a classic piece of EU regulatory state legislation, is also, as Chapter 5 has argued, reflective of post-regulatory state forms of governance in several of its key stipulations. This chapter has shown that EU Member States have accepted the proposition that self-regulatory governance structures should at the very least be given a try, though it is important to note that the somewhat experimental nature of these measures is being monitored by governmental authority, both nationally and within the EU dimension. Beyond this, should self-regulation fail, the formal legal system will be utilised to solve any disputes arising from e-commercial activity.

The chapter highlights also that the tentative nature of the extended form of European regulatory state activity epitomised in the DEC has, perhaps unsurprisingly, thrown up a series of difficulties. Some of these can be viewed as inadequacies of the European regulatory state in action. Most notably, the definition of the internal market clause, and consequently its interpretation at the national level, has been a widespread problem. Similarly, the definition of the scope of protection from liability granted to service providers has been considered to be too narrow. It is also clear from the ICSTIS case and the absence as yet of a European-level epistemic community of regulators to share best practice that the EU has only begun to develop the kind of robust system to deal with cross-national regulatory issues which the

DEC aimed to create. Finally, whilst there is to date only very limited evidence of self-regulation of e-commercial activity being practised as a consequence of the DEC, the examples of notice and 'take down' and 'put back' procedures should sound a note of caution. It is likely that the use of other self-regulatory methods, notably ADR, may face similar difficulties if and when adopted more widely and may require the kind of state (either national or EU level) 'regulated self-regulatory' framework which has been created for the dot eu TLD, as described in Chapter 4.

NOTES

1. France, the Netherlands and Portugal are the countries where the Directive had not been transposed fully although work was well advanced.
2. In addition to this the EU and its Member States are now participants in the 'Council of Europe Convention 180 of regulatory dialogue on Information Society Services' (http://europa.eu.int/rapid/e-commerce).
3. See http://europa.eu.int/comm/enterprise/ict/policy/b2b/wshop/fin-report.pdf
4. Although Member States have argued that notice and take down procedures need to be much simpler and clearer to make it easier for providers.
5. See http://europa.eu.int/comm/internal_market/en/ecommerce/index.htm
6. See http://www.stat.fi/tk/yr/tietoyhteiskunta/verkkokauppa_en.html
7. It is important to note that there are different views within the involved Ministries in Finland on regulating e-commerce. The Ministry of Transport and Communications supports a market-driven view and industry self-control, and thus argues for less regulation. The Ministry of Justice on the other hand is, by its very nature, in favour of greater protection for consumers and more regulation in order to achieve justice for consumers.
8. Others to be kept informed were the Ministry of Education, which had an interest in copyright matters, and the Ministry of Trade and Industry, which had a general interest because of the nature of the Directive (commerce).
9. The Finnish Constitution is available in English at:http ://www.finlex.fi/ pdf / saadkaan/E9990731.PDF. The opinion of the Constitutional Law Committee of the Parliament, PeVL 60/2001 vp, p.3, is available in Finnish and Swedish at www.eduskunta.fi
10. See http://www.dti.gov.uk/comp/competitive/main.htm
11. See http://www.statistics.gov.uk/downloads/theme_economy /ecommerce_ report_2004.pdf
12. See http://www.hm-treasury.gov.uk/Documents/Financial_Services/ Regulating _Financial_Services/fin_rsf_edirec.cfm?
13. http://www.dti.gov.uk/industries/ecommunications/electronic_cmmerce_Directi ve_0031ec.html
14. http://www.bakernet.com/ecommerce/germany-t.htm
15. See http://www.dti.gov.uk/industries/ecommunications /electronic_ Directive_0031ec.html

16. Under Section 120 of the Communications Act, Ofcom is responsible for setting the conditions under which premium rate service providers can operate, whilst ICSTIS is the body responsible for creating a Code of Practice and enforcing compliance. On 15 July 2004, ICSTIS announced plans for new rules requiring premium rate providers to pre-register with the regulator before offering Internet dial-up services. See http://www.icstis.org.uk/icstis2002/default.asp?Node=61
17. See http://www.legal500.com/devs/uk/it/ukit_119.htm
18. http://www.auswaertiges-amt.de/www/en/willko mmen/deutschlandinfo /nachric hten _dlt/nachrichten_archiv_html?wb=2
19. There was some dissatisfaction at the Ministry and from businesses with the informational requirements within the DEC because they indicated that a telephone number had to be supplied for customers. Many service providers however did not want to supply a telephone number, simply because they did not have the infrastructure to enable them to deal with telephone enquiries.
20. The federal government (the Bund) and the Laender both claim responsibility for establishing a legal framework for the Internet under their specific competences. The Bund considers Internet regulation to consist mainly of commerce and telecommunications, for which it has the power to legislate. The Laender, on the other hand, regard the Internet largely as a broadcasting issue in which they hold the power to legislate. See Koenig and Röder (1998).
21. LG Munchen, Judgment of 7 March 2005 - Az. 21 O 3220/0 (Heise).
22. BGH, Judgment of 1 April 2004 - Az. I ZR 317/01

7. The global governance of the electronic network economy and the EU

All the chapters of this book have referred at some point to the potentially global reach and commercial potential of the Internet economy. As has been illustrated in the analysis of the nature and scope of the EU's policies for core aspects of the electronic communications sector, the 'EU-isation' of the Internet has been very much contingent on an awareness of the need to take account of the international policy contexts within which the parameters of Internet governance have been developing since the late 1990s. This awareness has variously informed and enabled, but also constrained, the emergence of the key policy areas heretofore discussed (see in particular Chapters 2, 4 and 5).

This chapter develops in much greater detail the theme of the evolving global governance arrangements for the Internet and their relationship to the EU. Employing a chronological line of investigation, it develops along three inter-related lines. First, it focuses on three key institutional contexts within which global Internet governance is developing. Second, it highlights the key governance themes of a commercial nature that are evident in these institutional scenarios for policy deliberation on the Internet's future. In so doing, it picks up issues raised in Chapters 2 and 4 by considering the relationship which has developed between the EU and the Internet Corporation for Assigned Names and Numbers (ICANN) since the latter's inception in 1998. Thereafter, it draws on the themes of Chapter 5 on Internet-based commercial activity by exploring the emergence of the World Trade Organization (WTO) as an institutional forum within which the global governance of e-commerce has been considered. Finally, it chapter explores the institutional context of the United Nations (UN), specifically the International Telecommunications Union (ITU) – organised World Summit on the Information Society (WSIS), and the role which the EU has played in the 'WSIS process' and its key themes related to Internet governance, which began in 2001 and involved two summits, in December 2003 and November 2005, respectively. The third line of analysis of the chapter involves an identification of the patterns of global governance that are developing for the Internet, and their implications for the EU and its electronic network economy. This final line of analysis is approached with caution, since such patterns that are discernible are relatively new and often very loosely constituted.

Overall, the chapter argues that the EU has developed relatively quickly into an important actor in global Internet governance, something that is likely to persist. The relationship between the EU and relevant global institutional fora is an interesting dialectical one. On the one hand, the EU has had to accept, adopt and adapt to a number of the key norms and practices developed within the global institutional context. Yet there is also evidence that it has been able to advance and secure the accommodation of several of its policy preferences at key junctures. In any event, it is the case that the trajectory of EU policy for the governance of its e-economy, developed in considerable part 'internally' over the last decade or so, was broadly in line with the preferences of the early most influential actors at the global level.

However, there is also some important evidence of the EU acting recently as a respected global state actor in its pivotal role prior to, and at, WSIS II, in its claim to have brokered a compromise agreement between states whose views differed on the global institutional context within which key aspects of the Internet should be governed in the future. Just how significant this intervention proved to be will most likely be determined by the performance and longevity of the arrangement which was agreed by the world's powers at WSIS II in November 2005. Nonetheless, the emergence of the EU not only here but earlier in the contexts of ICANN and the WTO is highly significant.

Finally, the chapter argues that the global governance of the Internet, though only embryonic in nature at this stage, represents a conjunction of the traditional and the (relatively) novel. The global strategic economic and social significance of the Internet has meant that, despite the wishes of the early Internet pioneers and entrepreneurs, the state quickly asserted its authority in determining the key parameters of its governance (see Drezner 2004). However, the history to date of the global governance of the Internet is not completely about the exercise of state power. The private sphere – in the shape of the technical, commercial and (to a considerably lesser extent) civil society communities – has played a significant role and looks certain to continue to do so. To date at least, therefore, we argue that the 'model' evident at the global level is comparatively similar to that which the EU is developing internally for the governance of its Internet based e-economy: self-regulation overshadowed by state authority.

THE EU, ICANN AND THE MANAGEMENT OF INTERNET NAMING AND ADDRESSING

As Chapter 2 has noted, the creation of ICANN in October 1998 marked a landmark step in the internationalisation of the governance of the Internet's system of naming and addressing. Nonetheless, as the chapter also makes clear, despite a move towards sharing these essential aspects of Internet governance with other states, ICANN was fashioned according to US priorities and preferences – both those of its government and its computer science technical constituency. This was perhaps understandable. After all, the Internet originated in the US and was developed through several decades with US public finance. The functional heart of the Internet in technical and managerial terms grew up on US territory. The power and control leverage over an increasingly valuable asset – in commercial, cultural, political and broad social terms – that this afforded the US would have been the envy of any of the world's nation states and thus was yielded only gradually and with extreme caution. ICANN was therefore established on US soil and was subject to US (Californian state) law. The majority of its key personnel were initially American. Most important of all, the US, through the Department of Commerce, claimed the right to supervise and have ultimate authority over the development of ICANN in two key areas: its contractual relationship with Network Solutions Inc (NSI) and any changes to registry arrangements for the three key TLDs: dot com, dot net and dot org (see Chapter 2). The US government also secured the agreement of ICANN to assign to the Department of Commerce all rights which the former held pertaining to TLD Registry and Registrar relationships should the US government decide to de-recognise ICANN (European Commission 2000e p.14).

For the EU and its Member States, the evolution of the global governance of Internet naming and addressing arrangements in this manner was far from an ideal situation. Particularly on the commercial side, as Chapter 5 has shown, the EU was by the late 1990s very much aware of the manifold strategic importance of the Internet to the realisation of its Information Society (IS) policy objectives. The European Commission went as far as to suggest that, 'Indeed, *all* the initiatives envisaged in the…recent eEurope initiative depend in the last resort on the efficiency and economy of the Internet infrastructure' (emphasis in original) (European Commission 2000e, p.5). In many respects, the EU's support for the creation of ICANN was supplied more as an acquiescence than an agreement. Like all states, it was very much aware of its relatively weak position during the negotiations which led to the creation of ICANN. In this respect, it was happy to have secured, relatively late in the day, the US government's concession to see the creation of a Governmental Advisory Committee (GAC) for ICANN. On the other hand, the EU was a wealthy and burgeoning Internet marketplace which leading US e-commerce firms were keen to see quickly developed. EU Member States were viewed thus as an essential part of any new emerging global system of governance for the Internet. Further, the EU's version of neo-liberal free market competition, though exhibiting key differences from the US model, was also broadly in line with it. Thus, more than any other governmental entity, the EU had the potential to alter significantly the nature and functioning of ICANN more towards its own economic interests and governance preferences after ICANN's inception.

The European Commission, not least because of its role as representative of the EU in ICANN's GAC, was quick to articulate the areas in which the EU wished to see significant alterations to the governance of Internet naming and addressing. In 2000, it produced a key position paper which was notable for its concerns about US foreshadowing influence over ICANN and when its promise to relinquish complete control over ICANN would actually materialise. Related to this, the Commission made important reference to ICANN in two respects. First, it expressed its wish to see the then rather narrow membership of the GAC grow to what it viewed as truly global proportions.

The sub-text behind this assertion was the desire to shift the balance of power away from the US to a more multilateral context. It was argued that the 'necessary governmental oversight of ICANN should be exercised on a multilateral basis, in the first instance through the Governmental Advisory Committee' (European Commission 2000e, p.14). Second, the Commission made its feelings clear about the extent to which ICANN's decisions could infringe on governance territory it regarded as being the preserve of state governments, as opposed to private interest organisations such as ICANN. Whilst acknowledging the apparent preference of governments to adopt a 'back seat' role in Internet governance to that point, it cautioned that:

> Should ICANN extend its influence tacitly or de facto to other policy areas where governments found that the interests of their general public were being affected, or in the event of a significant disagreement between the Board and the GAC, then the current relationship would probably have to be re-visited (European Commission 2000e, p.8)

The Commission's view on the relationship between ICANN and the GAC provided evidence of a different perspective on the GAC from that envisaged by the US government. Whilst the latter was adamant that government should not interfere in the management of the Internet and found acceptable the *advisory* role of the GAC conceded to the EU to ensure its participation in ICANN (Mueller 2002), the EU made it clear that it considered the ICANN-GAC relationship to be a 'self-regulatory structure buttressed by active policy *oversight*' (our emphasis) (European Commission 2000e, p.9), suggesting a much more influential role for governments, even if they possessed no enforcement or veto rights over ICANN.

The Commission was also openly critical of a number of aspects of the evolving TLD market. It argued that the decision to allow 'open house' registration under the most popular TLDs – dot com, dot net and dot org – was a 'lost opportunity to manage the available domain name space in a responsible and efficient manner'. Equally, the Commission chastised the US government's proposal to create unilaterally a number of new TLDs as 'tending to confirm US authority and jurisdiction in such matters' (European Commission 2000e, p.12). It noted general European concern over the monopoly TLD registry position held by VeriSign, highlighting, in particular, the key problem of data protection for EU citizens. Finally, the Commission, keen to promote the influence of the EU in the domain of evolving global Internet governance, claimed a significant policy success regarding alternative dispute resolution. Here, it noted the acceptance by the TLD registrar industry of a uniform dispute resolution policy which the EU had advocated in a policy axis with the World Intellectual Property Organization (WIPO) which drew up the policy's procedures and guidelines. Here, it claimed that the 'policy promoted by the EU in March 1998 and sustained by the Commission and Member States throughout the intervening period has largely borne fruit' (European Commission 2000e, p.17).

The creation of the GAC to ICANN provided the EU with a crucial opportunity to exert influence on the emerging governance of naming and addressing on the Internet. However, at ICANN's inception, relative to those of the US, European interests were in a relatively weak position. The membership of the GAC reflected the extent to which the Internet was a salient policy issue for the world's states. Unlike other longer established international organisations, it was relatively small in size and was composed mostly of those states which were at the leading edge of Internet take up and usage. Since then, with growing awareness of the strategic importance of Internet domain names and Internet Protocol (IP) addresses, its membership has expanded.

The role and significance of the ICANN–GAC relationship has been contingent from its inception on the perspective on self-regulation held by participants in, and interests directly affected by, ICANN's functioning. Whilst both strong advocates of self-regulation for the Internet, a clear difference of emphasis was evident between European and US approaches. Here, it has been argued by Newman and Bach (2001) that the essential difference concerns the nature of the public monitoring of private interests, where US traditions of 'hands off' legalistic self-regulation stand in contrast to the more interventionist, coordinated self-regulation favoured by the EU. To some extent, this can explain the difference of attitude towards ICANN. However, much more significant are material circumstances associated with the emergence of the Internet and ICANN. As Chapter 1 has illustrated, from a US perspective, the powerful technical and commercial interests closely involved in the early management of domain names displayed a deep aversion to direct government intervention – at ICANN's inception, the creation of any form of hands-on governmental control would have been considered beyond the pale for these interests and thus difficult to implement, something which could have slowed considerably the expansion of the Internet. In any event, it is plausible to suggest that the US government did not need to create a more interventionist version of the GAC, nor was it in its interests to do so, since it held ultimate control over the technical hardware and software integral to the functioning of the Internet's domain name and IP addressing system.

For the EU, as Chapter 5 focusing on its approach to the regulation of e-commerce has shown, it was not the case that there was an aversion *per se* to the kind of legally mandated self-regulation which was more recognisable in US policy traditions. There was, however, a very real need for the EU to establish as firm a foothold as possible in the aspects of Internet governance under ICANN's authority from the outset. Whilst the GAC as was set up as a concession to the EU, albeit with an advisory remit only, the EU was careful to point out early on that it considered ICANN to be something of a work in progress. Here, shortly after ICANN's creation it was argued that 'the objectives which the European Union has set itself on domain name management cannot be regarded as having been met' (European Council of Ministers 2000c, p.1).

The delicate nature of the EU's position ensured that it had to proceed with caution. On the one hand, the relative weakness of its position in ICANN had to be addressed. On the other hand, there were at the time no other serious alternatives at the international organisational level that could readily be pursued and created for Internet domain name and IP address management. Even to attempt to do so risked hampering the growth of the Internet upon which the EU had settled as a key vector to deliver its IS policy. Nonetheless, the European Commission, as the representative of the EU has played a prominent role in the GAC throughout its short history. At its first meeting in 1999, the Commission tabled a paper which set out its position on the principles by which the GAC should operate (ICANN GAC 1999), though a year later, the EU still regarded the issue of the 'nature of, and arrangements for, balanced and equal oversight of some of ICANN's activities by public authorities' (European Council of Ministers 2000c, p. 1) as unresolved.

The European Commission continued to put forward its case for a more influential role for the GAC than was originally envisaged by the US government or considered tolerable by ICANN. Its principal negotiator with ICANN argued that the latter's relationship with the GAC was a public-private partnership in which the public input was primarily to guide and constrain private interests (Wilkinson C. 2000, p.6). It raised the issue of regional underrepresentation within ICANN as a means of promulgating its view that ICANN should not be allowed to exercise a free unilateral rein on key Internet management issues of global importance (ICANN GAC 2001a). It also attempted to inject greater operational energy into the GAC by criticising what it considered to be inadequate communication between its members outside formal meetings of the ICANN Board (ICANN GAC 2001b). On another occasion, a clear indication of the EU's vision for the GAC was evident in the Commission's request, made directly to the ICANN President, to consider how a better relationship could be developed between the GAC as adviser and ICANN as decision-taker, the less than veiled inference being that the latter should take greater account of the former.

There is evidence that the ICANN–GAC relationship has moved in a relatively short period towards a position more suited to the EU's views on how private interest self-regulation should function though it is not possible to say precisely to what extent this was directly because of the EU's influence or other GAC members, some of whom have been more overtly critical of ICANN's performance. ICANN has begun to refer to its relationship in terms of the public-private partnership envisioned by the EU (authors' interview 2004), in the light of a number of criticisms which it has faced, not least over its policy on the creation of new TLDs. This is evidenced in a series of GAC working groups whose role is to engage more closely with ICANN's supporting organisations (ICANN GAC 2003). Nonetheless, it is significant to note that the European Commission has expressed the view that the GAC should not be given a right of veto over ICANN decisions (ICANN GAC 2002). In a recently adopted amended set of GAC operating principles, the robustness of the 'advisory role only' for the GAC was very evident. Whilst the principles state that the 'advice of the Governmental Advisory Committee on public policy matters shall be duly taken into account by ICANN, both in the formulation and adoption of policies', it was also reaffirmed that the 'GAC is not a decision-making body' (ICANN GAC 2005, pp.1–3). A significant, more widely applicable, outcome of the self-regulatory experience of ICANN might be that often a public policy backdrop provides at least an important sounding board and often a useful support, and even a responsibility shifting forum, for tackling highly complex and politically sensitive issues.

Finally, it is important to note that whilst the European Commission acts as the EU's representative in ICANN's GAC, other EU Member States are also separately represented. Thus, the Commission arguably represents the EU position on an issue, but not necessarily that of all its Member States. A clear example of this was the decision by two of the EU's most influential Member states, France and Germany, to dissociate themselves formally from a recent GAC response on ICANN reform, supported by the EU, which advocated that the Chair of the GAC should sit on the ICANN Board in an ex-officio capacity. This proposal, along the lines of increasing cooperation between the two organisations without giving a voting right to the GAC on ICANN decisions, was clearly not far-reaching enough for France and Germany which issued a quite radical counter declaration suggesting that a different type of legally secured government involvement in ICANN's affairs might be required in the future. Further, they argued that other international organisations, notably the Organization for Economic Co-operation and Development (OECD), the ITU and WIPO had a right to take decisions in areas which ICANN currently considered that it had exclusive preserve (ICANN GAC 2002). This declaration gave a strong flavour of a growing movement that was gathering pace at the global level following the UN's decision in 2001 to hold a two Phase World Summit on the IS. This movement would ensure that Internet governance, and within this the future governance of the Internet's domain name and IP address system, occupied centre stage at WSIS.

The issue of EU national Member States' divergence of opinion from the European Commission within ICANN, aside from highlighting the challenge of coordination facing the EU, also highlights the extent to which ICANN is an organisation which is dominated by 'national-to-global' level relationships due to its administration of country code TLDs. Whilst the politics of these relationships go beyond the scope of this book, it is worth noting that, as Chapter 4 describes in detail, the EU has been successful in securing ICANN's agreement on the dot eu TLD which ensured that it has now created for itself a strong stake in discussions which take place within the GAC on ccTLDs. The reason for this is that dot eu is effectively the EU's own 'ccTLD'. A recent indication of the extent of the EU's involvement here is provided by the role played by the EU Commission's GAC representative in putting forward a paper outlining a series of proposed objectives for the process of updating the GAC ccTLD principles. However, it is interesting to note that, according to the French representative on the GAC, 'the European Commission has no competence in this field' (ICANN GAC 2004, p.13). By contrast, the EU had much earlier asserted its right to exercise its competition policy powers to scrutinise the structure and functioning of the ccTLD industry across the EU (European Commission 2000e).

THE GLOBAL GOVERNANCE OF COMMUNICATIONS TRADE AND THE EU

As Chapter 5 has shown, since the late 1990s, the EU has developed a series of legislative and other initiatives aimed at promoting the development of e-commerce activity across the SEM. However, whilst significant, this intra-EU context by no means captures the full economic potential of e-business which the growth of the Internet has made possible increasingly. Instead, those firms and their governments at the leading edge of e-commerce development began to look at the possibilities for the global expansion of such activity which in theory was eminently feasible as more and more users became connected to the Internet across ever greater expanses of the world's territory. Thus the global infrastructural expansion of the Internet in part served to facilitate the emergence of the global e-business sector. It was therefore natural that the globalisation of e-commerce soon became part of, and entered a mutually reinforcing relationship with, the agenda of broader economic globalisation which had gained weight and influence through the 1980s and into the 1990s (Simpson 2004).

At the core of economic globalisation lay the realisation of liberalised markets and free international trade pursued through attempts to create multilateral agreements in international institutional fora. The pursuit of free international trade had exercised the minds of states long before the current wave of globalisation. The unsuccessful attempt to create a global trade liberalisation forum in the shape of the International Trade Organization (ITO) led instead to a much more modest, though still highly significant, commitment by 23 states to the General Agreement on Tariffs and Trade (GATT) in 1947 (Wilkinson, R. 2000). GATT was constructed and thereafter dominated by the world's leading industrial states, many of which were in the process of relinquishing the colonial territories of the developing world which had helped to fuel in part their industrial development. Here, the countries which later came to make up the EU were prominent from the outset and were instrumental in ensuring that membership of GATT expanded to their ex-colonies with time, the latter of which were keen to develop a foothold in those international markets in which they had a comparative trade advantage.

Within a relatively short period, the leading protagonists from the industrialised world in GATT strove and were successful in securing a more liberalised international trade regime in the manufacturing and, eventually, high-technology goods sectors in which they progressively developed prime competitive positions (Wilkinson, R. 2000). As the current wave of globalisation, driven by the spread of neo-liberal ideology, began to build through the 1980s, the need to remove a series of impediments to international trade, in particular non-tariff barriers, fuelled, to a significant extent, efforts to create a new, more expansive system of international trade governance. The Uruguay Round launched in 1986 culminated in an agreement to create the WTO in 1994.

For the EU, the emergence of the WTO was vital for the development of international trade liberalisation in various respects. Very importantly, the conclusion of the Uruguay Round heralded the creation of the General Agreement on Trade in Services (GATS), an increasingly important part of EU Member State economies. It also resulted in two key agreements indirectly related to trade – the Trade Related Aspects of Intellectual Property Agreement (TRIPs) and the Agreement on Trade Related Investment Measures (TRIMs). These agreements laid a comprehensive basis for the EU to exploit its strengths in high-technology goods and services – not least in the burgeoning area of communications – since adherents to the Uruguay Round had to commit to adopt all three at once: the so-called Single Undertaking (Wilkinson, R. 2001). WTO agreements must be ratified at the national level and, thereafter, they are legally binding. The far from equivalent quid pro quo for leading-edge industrial states in this arrangement was an agreement on agriculture and textiles and clothing, areas where, amongst others, EU countries had been accused by their developing country counterparts – in possession of comparative trading advantages in these areas – of protectionism. The inclusion of new agreements as part of the Uruguay Round was championed by the US, heavily supported by its multinational business interests (Ostry 2004).

The launch of the WTO, in January 1995, heralded the emergence of a powerful new global institutional actor whose remit was essentially thus: to pursue, secure and enforce comprehensive trade liberalisation agreements in goods and services across as many sectors of the economy as possible. It was not long therefore before strident efforts were made to create global agreements in the electronic network communications sector, in which telecommunications, according to its proponents, appeared to be a tailor-made case for the development of a trade accord. As Chapter 3 has shown, many European states had embarked, since the mid-1980s, on progressive liberalisation of their once highly uncompetitive telecommunications sectors. This involved a complex process of harmonising and liberalising re-regulation, the vital legislative fulcrum of which was the EU which variously coordinated and led the fundamental changes which occurred (Humphreys and Simpson 2005). Underpinned by the rationale of creating a single, open and competitive Europe-wide market in telecommunications, it was inevitable that, the agreement to comprehensive liberalisation among EU Member States having been secured, thoughts would turn, around the time of the WTO's inception, to how this experience might be utilised to good effect in the global telecommunications market still highly balkanised but with huge potential in trade terms.

The EU, along with the US – with whom it developed something of a liberalisation policy axis – played a prominent role in the Uruguay Round in trying to promote a trade accord in telecommunications services. At the end of the Uruguay Round a modest, though significant, agreement to liberalise telecommunications was achieved among 57 signatory WTO members (Cameron 2004). It is important to note the schedules of commitments taken by participating states was not radical in that, for the most part, they involved liberalisation of VANS which were already open to competition domestically (Cameron 2004). However, the fact that these services would now, in theory, be open to competition from a much wider range of companies was a significant departure in the direction of liberalisation. Equally significant was that the snowball of international telecommunications liberalisation had started to roll and having gained momentum would soon grow much larger. That there was much more scope for further liberalisation was clear from the fact that only 19 states had included in their schedule of commitment to telecommunications, done as part of the GATS, any agreement to liberalise basic, that is voice, telecommunications services (Drake and Noam 1997). Specific sectoral liberalisations aside, the signing of the GATS was also highly significant in that it contained a number of attached annexes, one of which pertained to telecommunications. The Telecommunications Annex was not about liberalisation of telecommunications networks and services *per se* but was aimed at enabling the liberalisation commitments made by states in the range of industrial sectors covered by GATS. Here, states were required to ensure that public telecommunications networks and services were made available to any supplier of a service liberalised as part of that Member's schedule of commitments in GATS (Luff 2004). Though concluded before the Internet's global expansion had commenced, the Telecommunications Annex held very significant implications for the creation of trade liberalisation in e-commerce.

The combination of the telecommunications-specific schedules of commitments in GATS plus the practical requirement in its Telecommunications Annex ensured that the conclusion of the Uruguay Round was merely the commencement of the liberalisation process. By the mid-1990s, EU Member States had made a commitment to liberalise by 1 January 1998, all telecommunications infrastructures and services and, within the institutional context of the WTO, the EU soon made important strides in trying to ensure that its agenda of telecommunications was adopted more widely among WTO members. After the creation of the WTO in 1995, the EU, on behalf of its Member States, became involved in a vital series of negotiations whose outcome resulted, in February 1997, in the Agreement on Basic Telecommunications (ABT) which, as its name suggests, was a commitment by its 69 signatories (which later expanded to more than 80) to liberalise the provision of a range services which included voice telephony. From an EU perspective, the ABT was highly significant in two key respects.

First, it highlighted the growth of the EU as an institutional actor in global negotiating fora. From an 'internal' perspective, there was reticence initially about giving the European Commission the responsibility of acting as EU Member States' representative in telecommunications since, from a legal perspective, the doctrine of implied powers, stemming from the EU Treaties, to allow it to do so did not appear to cover certain key issues in the negotiations, notably the establishment of commercial presence in national Member State markets. However, Member States soon came to realise the utility of presenting a concerted negotiating position through the EU, with the caveat that they would have to be individually consulted before any commitment was made by the European Commission on their behalf (Young 2002). In the process, the EU established itself further as a prime political actor in the evolving global governance arrangements for the electronic communications sector.

Second, in terms of the substance of what was concluded, the ABT was a striking example of how the EU was able to export its policy model of liberalisation for the communications sector to the global level. On the one hand, the European Commission was successful in ensuring that audiovisual services were not included for EU Members as part of schedules of commitments made in either the Uruguay Round or the ABT. On the other hand, as well as the inclusion of a commitment on voice telephonic services, the ABT was vitally important for the adoption by a large number of its signatories of what became known as the Reference Paper. This paper related to a series of areas to be addressed by signatories to ensure that the ABT would be implemented fully (Fredebul-Krein and Freytag 1999). It was based on a set of principles related to ensuring pro-competitive behaviour, fair interconnection and licensing arrangements, and regulatory independence. In addition and by contrast, the Reference Paper commits its adherents, of which there were 57 at the ABT's inception, to the development of universal service (Blouin 2000). Overall, the ABT and the Reference Paper were very much a reflection of the kind of 'European-style managed capitalism' which Drake and Nicolaidis (1992, p.41) argued was becoming more influential in global trade negotiating circles. However, the fact that the substance of the ABT was acceptable to the US should not be underestimated in any consideration of why it became an important part of the WTO's portfolio of sectoral liberalisations.

THE EU AND NEGOTIATIONS ON E-COMMERCE IN THE WTO

The agreement of the ABT in 1997 and its subsequent adoption by additional WTO members had relevance not just for telecommunications, but also the Internet and e-commerce. As has been noted in Chapter 5, the EU was very much aware of the degree to which the expansion of the Internet (and thus e-commerce conducted through it) would be contingent on the availability of affordable good quality telecommunications. However, whilst the challenge of infusing the local telecommunications loop with competition was something which the EU could deal with readily (though this was still a persistent problem several years after the EU's 1998 liberalisation deadline), to ensure the kind of liberal market on a global scale that the EU believed to be necessary to realise the potential of e-commerce was a much more complex and daunting task, of which the ABT and its associated Reference Paper was merely a starting point. As early as 1997, a gathering of European ministers, from EU members as well as countries of the European Free Trade Area, central and eastern Europe and Cyprus noted the 'fundamentally transnational nature of the Internet' and 'underline[d] the opportunities which electronic commerce offer[ed] for both European enterprises and consumers' (European Ministerial Declaration 1997, paragraphs 3 and 11).

The enabling elements of associated telecommunications network and service liberalisation aside, it also soon became clear that e-commerce itself presented a gamut of issues in need of resolution before any trade agreement on it might be attained by anything resembling a critical mass of WTO members. Certainly, there was little doubt that the WTO was an appropriate forum in which to investigate the possibility of creating a legal framework to ensure global electronic free trade. However, around the period of the late 1990s, only the world's leading-edge ICT states could claim to have developed a strong e-business sector. In fact, even in these countries, it is arguable that it was the potential future worth of e-commerce – fuelled by the short-lived 'dot com' expansion which was about to reach its zenith as the 1990s closed – that motivated WTO members to consider e-commerce as a new policy area. Given the embryonic nature of global e-commerce development at the time, the initial WTO foray into the area was an exploratory one in the shape of a 1998 Work Programme established by the General Council in response to the Declaration on Global Electronic Commerce made at the 1998 WTO Ministerial Conference (WTO 1998a). This initiative entailed examination of e-commerce issues within the WTO's four key councils on goods, services, intellectual property and development. In an initial effort to evoke enthusiasm among those Members with little knowledge of the subject area nor infrastructural capability to support e-commerce systems, the WTO was keen to point out how potentially it could widen choice and reduce prices for developing economy consumers (WTO 1998b). As might be expected and as has been the case throughout the history of what has been essentially path-dependent post-1945 trade regulation, it is the advanced industrial states which have taken the lead on e-commerce development, an area in which they have most to gain (Simpson and Wilkinson 2003a). Here, the EU has continued to cement its position as representative of its Member States through playing a prominent role.

The WTO's consideration of the regulation of e-commerce trade has reflected the extent to which e-commerce relates to both the 'traditional' and the 'novel'. On the one hand, the cautionary nature of its approach is reflected in the major decision made to date by its Members on the matter – an agreement to introduce a moratorium on the imposition of customs duties on e-commerce transactions (Farrell 2003), the aim being to avoid the creation of international trade barriers in a nascent sector until a fuller understanding of its likely future development and revenue generating capabilities became clearer. The WTO also recognised the inter-issue complexity of e-commerce by establishing a series of cross-cutting meetings in its General Council. These have dealt with a range of issues, such as the fiscal implications of e-commerce, legal jurisdiction and e-commerce transactions, development and competition (WTO 2003). On the other hand, it has been argued by the WTO that e-commerce issues can be dealt with within existing global trade agreements, such as the GATS and TRIPs. The EU, keen to ensure the expansion of liberalised e-commerce trade, has expressed strong support for this position (WTO 2003) noting that it pertains to general obligations, such as those that might relate to Most Favoured Nation (MFN) and transparency, or specific commitments, such as those pertaining to market access or national treatment (WTO 1999a). Very importantly also, early on the EU argued that 'Internet access and network services are telecommunications services', that the obligations of the aforementioned GATS Telecommunications Annex apply to Internet access and network services, and that the specification of the GATS Reference Paper on Basic Telecommunications applies to suppliers of Internet access and network services as well as those providing telecommunications services over the Internet (WTO 1999a, p. 2).

The EU has played a prominent role in the deliberations undertaken to date by the WTO in e-commerce. Early on, it argued that the WTO had a crucial role to play in e-commerce trade regulation and urged other WTO members to undertake an evaluation of a range of important issues related to e-commerce. The EU was keen to ensure that its core interests were clearly enunciated from the outset. It urged WTO members not to impose 'any sort of duties on the import of services provided across border by electronic means...which would act in a similar form as customs duties on goods' (WTO 1998c, p.3). By contrast, the EU decided to impose a system of indirect taxation at the point of consumption in the area of e-commerce to serve, effectively, the dual purpose of revenue generation and industrial policy. In the latter case, the EU aimed to create a level playing field for EU e-commerce firms through ensuring they no longer had to impose VAT at the point of production which was placing them at a potential disadvantage against non-EU (particularly north American) competitors on price terms (Halpin and Simpson 2002).

The EU also advocated the creation of effective systems of data protection for consumers, citing articles III (on transparency) and XIV (on the adoption and enforcement of specific measures to protect privacy) of the GATS. It also noted the need to take measures to eradicate any anti-competitive business practices arising from e-commerce. It argued that the WTO should examine how e-transmission techniques might be used to enhance the facilitation, that is the simplification, of trade, a subject on which it produced a specific communication for the WTO's Council for Trade in Goods, arguing that 'there has to be a strong political commitment and a top-down driven approach to trade facilitation in which customs automation plays a part' (WTO 1999b, p.3). The EU highlighted the need to ensure that public sector e-procurement was conducted with transparency and fairness, especially for potential foreign suppliers and in general advocated the creation of internationally agreed standards to promote free competition (WTO 1998c). In addition, some important policy statements were made about the institutional treatment of the complex area of intellectual property rights in the electronic trading context. Centrally, it contended that the existing TRIPs agreement was applicable in principle to the technologies which are used for e-commerce and advocated that it be extended if and when necessary. The EU noted the importance of past and ongoing work done in WIPO in the area of intellectual property, in the process expressing support for a closer liaison between WIPO and the WTO on relevant matters (WTO 1999c, 2000).

In 2001, the WTO argued that the provisions of the GATS are directly relevant to international commercial transactions conducted through electronic communications networks (WTO 2001). This is a position that the EU has supported, going as far as to issue a strongly worded submission on the matter and suggesting to some that the EU does not believe that e-commerce needs separate trade regulation (Carden 2003). In particular, the EU was concerned about the possibility of WTO Members drawing on the provisions of the GATT to apply them to digital goods. The significant point here is that so doing would allow a state to impose customs duties on the good in question and the EU was keen to ensure that the temptation to do this did not grow among the less neo-liberal WTO Members. This option might have been particularly alluring for developing economies, desperately in need of foreign trade tax revenue, in most cases. The line adopted by the EU was one of definitional misnomer. It argued very strongly that GATT had not in the past been used to cover cross-border digital information transmitted via telecommunications networks as part of a commercial transaction. Basing its argument on the fact that so-called digital goods were in fact electronic commerce services and thus covered by the GATS, the EU argued quite dramatically that the 'notion of "digitised products" is misleading, and its interpretation has led to ideas that would wreak havoc in the WTO architecture' (WTO 2003, p.2).

One particular problem highlighted was the fact that 'anything physically crossing a border has to be treated under GATT...includ[ing] the outcome of services, such as architectural or industrial designs...where WTO Members have to apply both the GATS (to the supply of the service) and the GATT (to the physical outcome)'. Here, the EU, somewhat vaguely, called for 'consistency between the national treatment commitments made under the GATS for such services and the possible tariffs collected on the good delivered' (WTO 2003, p.4). Finally, in its submissions on e-commerce trade, the EU has been keen to highlight the need to enable developing economies to take part in the global e-economy. This is important, not just for a typical developing economy itself but also for forerunner economies like those of EU Member States which stand to benefit much more in relative terms from a widening of the international trading environment for e-commerce.

Despite this considerable amount of what is best described as preliminary activity since the late 1990s, to date WTO Members have not reached a stage where they have undertaken formal negotiations on e-commerce. There are several reasons for this. First, despite being an agenda item at the WTO Ministerial Meeting in Cancun, Mexico, in September 2003, no negotiations were begun on e-commerce. Instead, Members resolved to undertake further work in a number of areas notably the classification of electronically transmitted content as goods or services (or both); the fiscal aspects of e-commerce; development issues related to e-commerce; and jurisdictional and applicable law issues (Simpson and Wilkinson 2003b).

This Ministerial meeting and subsequent efforts among WTO Members to advance trade liberalisation have been focused on the highly controversial area of agriculture in which countries from the northern and southern hemispheres have been at loggerheads. It is unlikely that WTO Members will commence negotiations in other areas if, and until, problems in this domain have been resolved, something which at the time of writing has not occurred. In the meantime, since Cancun, there is very little evidence of much further policy activity on e-commerce having been conducted in the WTO, bar a recent proposal from the US for a software liberalisation agreement to be considered at the Hong Kong Ministerial meeting in December 2005 (WTO 2005). Second, it is the case that e-commerce has not expanded internationally at the rates envisaged in the late 1990s when the WTO first put forward its work plan. Whilst nevertheless having developed at a significant rate, the urgency with which global e-commerce trade liberalisation was viewed in the late 1990s no longer exists. Here, it is also important to realise that as many as 80 per cent of WTO members are neither rich nor heavily industrialised (Ostry 2004).

In any event, and third, it is not necessarily the case that the WTO's main remit in e-commerce was to secure a trade agreement. It is arguably the case that the main policy objective among those at the helm of e-commerce development was to ensure that no extra impediments to the free flow of global electronic trade were put in place. As has been shown, the EU has been a leading actor here and has been successful, on the whole, in achieving a prominent position, at least, for its objectives. Fourth, whilst the WTO is undoubtedly a vital (and possibly will in the future be the most important) actor in the development of a governance framework for the global electronic economy, since 2001 a new initiative has emerged in the shape of the UN World Summit on the IS. Whilst having a remit stretching beyond arrangements for global Internet governance, this issue area eventually came to dominate the politics of WSIS, in the process absorbing the policy energies of governmental, commercial and civil society interests over the recent period.

WSIS, GLOBAL GOVERNANCE OF THE INTERNET ECONOMY AND THE EU

The origin of WSIS lies in resolutions of the ITU's Plenipotentiary Conference (1998) and Council (2001). The initiative was soon thereafter endorsed by the UN (of which the ITU is a specialised agency) which authorised the ITU to play a leading role in the preparation of the summit (United Nations 2002). Politically, the proposal for a summit can be viewed as part of an attempt by the ITU to re-establish itself as the premier organisation for the global regulation of communications. It had lost considerable ground through the 1990s since many of its practices – most notoriously the system of international telephone accounting rates – were viewed as highly traditionalist and 'old order', anathema to the neo-liberal policy agenda of telecommunications being widely pursued by the world's most powerful governments and communications business interests. Equally significant, despite its best efforts, the ITU found itself deliberately 'sidelined' in negotiations which took place on the governance of the Internet's domain name and IP address system which eventually resulted in the creation of ICANN, an organisation which was quintessentially polar in make-up to the ITU (see Mueller 2002).

Like the UN and the ITU, the agenda of WSIS was fundamentally 'globalist' in nature, encompassing a wide range of issues which had rapidly come to be associated with the international IS policy agenda. This was reflected in the outcomes of its first phase, held in Geneva in December 2003. Here a complementary – though often confusingly overlapping – Declaration of Principles and Draft Plan of Action were produced. In the former – a document which also addressed a wide range of issues related to the introduction and use of ICT, *inter alia*, the promotion of ICT for development purposes, ICT infrastructure, access to information and knowledge, and cultural and linguistic diversity and identity – specific treatment was given to the core issues of the Internet governance. Very importantly, it was declared that the:

> international management of the Internet should be multilateral, transparent and democratic, with the full involvement of governments, the private sector, civil society and international organisations. It should ensure an equitable distribution of resources, facilitate access for all and ensure a stable and secure functioning of the Internet (WSIS 2003a, p.7).

The WSIS Draft Action Plan set out a series of Action Lines which, like the Declaration of Principles, had a broad focus part of which concerned Internet governance under a heading termed the enabling environment. Here a consideration of legal, regulatory and policy issues related to the IS occurred. It was resolved to set up a Working Group on Internet Governance (WGIG) whose main tasks were to produce a working definition of Internet governance; highlight relevant public policy issues around Internet governance; and to work towards creating a common understanding of the roles and responsibilities of a range of public and private actors in Internet governance, notably governments, intergovernmental and international organisations, the private sector and civil society (WSIS 2003b, pp.7– 8). This action line also made reference to the need to develop the conditions to promote e-commerce and made specific separate mention of the promotion of alternative dispute resolution.

The WGIG contained a quite eclectic international membership, variously from national and international government and intergovernmental organisations, business, academic and civil society quarters. The report which it produced in June 2005 was predictably tentative and somewhat generalised given how controversial and contested the issue of Internet governance had become, making it, alongside financial mechanisms, the most high-profile issue leading up to the second phase of WSIS held in Tunis in November 2005. In line with its core remit, WGIG (WGIG 2005, p.4) defined Internet governance as 'The development and application by Governments the private sector and civil society, in their respective roles, of shared principles, norms, rules, decision-making procedures, and programmes that shape the evolution of the Internet'.

WGIG was keen to point out its view that Internet governance encapsulated more than the work currently undertaken by ICANN, whose remit and (in particular) relationship with US government rapidly accelerated into the most politically controversial element of the negotiations leading to the second phase of WSIS. The report went on to refer briefly to a range of relevant public policy issues relating, *inter alia*, to the management of Internet domain names and IP addresses; Internet security, capacity building, freedom of expression and data protection and privacy. However, the coverage of these issues was broad-brush and scant. More significantly, this section of the report also referred to what it termed 'meaningful participation in global policy development' noting key impediments to the sharing of global Internet governance responsibility. WGIG bemoaned the absence of a suitable global participatory governance mechanism and 'lack of transparency, openness and participatory processes' with, in particular, limited developing economy involvement (WGIG 2005, p.6). The group went on to list a series of responsibilities which government, the private sector and civil society should assume when addressing Internet governance though these were not described in any detail and, with regard to the role that governments should exercise, were overlapping in nature.

For example, it was noted that governments should engage in policymaking, coordination and implementation. Yet, it was separately claimed that governments should exercise oversight functions, the development and adoption of laws, regulations and standards and, yet again, the making of treaties. Overall, this brief set of responsibilities was little more than a re-statement of, on the one hand, the kinds of interactions that have developed to date in an often ad hoc way in international Internet governance alongside some worthy and aspirational, though rather vague, exhortations often associated with more idealistic visions of the IS in action.

The most significant element of the WGIG report was its recommendations for the creation of a global forum for Internet governance which would provide 'a new space for dialogue for all stakeholders on an equal footing on all Internet governance related issues' (WGIG 2005, p.10). It was clear that the Forum aimed to address the concern of developing economies about being excluded from participation in Internet policy-making at the international level, the magnitude of which became clear during, and in the aftermath of, the first phase of WSIS. The Working Group recommended that the Forum be linked in some way to the UN, though was careful to point out that it should not duplicate the activities of other international institutions which deal with Internet governance, though it is difficult to envisage how this might be achieved in practice given that within the Forum 'any stakeholder could bring up any Internet governance issue' (WGIG 2005, p.11).

WGIG's report went on to posit four governance models, within each of which the forum would occupy a, though not the, central position. The aim of each model was to define and locate the role that governments might play in the evolution of Internet governance, the difficulty and complexity of which was reflected in each of the models which contained ambiguous and contradictory elements, in considerable part.

In the first model, a Global Internet Council (GIC) would be created as part of the UN, made up of governments and what were described as 'other stakeholders'. The GIC would assume the oversight role exercised by the US Department of Commerce over ICANN, in the process also replacing ICANN's GAC, though it appears that ICANN by implication would be retained in its current form. The GIC was to be government-led, with only an advisory role assigned to the private sector and civil society. It was not stated explicitly whether the GIC would run alongside, or would be an incarnation of, the Forum referred to by WGIG initially.

The second model advocated was the least radical of the four. It argued merely for the possibility of an enhanced role for ICANN's GAC 'in order to meet the concerns of some governments on specific issues' (WGIG 2005, p.14), though neither the concerns in question, nor the nature of the enhancement were specified in any way. The model placed central emphasis on the role of the Forum advocated earlier in the Report, which would be a context for deliberation only, and would produce analyses and recommendations on particular issues. By implication, this model would maintain the US government's unilateral control over what the Report termed the Internet's critical technical resources.

By contrast, the third model, based on the premise that 'no single Government should have a pre-eminent role in relation to international Internet governance' (WGIG 2005, p.14) argued for the creation of an International Internet Council to undertake governmental functions, *inter alia*, related to ICANN, as well as unspecified issues related to 'Internet resource management and international public policy issues that do not fall within the scope of other existing intergovernmental organisations'. In these cases, a lead role for government would be accompanied by input in an advisory capacity from the private sector and civil society. Very importantly, the model, with indirect reference to the thorny issue of US's unilateral oversight role of Internet management, advocated the creation of an 'adequate host-country agreement for ICANN' (WGIG 2005, p.14), though not even the broad parameters of this, let alone its precise nature, were specified. The model made no direct mention of the aforementioned Forum or its relationship to the proposed IIC.

The final model put forward by WGIG was the broadest of the four, advocating the creation of three major international institutions to deal with: decision-taking by governments on global Internet public policy issues; oversight of that part of Internet management presently undertaken by the private sector; and, third, global coordination of Internet policy development through deliberation between government, the private sector and civil society. In terms of the first function, a government led Global Internet Policy Council (GIPC) would take over responsibility for Internet public policy decision-taking from existing intergovernmental organisations, as well as assume responsibility for unspecified issues of a cross-institutional nature. This change would suggest that the GIPC should take responsibility for issues such as trade and intellectual property in respect of the Internet arguably diluting the power of the WIPO and the WTO.

In terms of the second function, the model advocated the creation of a private sector led World Internet Corporation for Assigned Names and Numbers (WICANN) to deal with technical and economic issues in relation to the Internet – effectively a UN-linked internationalised version of ICANN. Governments would play two key roles here. First, through an Oversight Committee, they would assume the current role played by the US government and would be responsible to the intergovernmental GIPC referred to in the first part of the proposed model. Second, governments would exercise an advisory role similar to that currently undertaken by ICANN's GAC. It was also stipulated that WICANN would have a host country agreement, though no more detail on this potentially controversial issue was specified. The third part of the proposed three-fold governance framework was a Global Internet Governance Forum which essentially would undertake deliberation and coordination on Internet public policy issues in which governments, the private sector and civil society would participate on an equal footing (WGIG 2005), suggesting that this would be an incarnation of the Forum set out by WGIG earlier in its report. The specification of a clear relationship between the three organisations in the model was notable by its absence.

THE EU AS AN INTERNATIONAL POLITICAL ACTOR IN WSIS

The EU strove to ensure that it played an important role in WSIS as early as possible. Keen to establish its global political credentials, in the months preceding the first phase of WSIS it went as far as to claim global leadership in the development of the IS and its public policy agenda. The European Commission opined that WSIS was 'the single most important political event in this area since the term IS was coined by the European Union in the mid-1990s'. It also claimed that 'most countries are rethinking their economic and social policy approaches and have expressed their interest in the EU approach' (European Commission 2003c, p.2) citing dialogue and partnership agreements wrought with countries in Asia, Latin America and the Mediterranean.

The months leading up to each phase of WSIS witnessed a process known as Prepcom, involving an attempt to construct a text which might be agreed formally by participating Heads of State at the respective summits. Unsurprisingly, the EU was keen to establish and promote its positions through the Prepcom process. For the Geneva summit in 2003, it laid out a series of proposed positions relating to both the Declaration of Principles and Plan of Action. In terms of governing the e-economy, the EU argued for the promotion, development and implementation of clear, secure and even-handed legal and regulatory provisions in the field of electronic network communications. It also argued for the expansion (in terms of increasing the number of signatory states) of the WTO's Information Technology Accord and Agreement on Basic Telecommunications, areas in which it would be set to gain significant trade benefits were liberalisation to be extended. Importantly, the EU argued for the creation of greater inclusiveness in global governance fora that consider IS issues, making a pointed reference in the process to Internet governance. The EU also urged the creation of 'appropriate frameworks for e-commerce' (European Commission 2003c, p.14), something which, as noted above, it has been keen to promote in the WTO. To galvanise its input, the EU secured a common position among its Member States for the first phase of WSIS in the Telecommunications Council (European Commission 2004c).

In the aftermath of the first phase of WSIS, the EU was again keen to point out its significance as an international political actor in IS policy-making. Rather boldly, it argued that the aforementioned agreements made in Geneva were 'largely inspired by the EU approach to an "IS for All" developed in the context of the Lisbon strategy' (European Commission 2004c, p.2). Noting the commitment made by states at WSIS to develop e-strategies, the European Commission put forward the EU as an exemplar of good practice, arguing for a global collaboration built on its own model of the Open Method of Coordination (OMC). The Commission even posited that its 'core of experience in common target setting, indicators and benchmarking and in exchange of best practice could be broadened to a progressively wider collaboration (European Commission 2004c, p.3). This soon became incorporated as part of the EU's formal negotiating position on how to implement agreements that would be made at the second phase of WSIS (European Commission 2005a). Regarding the specific issue of Internet governance, the Commission merely reiterated its earlier position of the need to develop further a multi-stakeholder approach which would be primarily bottom up and would be inclusive of developing economies. It also advocated the creation of an EU High Level Group on Internet Governance to develop a coordinated EU negotiating position (European Commission 2004c). Interestingly, the European Commission argued that the EU's approach to IS policy development involved the pursuit of "'regulated globalisation'" (European Commission 2004c, p.3).

As it became clear that Internet governance was becoming one of the most high-profile and potentially controversial issues on the agenda for the second phase of WSIS, the EU quickly developed and posited its own clearly articulated strategy. The Council of Ministers urged that Member States should work to ensure coordinated EU positions in forthcoming debates and negotiations, the WGIG having been given specific mention. Here, adherence to a set of Guidelines on Internet Governance, adopted by the EU in October 2004, was advocated. The Council of Ministers also appealed for discussion, which would lead to a uniform EU position, to take place within the Council's Working Group of Telecommunication and IS and the EU's High Level Group on Internet Governance which was chaired by the European Commission (European Council of Ministers 2004). The Council of Ministers continued to emphasise the EU's core position on the IS, first articulated in the Bangemann Report and affirmed by the EU's IS Commissioner at the Geneva summit (Liikanen, 2003), that the necessary ICT infrastructure would be delivered for the most part by the private sector, thus requiring the public sector to ensure that a legal and regulatory framework appropriate to this was created.

In the months leading up to the second phase of WSIS, the EU began to articulate its negotiating position on future Internet governance. It soon became clear that it favoured 'a new cooperation model' (European Commission 2005b, p.8) founded on 'a more solid democratic, transparent and multilateral basis, with stronger emphasis on the public policy interest of all governments' than currently existed (European Council of Ministers 2005, p.1). Importantly, however, the EU advocated change to the development of existing arrangements to create a 'public private cooperation model' (European Commission 2005b, p.8; see also European Commission 2005a) rather than a radical overhaul of current structures and processes, in which government would address public policy issues but would not get directly involved in operational matters.

In other words, the EU was aiming to promote globally the approach to the electronic network economy which it had been developing since the late 1990s 'domestically'. In this way, it soon found itself in something of a middle ground position between those interests, on the one hand, which wanted a system in which control over the Internet and public policy issues surrounding its development were placed in the hands of a new multilateral forum and, by contrast, those primarily US interests which were concerned about relinquishing control over the core technical elements of the Internet (notably those related to its system of naming and addressing) to a global governance authority. Consequently, the EU was able to position and promote itself in a way which heightened its profile as a political actor in global ICT governance to an extent not witnessed heretofore.

The centre point of the controversy surrounding future Internet governance arrangements concerned the US government Department of Commerce's continued oversight role of ICANN and, associated with it, the location on US soil of the majority of the key elements of the technical architecture (principally root servers and name and address databases) underpinning, and controlling ultimately, the functioning of the Internet. Here, the political stakes were 'upped' quite dramatically by a US government statement, issued in June 2005, declaring support for ICANN and its intention to 'maintain its historic role in authorizing changes or modifications to the authoritative root zone file' thus 'continu[ing] to provide oversight so that ICANN maintains its focus and meets its core technical mission' (US Government 2005, p.1). It merely offered to work with other states whose right to raise concerns regarding their own country code TLDs it acknowledged. Equally important, the US statement appeared to signal no support for the creation of a single Internet governance forum of the kind envisaged by WGIG, arguing instead that 'dialogue related to Internet governance should continue in relevant multiple fora' given the range of topics on the Internet governance agenda, in which the US would continue to support strongly market principles and industry leadership (US Government 2005, p.1).

The EU's position on future Internet governance had much in common with, though also differed significantly from, this position. Whilst it favoured development of the current ICANN model, which it described as a public-private partnership, a loose term open to differing interpretation, it also argued for the creation of a new global deliberative forum to be created. Equally significant was the EU's position on internationalisation of oversight of the domain name system. Here, the EU Commissioner for IS and Media was unequivocal, declaring in a speech made in October 2005 that the earlier June US declaration was 'announced without warning', was 'a recipe for stalemate' and was 'very disappointing to Europe and others who have worked towards a cooperative global approach since 1998' (Reding 2005a, p. 4). Nonetheless, illustrating the key high-profile position which the EU considered itself to be in, Reding (ibid.) also argued that:

Europe, far from being in an extreme position, is in the middle between US unilateralism and much stronger demands from other countries for multilateralism. But our position of deal broker cannot work unless the US recommits to its historic compromise to internationalise the Internet governance regime.

Despite this, care was also taken to assert that the EU position was 'mostly similar and often identical to that of the US' (ibid.). The EU's full support for

ICANN was also asserted. In an earlier speech to ICANN, Reding clearly articulated the strategic significance of what was at stake for the EU arguing that 'considering the economic importance of the Internet for Europe, notably its increasing weight in our trade relations with our economic partners...it would be in our interest to jointly work on realistic solutions' (Reding 2005b, p.1).

In its self-styled role as global inter-state deal broker, the EU put forward skilfully a proposal which included three core elements allowing a compromise position to be reached prior to the second phase of WSIS, held in Tunis in November 2005. First, the EU advocated the creation of a new global forum for deliberation on Internet public policy issues, thus appealing to those states that advocated a significantly new approach. It also acknowledged, and drew on, the work done by WGIG. Second, the forum was not intended to replace, but rather to complement, existing structures and processes of Internet governance, thereby addressing US concerns, but also leaving open the possibility for change in the future through further negotiation. Third, the EU proposal expressed strong support for continued private sector leadership heightening the chances of securing the support of some of the most powerful business interests in industrial capitalism, many of which could exert strong influence over government policy at the national and international level. Shortly before the commencement of the Tunis summit, the EU declared a major policy success for its initiative claiming that 'the compromise text agreed [by participating states in WSIS] was based largely on EU proposals' (European Commission 2005c, p.1) though this was perhaps somewhat misleading. Though a significant proportion of the agreed text on Internet governance is open-ended and requires further action, it is clear that the agreement is more akin to an interface than a compromise, certainly at this juncture. In it, states declared that the international management of the Internet should be multilateral, transparent and democratic, with the full involvement of governments, the private sector, civil society and international organisations. To assist with this, states invited the UN to create a new multi-stakeholder forum for policy dialogue, rather than decision-making, on core elements of Internet governance. The Internet Governance Forum (IGF), as it was named, was required to have its first meeting by the mid 2006.

However, it appears that the IGF, whilst possibly able to exert influence on Internet governance, will have no decision-making authority invested in it. In particular, it was clearly stated that the IGF 'would have no oversight function an would not replace existing arrangements, mechanisms, institutions or organisations...[and] would be constituted as a neutral, non-duplicative and non-binding process. It would have *no involvement in day-to-day or technical operations of the Internet*' (our emphasis) (WSIS 2005a, p.12). Despite the policy success claimed by the EU, it was clear that a September 2005 proposal to WSIS arguing that there should be 'international governance at the level of principles' over a range of matters to do with the Internet's naming and addressing system was not incorporated into the final agreed WSIS text (WSIS 2005b).

Thus whilst, as the EU rightly claimed, much of the language and form of the agreement was derived from its input, the real politik of the outcome was such that neither the EU nor other states in favour of doing so were able to secure a commitment from the USA to internationalise the direct governance control of the Internet's naming and addressing system. Nonetheless, it is clear that the widespread call for change in the US-ICANN relationship has had some practical effect. The stimulus for this development was the need to renew or otherwise, in October 2006, the contract between ICANN and the US Department of Commerce. Here, a new 'Joint Project Agreement' was announced between the two parties to run until 2009 in which, significantly, ICANN would now have, in theory at least, the right to determine its own programme of work free from any direct US prescription. Furthermore, rather than having to report on a six monthly basis to the US Department of Commerce as per the previous contractual arrangement, now ICANN was bound merely to issue an annual report which would be addressed not just to the US but to the whole of the Internet community (European Commission 2006).

What will happen after 2009 is impossible to determine at this stage. According to the UK BBC (2006, p.1), as part of the new arrangements, the 'US government has pledged to cede control of the net to private sector hands at an unspecified future point'. However, the EU's interpretation of these events was much more forthright. Here, it was claimed that the old contractual arrangement had 'now been replaced by arrangements intended to end *definitely* by 2009' (our emphasis) the inference being that this would signal an end to the unilateral control exercised by the US over ICANN. Giving a flavour of the EU Commission's currently favoured position on what kind public policy relationship might be developed between states and ICANN, Vivane Reding, the Information Society and Media Commissioner, argued for "'a reformed Governmental Advisory Committee to ICANN playing and increasingly important role'" (European Commission 2006, p.2). Clearly, were such a scenario to materialise, it is likely that the EU would expect to play a prominent role, not least because of its experience in hosting the Secretariat of the GAC.

CONCLUSION

This chapter has illustrated the increasingly significant role which the EU has played in the arrangements which exist, and are still emerging, to govern economic aspects of the Internet at the global level. The prominent presence of the EU in the key global fora analysed in this chapter is in no doubt. Its voice has been heard clearly in ICANN's GAC, in the Councils of the WTO which have examined e-commerce and, lately, during the WSIS process. Here, the European Commission has played a key role in representing and articulating a unified EU perspective vital in order to enhance the EU's status as a heavyweight political actor in global Internet governance. For this to hold, the EU will need to continue to ensure that wherever it sits alongside its Member States in global institutional contexts, coordination takes place to create common viewpoints on key issues. In ICANN's GAC, notably, there is already some evidence of divergence of opinion between the European Commission and key states such as France and Germany on issues such as country code TLD governance and the future remit of the GAC (Christou and Simpson 2004).

However, aside from determining the degree to which the EU has engineered for itself a prominent position in global Internet governance, it is also important to consider how effective it has been in practice in ensuring that its preferences are incorporated within policy-making processes. Here, unsurprisingly, the picture is more mixed. Whilst the role of the GAC has shifted more towards the so called 'co-regulatory', or more accurately state-shadowed regulatory, model preferred by the EU, there is no doubt that, officially at least, no direct oversight function of the kind first envisaged by the EU takes place, though the EU now eschews us an interventionist model anyway. It is also uncertain whether the more influential role adopted by the GAC in recent years is due to state pressure or to a realisation by the technical elite in ICANN that public policy responsibility for contentious matters could be usefully offloaded to states leaving the more straightforward technical matters in ICANN's hands.

The WTO, by contrast, is very definitely an inter-state institutional affair of the more traditional kind. Here, the EU's preferences have to date been largely realised, mostly through the acceptance by WTO members not to put in place customs duties on electronic trade items. It also seems likely that WTO members will continue to accept that e-commerce matters can be dealt with within existing treaties, such as GATS and TRIPs. The fact that the EU's interests are largely in line with that of the US is in no small measure a reason for the current position (Humphreys and Simpson 2005). However, by contrast, differences between the two have been evident in the recent negotiations leading to WSIS. As shown, the EU positioned itself skilfully as a compromise broker which certainly enhanced its international reputation as a player in global Internet governance, though its preferences, as shown above, were only partly realised, most obviously because of the decision made by the US to maintain its unilateral oversight role over the Internet's naming and addressing system.

Finally, the chapter provides some evidence of the patterns of governance emerging for the commercial aspects of the Internet at the global level. Here, only a nascent, inchoate picture is apparent. It is certainly the case that the state has been a very prominent actor (Drezner 2004), something which will persist as long as there is strategic economic and political value in the Internet. Activity in the WTO and WSIS is classic inter-state interaction. Whilst ICANN provides some indication of novel governance arrangements for the Internet through not-for-profit private sector self-management of technical issues, two points are worth noting. First, the world's most powerful state, the US, still maintains ultimate control of the technical resources integral to the Internet's functioning which were developed on its territory before the years of global Internet expansion. Second, it is also clear that the majority of the world's states have expressed the preference to be able to exert influence over the affairs of ICANN, aside from their displeasure at the US decision to maintain its control over the Corporation, albeit in a recently modified 'softened' version. What will emerge in the future as a result of the new forum to be set up in the light of phase two of WSIS is uncertain. At the moment, it seems likely that the GIF, though global and multi-stakeholder, will amount to little more than a 'talking shop' in which continued pressure will be exerted for the US to agree to multilateral governance of the Domain Name System (DNS). In any event, hardly radical state-shadowed self-regulation is likely to be the dominant form of global Internet governance for the foreseeable future, in which the EU is likely to continue to be a significant player and to prosper as a global political actor.

8. Conclusion: the EU and the evolving electronic marketplace

The governance of Internet based commercial activity has become, in a relatively short space of time, a most significant domain of economic and communications policy in Europe. This book has explored the role that the EU has played as an international institutional actor in the development of policy positions and regulatory instruments aimed at shaping the European Internet-based e-economy. Given both the newness and complexity of Internet governance across the EU and at the global level, conclusions which can be drawn on the significance of the EU and the governance measures that it has created must be tentative. Nonetheless, as the book has shown, there is evidence both of the form and processes of EU governance of commercial activity based around the Internet in the EU's 'domestic' space as well as the global policy context.

This chapter has two purposes. First, it aims to draw together the main themes of the book's preceding chapters, in the process reflecting on the extent to which the EU has developed new governance approaches not hitherto employed for elements of the electronic communications sector. Contending that EU Internet governance is more akin to the well-established and traditional, rather than the radically new, the chapter illustrates the degree to which governance characteristic of the European regulatory state is being deployed alongside alternative forms, such as post-regulatory state governance. In complement to this, it examines the degree to which it is possible to discern a clear pattern of modes, or practices, of Internet commerce governance, such as network or legalistic regulation, in the policy measures formulated and deployed by the EU in the areas considered in the book. The chapter's second purpose is to debate the likely future development of EU policy for Internet commerce. Here, three issues are explored briefly, two of a domestic and one a global policy nature: recent EU proposals for the next phase of its IS initiative; the possible extension of the EU's Electronic Communications Regulatory Framework (ECRF); and possible future developments in the light of the conclusion of World Summit on the IS and the EU's role here.

IS A CLEAR GOVERNANCE FORM DISCERNIBLE IN EU POLICIES FOR INTERNET-BASED COMMERCE?

Chapter 1 explored a number of theoretical approaches and conceptual models whose features appeared to have at least some relevance to an explanation of the form of Internet commerce governance discernible in the EU. On the surface, the Internet represents a classic example of the kind of global economic phenomena which have been important stimuli to the rise of the competition state (Cerny 1997) and the regulatory state (Seidman and Gilmour 1986) at the national and EU levels across Europe. The decline of the corporate state and the rise of international regulatory cooperation has created a new dimension in the legal system developed for transnational market activity (Teixeira 2004), a classic example of which is the EU. The growth of new public regulatory agencies as part of the regulatory state has even led to them being described as the fourth branch of government, the other three being the executive, legislature and the judiciary (Woolcock 2003).

As a number of chapters have illustrated (notably Chapter 5), the EU's policy rhetoric on the development of the Internet commerce is reminiscent of the neo-liberal liberalisation discourses which underpinned the emergence of European regulatory state governance forms in the related and often overlapping sector of telecommunications. Competition state behaviour is also in evidence in the desire to promote a strong European capacity in liberal market Internet commerce. The EU has instigated a series of measures through its directive on e-commerce and dot eu TLD regulation aimed at enhancing European firms' ability to capitalise on the expanding European domestic and international e-commercial environment.

However, as the book has shown, the nature of EU Internet commerce governance can only be explained partially with reference to the European competition state and European regulatory state. It is certainly the case that the Internet's emergence, since the mid-1990s, can be considered as an important example of globalisation, even adding another dimension to it (Friedman 2004). Cerny's (1999) definition of globalisation as an interactive process involving closer economic relations among states (internationalisation), and across states (transnationalisation) is recognisable in the growth of the Internet which both facilitated processes such as these and was in turn shaped by them. The well-established tendency of globalisation to undermine the ability of the state to provide directly regulatory public goods relating to the interactions of market and non-market based institutions, thus leading to the need to create new institutional frameworks at the supranational level can clearly be seen in the Internet's global growth. The ideological argument propounded from neo-liberal quarters that There Is No Alterative to market expansion in the face of globalisation (Tsakalotos 2003), nonetheless merely calls for a modification of state interventionist behaviour and influence rather than a reduction in it.

Whilst neo-liberal arguments underpinning the emergence of both the competition and the regulatory state are evident to some degree in the EU's policy discourses on Internet commerce, as the book has illustrated, these have not resulted in a form of governance characteristic of the regulatory state (which tends to flow 'naturally' from the pursuit of the competition state) in other sectors of the economy. The regulatory state can be viewed as having been born from the corporate state era, in which the functioning of key industrial sectors, subject to economic globalisation was decoupled from nationalistic state ownership. Since the Internet (and commercial activity conducted through it) emerged outside Europe, namely in the US, and began to be globalised relatively quickly from this formative 'base', the transitory process from the corporate to the competition state and the regulatory state in communications, in order to fulfil the exigencies of neo-liberally ordered globalising economic sectors, was not required in Europe. Instead, a different model of governance has developed from that recognised in the growth of the competition state and the regulatory state. As Chapter 4 illustrates, only some elements of the European regulatory state in communications have been incorporated in the system of governance for the dot eu TLD. Here, the European regulatory state, through the EU, has attempted to assert its influence in steering the direction of evolution of an initiative with European 'nationalistic' industrial policy concerns inextricably linked to the global level through the jurisdiction over TLD governance held by ICANN. The chapter also illustrates how this EU policy initiative has been characterised by regulatory principles and measures developed in the international Internet technical and policy-making communities. It is too early to be able to determine whether this governance form proves coherent enough to be effective in the EU's domestic environment, though it is illustrative of how the Internet's emergence has called forth novel governance forms to be developed in European communications regulation (Christou and Simpson 2006).

As Chapter 5 has shown, the governance of e-commerce across the EU, through the directive on e-commerce, is developing in a different form. Here, the 'classic' delegated legalism of the European regulatory state, exercised through its legislative process, has been deployed to shape as liberal and uniform a market for e-commerce as possible across the EU. EU policy activity in this area of Internet commerce can be viewed as characteristic of the regulatory state, since EU Members have agreed to delegate (partially) responsibility for e-commerce governance to the EU institutional level. EU governance is also of the procedural kind emblematic of the regulatory state. However, as Chapter 6 illustrates, unlike other parts of communications, there is very little evidence of sector-specific regulation by independent National Regulatory Authorities in the directive's transposition and implementation. E-commerce will, as far as possible, be governed in a 'generalist' framework within which competition and consumer law will be used to regulate the market's development. That said, an equally important element of this system, like the one being developed for the governance of the dot eu TLD, comes from the Internet community, in the form of self-regulation. Here, the development of codes of conduct and Alternative Dispute Resolution (ADR), in particular, are encouraged (though not made compulsory), and legally protected through the directive (and its transposed versions at the national level) as alternatives to the use of consumer and competition law in the judicial system. Liberal market electronic commerce will be delivered, therefore, through the self-management of 'soft law' with a 'hard' legal backdrop.

To what extent, then, do the emerging forms of governance for the aspects of Internet commerce governance covered in this book reflect a movement beyond the regulatory state, the dominant governance paradigm of the last 25 years? Specifically, does the evidence suggest that, in the communications sector at least, the European 'post-regulatory state' is emerging? Green-Cowles (2004) has argued that the role which the EU has come to play as a promoter of, and a shield against, global economic activity is suggestive of the need to consider the role of firms and other non-state actors in the EU political economy. The use of the 'soft' methods of self-regulation, such as ADR and codes of conduct, has not been characteristic of the regulatory state at the national level nor the European regulatory state as they have developed recently in the communications sector. However, ADR and codes of conduct are by no means novel in the European political economy. In the communications sector itself, self-regulation has been the bedrock of the press system for many decades. Thus, these kinds of governance practices are hardly radical in nature. When added to evidence of the strong EU influence which will be exerted in the implementation of the dot eu TLD and the Directive on E-Commerce (DEC), then the most that can be said is that Internet commerce governance provides an (albeit tentative) example of a significant modification of the European regulatory state, rather than the transition to a form of governance more akin to the post-regulatory state.

Internet commerce governance points, therefore, to two new methods of governance to add to Knill and Lenschow's (2004) typology considered in Chapter 1. First, the dot eu system of regulation suggests delegation of governance responsibility to public (the European Commission) and private (principally the dot eu registry, Eurid) agents – a system of legally mandated public-private European transnational governance. An important element of private governance here is ADR. The public dimension involves hierarchical shadowing, indicative of well-established European governance practices. Second, the regulation of e-commerce is orchestrated through the directive on e-commerce whose 'hard' legal character, despite the considerable discretion given to Member States in transposition of its measures (see Chapter 6), contrasts with the ADR and codes of conduct measures which it specifies. It has been argued that the creation of private authority in any sphere of governance makes the use of soft law – that is law which is not legally enforceable – of some kind or another inevitable (Morth 2004). These self-regulatory elements, whilst legally protected through the directive are not *mandated* by it – as Chapter 5 notes, Member States are merely encouraged to set them up. Should they not be operationalised, the alternative traditional mechanism of 'hard law' delivered through European and national level courts will be employed to address problems arising from e-commercial activities. In the transposition of the directive on e-commerce, there is only some evidence, from Finland, of the European regulatory state-like National Regulatory Authorities (NRAs) in telecommunications having assumed any responsibility for the directive's implementation. In fact, evidence elsewhere, notably in the UK and Germany, shows a deliberate strategy of separation of the regulation of e-commerce from the purview of these classic embodiments of the regulatory state in the communications sector.

Despite its comparability with and, as it expanded, close reliance on, traditional communications networks, it can be argued convincingly that the Internet is a *sui generis* development in international communications. Its innate (functionally derived) internationality, though trumpeted more than was actually the case in the latter half of the 1990s, has presented national and regional governments with policy challenges from the outset which are only beginning to be addressed fully. Not least amongst these is how to position national and regional governance traditions and practices in relation to a global phenomenon which developed significantly beyond these jurisdictions' 'consciousness'. The EU, unlike the majority of the world's states, because of its prominent techno-industrial position, felt the incumbency of this particularly acutely. Thus, as Chapters 2 and 4 illustrate, it has undertaken a careful process of developing a negotiated response to the features of Internet governance nurtured and promulgated within the international Internet community, primarily composed, in the first instance, of US elites from the technical, academic and business spheres. As Chapters 4 and 7 point out, the EU has aimed also to assert its interests in global fora, notably ICANN but also the WTO, and has been to some degree successful in doing so. However, the EU has also absorbed ideas around the form of self-regulation to be deployed for the Internet and customised these, a phenomenon recognised elsewhere (see Schmidt 2002). This is most evident in the dot eu system of governance but the e-commerce directive too, as Chapter 6 has shown, gives considerable scope for national discretion in the form of self-regulation though it is too early to comment authoritatively on the extent to which embedded variation exists at national level, not least because of the slower than expected growth in the European electronic network economy. Thus, the role of the EU in key global institutional fora can be viewed as a form of the European competition state in which liberal market Internet commerce governance is pursued with the aim of skewing arrangements favourably towards European traditions and interests as much as possible. This has called forth, necessarily, a form of behaviour recognisable in extensions of the European regulatory state in the manner discussed above. The modalities of these forms of governance – self-regulation through ADR and codes of conduct, public-private governance through networked agencification and the use of EU level and domestic competition and consumer law – are varied in nature and it remains to be seen the extent to which they exhibit compatibility and, following from this, coherence.

THE MODALITIES OF INTERNET COMMERCE GOVERNANCE IN THE EU

The debate on the relevance and role of well established forms of state-led governance in situations of widening global economic activity has led to a consideration of possible alternatives for the provision of sectoral governance internationally. If, as claimed, globalisation has realigned the interests of governments with the corporate sector, alternative modes of regulation such as codes of conduct might be considered as equally effective as government intervention. For Sassen (2004, p.65), 'the growing importance and formalization of what is now generally referred to as private authority is yet another component of the new privatised institutional order through which the global economy is governed and organized'. As a consequence of this activity, Baker et al. (2005, p.222) stress the need to 'rethink, or even jettison...hierarchically informed analyses that attempt to establish the primacy of any one level, attributing causal significance to developments at that level, and instead focus on the interactive and mutually reinforcing relationships between different levels, as well as the net consequences and outcomes of those interactions'. The globalising Internet, as this book has shown, is a context for precisely such a consideration, not least within the EU. Policy outcomes here, though far from radical, provide some evidence of the emergence of private authority governance. Such a development exemplifies specifically part of a wider trend identified by Green-Cowles (2004, p.32) where 'one increasingly finds a complementary relationship between public and private actors...[which]...is not merely an augmentation of public governance, but a qualitatively different kind of governance'.

First, non-state actors can influence the decisions of those with authority to delegate to them. Second, they can participate in the process of shaping policy proposals, prior to, during and after the delegation of authority. Third, they can assume responsibility – traditionally undertaken by the state or other governmental institutions – to monitor and enforce international agreements. Finally, they can provide legitimacy to supranational institutions which have been delegated power by their principals (Green-Cowles 2004, pp. 29–30). Chapters 5 and 6 illustrate the EU's preference in e-commerce for alternative self-regulatory governance methods such as codes of conduct, declarations, communications and recommendations – classic soft law measures (Frykman and Morth 2004, p.156). By contrast, Chapter 4 illustrates the emergence of, albeit embryonic, public–private authority trans-European network governance related to the dot eu TLD. These modes of self-regulatory governance raise the important question of the extent to which multidimensional governance is more a consequence of the nature of the EU and European integration than forces of globalisation (Baker et al. 2005). This issue, raised in other sectors, not least other parts of the communications sector, notably telecommunications, suggests that the EU and its Member States are developing the ability to customise trends which emerge at the global level, candidly illustrated in our case through both the dot eu and e-commerce initiatives. In the case of the former, the EU regulatory state has mandated private authority in the shape of Eurid, whereas in the latter case the directive on e-commerce provides a formal legal context for self-regulatory modes, namely codes of conduct and ADR, to develop.

In this respect, EU Internet commerce governance is suggestive of Kirton and Trebilcock's (2004) assertion that hard law and soft law might be best viewed as a continuum and may be complements rather than alternatives, though it is too early to make a concrete argument to this effect in the case of the emerging governance of the European electronic network economy. Alternatively, the system of governance for the dot EU TLD may be regarded as evidence to extend the scope of principal-agent theory (Kassim and Menon 2005) on two grounds. First, dot eu involves delegation from public interests to private interests rather than between public interests. Second, the kind of agencification in the dot eu governance network brings into focus a unique dual role played by the European Commission. On the one hand, as shown by Chapter 4, the Commission can be viewed as the agent of its Member States in dealing with the procedural governance aspects of dot eu. On the other, however, the Commission also plays the role of a principal in its relationship with Eurid, to whom it has delegated responsibility for much of the governance of dot eu. According to Schmidt (2004), the development of network-based regulation like this can result in interdependence, enduring relations and strategic action.

The penchant of the EU, in particular the European Commission, for exploring alternative regulatory forms for Internet commerce, provides more evidence of willingness to introduce and possibly incorporate new governance practices in key economic sectors. As early as 1995, EU Member States agreed a protocol on the principles of good Community regulation attached to the 1995 Amsterdam Treaty. Drawing on this, the 2000 Lisbon Council advocated the exploration of alternatives to existing forms of regulation drawing in relatively new actors such as those from the civil society quarters (EU Committee of the American Chamber of Commerce 2002). In the light of the Lisbon Summit, the Commission undertook a study of the matter, predicated in part on the changing regulatory environment of the developing electronic economy, as well as economic globalisation. An indication of the extent to which the EU was moving in the direction of alternative regulatory forms is evident from the commissioning, in 1999, of a study, undertaken by Lex Fori, a group of independent law firms, on the role of soft law in the EU. The influence of this study can be seen in areas beyond those which it was considered immediately relevant for. Three principles for alternative regulation were laid out – information, independence and participation – as well as three 'elements' namely, drafting and definition, performance monitoring and sanctions. The study advocated the employment of a combination of alternative techniques and made an important reference to the role(s) which might be played by the European Commission. Here, six categories were considered important: catalyst; facilitator; supporter; organiser; negotiator and legislator (EU Committee of the American Chamber of Commerce 2002). As this book has shown, many of these features are recognisable in the strategies that the EU is developing for the governance of the European electronic network economy.

The EU's White Paper on European governance also resulted in the creation of a working group on European governance that produced a report arguing for seven core principles to be considered in order to provide 'better regulation', namely proportionality, proximity, coherence, legal certainty, timeliness, high standards and enforceability. Very importantly, the report also defined co-regulation as a system that would combine legislation and alternative methods, necessitating participation, at some point, of civil society interests. In a similar vein, in 2001, the Mandelkern Group made its input into the EU debate on alternative regulation through the identification of seven core regulatory principles which echoed the views of the earlier white paper: necessity, proportionality, subsidiarity, transparency, accountability, accessibility and simplicity. The group's report recommended consideration of a number of criteria when deciding on the choice of regulatory instrument namely: authority, equality of treatment, ability to impose sanctions, length of regulatory process, cost of drafting and implementation, degree of removal of responsibility from market players, and credibility of the regulatory process. This report too took up the idea of co-regulation, stipulating various degrees of involvement of private stakeholders in either 'top-down' or 'bottom-up' policy formation scenarios.

In 2002, a Better Regulation Action Plan (European Commission 2002) was produced by the European Commission, which launched three initiatives, respectively on consultation, simplification and impact assessment. Regarding consultation, the same set of principles as those highlighted in the White Paper on governance were extolled. In respect of simplification, the Commission stated that any use of co-regulation would require a formal act by Member States and the European Parliament to allow the instrument in question to become part of the Community legal order. This part of the EU's policy also advocates the use of alternative regulatory forms. The dot eu policy initiative may be regarded as an example of the EU's attempt to mobilise governance in this manner.

However, to what extent are self-regulatory practices being developed by the EU, typified in its treatment of the governance of Internet commerce, likely to be superior to traditional methods? It is important to reiterate that the EU's movement into this terrain of governance is at most tentative as witnessed by the more familiar 'backstop' regulation which remains part of new initiatives. The extent to which novel regulatory practices develop will depend on the demonstrable efficacy of self-regulation compared to better established governance forms. Ladeur (2004, p.10) contends that 'it is increasingly important to use public-private partnerships, the "regulation of self-regulation" and other indirect forms of stimulating the productive exercise of state power in order to allow for an experimental, proactive and open conception of private intervention'. This general reflection on governance in the 21st century would appear to lend support for the kind of experimental governance in EU Internet commerce, typified by the dot eu system analysed in detail in Chapter 4.

Nevertheless, the use of soft law may result in compromise outcomes lower than could have been attained through more traditional government intervention and there may be ambiguity about compliance costs (Kirton and Trebilcock 2004). Other key issues around the performance of self-regulation concern reliability, transparency, and accountability which according to Marcussen (2004) emphasise Weberian bureaucratic principles as opposed to the efficiency criterion characteristic of neo-liberal New Managerialism. It has been suggested that the EU's consideration of alternative regulatory forms in its 'better governance' agenda deals with participation in instrumental terms, that is the extent to which it will fulfil set functional goals, rather than in democratic terms (Frykman and Morth 2004). On the other hand, if the EU is what Ahrne and Brunsson (2004, p.180) term a meta-organisation, it may be 'more restricted in [its] organisational elements than are most organisations with individuals as their members...[where]...often open conflict about regulation...given the relatively weak central authority in meta-organisations...[is]...difficult to solve. Instead, conflicting interests lead to the use of regulation on the soft end of the scale'.

CURRENT ICT POLICY DEBATES IN THE EU AND INTERNET COMMERCE GOVERNANCE

As noted in Chapter 5, the EU has, since the mid-1990s, emphasised as part of its IS policy the importance of the Internet, not least its role as a vehicle for commercial activity. Recent evidence suggests that this is likely to continue into the medium-term future. In 2004, the European Commission argued that as much as 40 per cent of the EU's productivity growth between 1995 and 2000 could be attributed to ICT. However, the Commission also complained that there continued to exist a series of significant regulatory impediments to the development of new ICT services and content, highlighting in particular the e-commercial area of financial service payments across mobile communications networks (European Commission 2004d, pp.4–6). A subsequent Commission statement put forward a proposal for the next phase of the EU's IS policy, named i2010 (European Commission 2005d). One of the main themes of this proposal was the need to instigate measures which would result in policy convergence across the ICT sector, whose most recent policy origins, as Chapter 3 has illustrated, are the European Commission's controversial 1997 Green Paper on convergence (European Commission 1997a).

The Commission proposed three priority areas for the EU, one of which was the completion of what was termed the Single European Information Space. Here, the further development of Internet-related activities was considered essential. Noting predictions for healthy growth of European online markets, not least in the business-to-consumer sphere, the Commission advocated action in four areas: ensuring the deployment of faster Internet services through broadband technology; providing a regulatory environment conducive to the further development of new content-rich ICT services; providing appropriate conditions to allow interoperability between different networks and devices used on them; and further enhancing the security of the Internet. Noting the range of policy areas covering the so-called European Information Space – involving audiovisual media, digital television, online trading and content support measures – the Commission resolved to have completed its examination of regulatory provision and put forward proposals, where necessary, by 2007. It is significant to note that the directive on e-commerce was highlighted as a legal measure which reflected digital convergence (European Commission 2005d, pp.4– 5) though as Chapter 5 has shown, it is far from being free from ambiguities and (potential) operational problems.

Any moves towards increasingly convergent regulatory activity will certainly impact on the EU's currently rather limited convergence regulatory package, the ECRF. As Chapter 3 has shown, the EU's debate on convergence which led to the ECRF, more than anything else pointed out the reluctance of Member States to regulate ICT content services convergently at the EU level (see also Humphreys and Simpson 2005, Chapter 6). It is a quite remarkable testament to the persistence of the Commission as a political actor that the proposals in the i2010 initiative, though tentative, appear to herald yet further attempts to Europeanise the convergence policy agenda. Reminiscent of the tone of its 1997 Green Paper, the Commission noted recently that '*Digital convergence* calls for a consistent system of rules for information society and media' (emphasis in original) (European Commission 2005d, p.5). This clearly suggests an expansion of the remit of the ECRF as currently constructed. It is once again reflective of the technological 'inevitabilism' which has accompanied EU statements on the development of ICT markets and regulation since the days of the Bangemann Report and before. Perhaps the biggest driver in the continued pursuit of convergence has been the Internet. As noted in Chapter 3, so-called IS services – which includes e-commerce – were excluded from the ECRF, despite the Commission's recent assertion that the directive on e-commerce reflects convergence, something which might be regarded as a piece of policy 'revisionism'.

However, the development and growth of the Internet through the last five years, although slower than the unrealistic predictions of the 1990s, has resulted, as Chapter 5 has shown, in it becoming the centrepiece of the EU's IS strategies. The Internet, not least because of its interoperative flexibility, has become more and more a technological platform epitomising convergence of telecommunications, broadcasting and IT (software) content and has led to what can be regarded as the beginning of the Commission's 'third phase' push to secure a comprehensive convergence regulatory framework at EU level. It is not possible to predict at this stage how successful it will be or indeed the timeframe for any change which may be proposed. It is, however, accurate to say that the arguments which were articulated so vociferously and forcefully regarding the regulation of public service broadcasting content in the late 1990s (see Chapter 3) still remain and will form an important part of any future deliberations by Member States.

Aside from whether it is further extended as a result of any future regulatory debate at EU level, the ECRF has had two important consequences for the development of the commercial aspects of the Internet across the EU. First, as Chapter 5 has shown, the EU's initiative to unbundle the local loop and to promote competition in the telecommunications market in general has assisted the uptake of the Internet through making it more affordable. Second, the EU has been keen to encourage the development of Voice over Internet Protocol (VoIP) services in as liberal a market environment as possible, something recently endorsed by the European Regulators Group (ERG). However, whilst the development of Internet telephony is the current convergence service 'cause celebre', it is clear that the EU's future ambitions stretch further than this. In a recent speech on VoIP, the EU Commissioner for DG IS and Media, Viviane Reding, noted that it 'was just the tip of the iceberg. IP-based networks and services will be the basis for a whole new range of communications services...as the market develops, the European Commission and national regulators will jointly ensure that throughout the EU, the roll-out of new IP services will not be hindered by regulatory hurdles' (European Commission 2005e, p.1). This provides a clear illustration of both the importance of the Internet in the Commission's thinking on the future of ICT convergence and the role that EU regulation should play in it.

THE FUTURE GLOBAL GOVERNANCE OF THE INTERNET AND THE EU

The process leading to WSIS, and the summits themselves, illustrate several key points about the current state of the politics of global Internet governance. Most strikingly, WSIS provides very strong evidence of the extent to which the nation state has reasserted itself in the global politics of Internet governance. More particularly, the role played by the two most high-profile political forces here – the EU and the USA – affirms the assertion made by Drezner (2004) that the world's most dominant economic and political state players have exercised the decisive roles in how Internet governance has evolved in the 21st century. By the early part of the 21st century, the insistence of the Internet business constituency that the market should act as regulator of Internet commerce – voiced so strongly in the latter part of the 1990s – was clearly less acceptable to governments which quickly and decisively reasserted their regulatory authority (Bayne and Woolcock 2003). The 'second coming' of the state in Internet governance must raise a significant doubt about the chances of developing new kinds of private governance floated by a miscellany of political activists, politicians and academics over the last decade. For example, Teubner (2004) has argued that globalisation has moved law-making from its historically institutionalised context of the nation state (in legislature and judiciary) to the fringes of law and thence to the boundaries between legal and other actors which have become globalised themselves. In the early years of the Internet's phenomenal growth, expectations were high that it represented a scenario for a truly novel form of governance. Menzel (1998, p.225, cited in Teubner 2004) was moved to comment that 'new international systems have also arisen that are able to more or less escape the grip of the State, think only of the regulatory systems for...the Internet'.

The EU provided further evidence of its growing political maturity in global Internet governance through the way it positioned itself in the lead-up to the second phase of WSIS. As Chapter 7 notes, on the one hand, it challenged the US to relinquish exclusive control of the Internet's root computing resources in quite bold fashion, most publicly through the interventions of the Head of the European Commission's DG IS and Media. Here, it presented itself as the most prominent 'state' in the vanguard for change to the global governance arrangements for the Internet and, in so doing, increased the possibility of gaining enhanced standing and legitimacy in the international communications policy community. Yet, the EU, through the European Commission, showed its political sophistication by simultaneously taking great pains to declare how closely allied to the US it was on the vast majority of the detail of Internet governance, not least the maintenance of a (neo-) liberally ordered (in terms of economic and social issues) and functioning Internet. As Chapter 7 notes, this positioning in the debate led it to promote itself as a compromise deal-broker. Thus, whilst in material terms the EU did not achieve fully its aims on Internet governance, the episode certainly ensured that its profile as an actor in the realm of global Internet governance was enhanced, part of a process which it has engineered since ICANN's inception and before.

The creation of the Internet Governance Forum (IGF) from the WSIS process raises the question of the extent to which the novel forms of (self-) governance propounded at the outset of the Internet's globalisation are still relevant. If as Cerny (2005, p. 47) argues 'the flexibilisation of governance is the main consequence of globalization' then this has yet to manifest in the global governance of the Internet, though there are signs emanating from WSIS, in particular, that it may possess some potential to do so. The new global institutional governance context that is developing may be akin to that of the OECD in terms of procedure, if not make-up. Here, though legal texts have been adopted through a formal decision-making process, they are non-binding in nature (Marcussen 2004). However, normative governance may also be developed in the new organisation through processes of theoretical statement and moral guidelines for behaviour. It has been argued by Morth (2004) that soft law can often be a precursor to binding legislative forms. However, it can also be an independent method of regulation, in which case it tends to be linked with network governance. In an instance of globalisation, such as that presented by the Internet, where traditional command and control regulation may be open to reappraisal, there can be a case made for the development of some kind of network governance. Here, soft law forms can create the kind of relationships between public and private actors that might 'open the door to intersectional agreements that do not make it clear who is regulating whom. Instead, states, international organisations, business corporations and non-governmental organisations may be simultaneously involved in the formation of regulations and may be subject to regulations that are formed in networks' (p.196).

The EU's recent suggestion that its Open Method of Coordination (OMC) be adopted at the level of global Internet governance is an interesting one in a number of respects. First, it shows how the EU has matured as a political actor on the global governance stage, epitomised by its recent role in the second phase of WSIS, as Chapter 7 has pointed out. Second, this method of governance would appear to be in line with the main decision to create the new Global Internet Forum. The OMC's flexible forms of soft governance rely on guidelines, timetables for goal achievement; bench-marking using quantitative indicators; national level action plans based on globally developed guidelines; and multilateral surveillance to review and evaluate the extent to which convergence towards agreed practice has occurred (Schelke 2004, p.151). However, implementing a system like this would prove a huge policy challenge and, like the (partial) private governance forms set up by the

EU in the areas of Internet commerce examined in this book, could prove controversial. For example, according to Baker et al. (2005) forms of multi-level governance have been viewed as a solution to governance problems arising from globalisation, something which has meant that problem-solving has taken much more prominence than democratic accountability as an issue.

In examining the modalities of global governance, Slaughter (2004) explores the nature of global transgovernmental regulatory networks, ideas which might be applicable to the current challenges of creating an acceptable system of global Internet governance. She argues that a key future challenge for those concerned with global governance issues is to consider holistically issues of delegation, transgovernmental deliberation, and horizontal democracy in order to accommodate appropriately both the role of the state and various forms of private authority. Achievement of such a task would address concerns of accountability. This idea springs from evidence of private governance forms and the adoption of rule-making through setting best practices. It also draws on the postmodern idea that self-government may develop in contexts that are neither wholly public nor private and would create transgovernmental networks with both public and private actors.

In a similar vein, Ladeur (2004, p.19), contemplating general problems of global governance, calls for new network based governance systems involving public and private actors working within and beyond states in the context of 'a new multi-polar (not multi-level) public order which is not separate from private ordering'. It seems highly unlikely, given the decisive roles played by states, including the EU, throughout the WSIS process, that a such a system of global governance will emerge for the Internet in the foreseeable future. Perhaps more realistically for our case, whilst acknowledging that the nation state will remain indispensable in future global governance, Vesting (2004, p. 265), making particular reference to networked economic activity, the kind of which has been the subject of this book, argues that whilst:

> the term 'global public-private governance' is often, perhaps justifiably, described as fuzzy, the term aptly describes the way the new world order follows the 'logic of networking', that is a logic in which order must be generated under the conditions of displacement of earlier stable boundaries...new regulatory networks will be based on time-dependent stability, will no longer be ordered territorially but *functionally*, and will largely proceed from co-operation with private actors' (emphasis in original).

CONCLUSION

As illustrated throughout this book, the growth of the Internet-based European electronic network economy, from its embryonic origins of the mid-1990s, has for the EU brought issues of online governance to the heart of communications and economic policy and regulation. Despite claims, couched amidst a wealth of hype, EU Internet commerce policy is far from radical, with core characteristics of the well-established, even traditional, rather than the new. Those novel elements of governance, generically involving variations of private self-regulation, are couched within, validated and delimited by, the overarching presence of public regulatory strictures. If as Vesting (2004, p.282) argues practical issues raised by the growth of the network economy require 'making possible and drawing together an intelligent collaboration of market, competition, autonomous rule creation, self-regulation and public regulation into functional regulatory networks', the EU faces three major challenges in the foreseeable future.

First, the practical efficacy of the chosen governance modes for Internet commerce development remains to be proven. As shown in this book, the public–private network model chosen by the EU for its TLD has barely become operational. In this and other aspects of e-commerce, the legally sanctioned practice of ADR, as well as codes of conduct, coordinated across an EU-wide governance network, have scarcely begun to develop.

Second, and related to the first issue, governance of the electronic network economy will only become important to the extent that there is activity in need of governing. How popular the dot eu TLD will be to Europe's enterprises is at present unclear. Much will hinge on the continued growth of e-commercial activity. Whilst positive growth trends are apparent, this part of the 'new' economy continues to be dwarfed in relative terms by its traditional counterpart. On the global Internet governance stage, the EU's continued ability to exert its influence will be a core issue. Thus far, rhetoric and posturing, carefully positioned closely enough to the US policy position, have to some extent ensured its prominence as a political actor. The challenge for the EU is how to capitalise on this to practical effect.

Finally, this book through its examination of intra- and extra-EU policy contexts for Internet commerce governance highlights the limited, though still significant, extent to which delegated governance to private agents has become part of international and global communications policy agendas. Practical concerns of functional efficacy aside, it is core issues of state material interest maximisation, and normative questions of legitimacy and accountability which may mean that, both within and beyond the EU, the governance of Internet commerce will evolve to resemble regulatory behaviour from present and recent past eras much more than something radically different to them.

References

Ahrne, Goran and Nils Brunsson (2004), 'Soft Regulation From an International Perspective' in Ulrika Morth (ed.) *Soft Law in Governance and Regulation: An Interdisciplinary Analysis*, Cheltenham, UK and Northampton, MA, USA: Edward Elgar, pp.171–88.

Ayres, Ian and Braithwaite, John (1992), *Responsive Regulation: Transcending the Deregulatory Debate*, Oxford: Oxford University Press.

Baker, Andrew, David Hudson and Richard Woodward (2005), 'Conclusions: Financial Globalization, Multi-level Governance and IPE' in Andrew Baker, David Hudson and Richard Woodward (eds) *Governing Financial Globalisation: International Political Economy and Multilevel Governance*, Oxon: Routledge, pp.213–22.

Baldwin, Robert and Martin Cave (1999), *Understanding Regulation: Theory, Strategy and Practice*, Oxford: Oxford University Press.

Barbet, Philippe (2001) 'E-commerce and the International Regulatory Framework', Université de Paris, CEPN.

Barlow, John Perry (1996), 'A Declaration of the Independence of Cyberspace', http://www.eff.org/-barlow/Declaration-Final.html

Bartle, Ian (1999), 'Transnational Interests in the European Union: Globalization and the Changing Organization in Telecommunications and Electricity', *Journal of Common Market Studies*, 37 (3), 363–83.

Bartle, Ian (2002), 'When Institutions no Longer Matter: Reform of Telecommunications and Electricity in Germany, France and Britain', *Journal of Public Policy*, 22 (1), 1–27.

Bartle, Ian (2005), *Globalisation and EU Policy-making: The Neo-liberal Transformation of Telecommunications and Electricity*, Manchester: Manchester University Press.

Bayne Nicholas and Stephen Woolcock (2003), 'Economic Diplomacy in the 2000s' in Nicholas Bayne and Stephen Woolcock (eds) *The New Economic Diplomacy: Decision-making and Negotiation in International Economic Relations,* Aldershot: Ashgate, pp.287–99.

Beat Graber, Christoph (2004), 'Audiovisual Policy: The Stumbling Block of Trade Liberalisation?' in David Luff and Damien Geradin (eds), *The WTO and Global Convergence in Telecommunications and Audiovisual Services*, Cambridge: Cambridge University Press, pp.165–214.

Bell, Daniel (1974) *The Coming of the Post-Industrial Society*, London: Heinemann Educational.

Bernstorff, J. von (2003), 'Democratic Global Internet Regulation? Governance Networks, International Law and the Shadow of Hegemony', *European Law Journal*, **9** (4), 511–526.

Better Regulation Task Force Review of E-Commerce (2000) 12, Cabinet Office, UK Government, October.

Bislev, Sven and Mikkel Flyverbom (2005), 'Global Internet Governance: What Roles do Businesses Play?' Paper presented at the Joint Sessions, ECPR workshop 23: 'Transnational Private Governance in the Global Political Economy', Granada, Spain, 14–19 April.

Biukovic, Ljiljana (2002), 'Unification of Cyber-jurisdiction Rules: Just How Close are the EU and the US', *Telematics and Informatics,* **19** (2), 139–157.

Blouin, Chantal (2000), 'The WTO Agreement on Basic Telecommunications: a Reevaluation', *Telecommunications Policy*, **24**, 135–42.

Bonfatti, Flavio and Migual Borras (eds) (2005), *The Single European Market in the Perspective of the i2010 Strategy,* http://www.seemseed.net/hShared%20Documents/SEEMseed_booklet_1_v2.pdf

Borrás, Susana and Kerstin Jacobsson (2004), 'The OMC and New Governance Patterns in the EU', *Journal of European Public Policy*, **11** (2), April, 85–208.

Boyer, Robert and Daniel Drache (eds) (1996), *The Power of Markets and the Future of the Nation State*, London: Routledge.

Brants, Kees and Karen Siune (1993), 'Public Broadcasting in a State of Flux' in Karen Siune and Wolfgang Truetzschler (eds) *Dynamics of Media Politics: Broadcast and Electronic Media in Western Europe*, London: Sage, pp. 100–15.

Cameron, Kelly (2004), 'Telecommunications and Audiovisual Services in the Context of the WTO: Today and Tomorrow' in David Luff and Damien Geradin (eds) *The WTO and Global Convergence in Telecommunications and Audiovisual Services*, Cambridge: Cambridge University Press, pp.21–33.

Carden, Richard (2003), 'The World Trading System Actors' in Nicholas Bayne and Stephen Woolcock (eds) *The New Economic Diplomacy: Decision-making and Negotiation in International Economic Relations*, Aldershot: Ashgate, pp.275–84.

Castells, Manual and Pekka Himanen (2002), *The Information Society and the Welfare State: The Finnish Model*, Oxford: Oxford University Press.

CENTR (Council of European National TLD Registries), 'Response to the European Commission's .EU Proposal', 3 April 2000, http://www.centr.org/docs/2000/04/response-doteu.html

Cerf, Vinton (1995), 'Computer Networking: Global Infrastructure for the 21st Century', http://www.cs.washington.edu/homes/lazowska/cra/networks.html

Cerny, Philip G. (1995), 'Globalization and the Changing Logic of Collective Action', *International Organization,* **49** (4), 595–625.

Cerny, Philip G. (1996), 'Globalization and Other Stories: The Search for a New Paradigm for International Relations', *International Journal*, LI, 617–637.

Cerny, Philip G. (1997), 'Paradoxes of the Competition State: The Dynamics of Political Globalisation', *Government and Opposition*, **32** (2), 251–74.

Cerny, Philip G. (1999), 'Globalization, Governance, and Complexity' in A. Prakash and J.A. Hart (1999), *Globalization and Governance*, London and New York: Routledge, pp.188–213.

Cerny, Philip G. (2000a), 'Political Agency in a Globalizing World: Toward a Structuration Approach', *European Journal of International Relations*, **6** (4): 435–63.

Cerny, Philip G. (2000b), 'Structuring the Political Arena: Public Goods, States and Governance in a Globalizing World' in R. Palan (2000) *Global Political Economy: Contemporary Theories*, London and New York: Routledge, pp.21–36.

Cerny, Philip G. (2000c), 'Restructuring the Political Arena: Globalization and the Paradoxes of the Competition State' in Randall D. Germain, *Globalization and its Critics*, London: MacMillan, pp.117–138.

Cerny, Philip G. (2005), 'Power, Markets and Accountability: The Development of Multi-Level Governance in International Finance' in Andrew Baker, David Hudson and Richard Woodward (eds) *Governing Financial Globalisation: International Political Economy and Multilevel Governance*, Oxon: Routledge, pp.24–48.

Christou, George and Seamus Simpson (2004), 'Internet Policy Implementation and the Interplay between Global and Regional Levels: The Internet Corporation for Assigned Names and Numbers (ICANN) and the European Union', Research paper presented at the ECPR Joint Sessions, Uppsala 13–18 April, 'Policy Implementation by International Organizations' Workshop.

Christou, George and Seamus Simpson (2006), "The Internet and Public-Private Governance in the European Union. *Journal of Public Policy*. Vol 26, 1, 43-61.

Collins, Richard (1994), *Broadcasting and Audio-visual Policy in the European Single Market*, London: John Libbey.

Crouch, Colin and Wolfgang Streek (eds) (1997), *Political Economy of Modern Capitalism: Mapping Convergence and Diversity*, London: Sage.

Cutler, Claire A., Virginia Haufler and Tony Porter (1999), *Private Authority in International Affairs*, Albany: State University of New York Press.

DENIC, '.net application, Registry-Registrar model proposal' http://www.denic.de/media/pdf/net/part_2-5-b-iv.pdf

Dickie, John (2005), *Producers and Consumers in E-Commerce Law*, Oxford: Hart Publishing.

Doyle, Gillian (2002a), *Understanding Media Economics*, London: Sage.

Doyle, Gillian (2002b), *Media Ownership*, London: Sage.

Drake, William and Kalypso Nicolaidis (1992), 'Ideas, Interests and Institutionalism: "Trade in Services" and the Uruguay Round', *International Organization*, **46** (1), 37–100.

Drake, William J. (2004), 'Framing "Internet Governance" Policy Discourse: Fifteen Baseline Propositions', International Telecommunications Union Workshop on Internet Governance, Geneva, 26–27 February.

Drake, William and Eli Noam (1997), 'The WTO Deal on Basic Telecommunications – Big Bang or Little Whimper?', *Telecommunications Policy*, **21** (9/10), 799–818.

Drezner, Daniel W. (2004) 'The Global Governance of the Internet: Bringing the State Back In', *Political Science Quarterly*, **119** (3), 477–498.

Dyson, Kenneth and Peter Humphreys (1990), 'Introduction: Politics, Markets and Communication Policies' in Kenneth Dyson and Peter Humphreys (eds) *The Political Economy of Communications: International and European Dimensions*, London and New York: Routledge, pp.1–32.

Eberlein, Burkard and Dieter Kerwer (2004), 'New Governance in the European Union: A Theoretical Perpective', *Journal of Common Market Studies,* **42** (1), pp.121–42.

Economist Intelligence Unit (2002), E-readiness Rankings, http://store.eiu.com/index.asp?layout=pr_story&press_id=890000689&ref=pr_list

EC-POP (2000a), 'The dot eu Registry Proposal', http://www.ec-pop.org/1009prop

EC-POP (2000b), Interim Steering Group on the Proposed Dot eu Registry, http://www.ec-pop.org/0511/

Eliassen, Kjell, A. and Marit Sjøvaag (1999), *European Telecommunications Liberalisation*, London: Routledge.

'EU brokers deal on progressive internationalisation of Internet governance at Tunis World Summit', http://europa.eu.int, December 2005

EURID, http://www.eurid.org
  Accredited Registrars:
  http://www.eurid.eu/en/registrarInfo/ listOfRegistrars.html
  Articles of Association:
  http://www.eurid.org/en/home.php?n=3
  Dot eu timetable:
  http://www.eurid.eu/en/euDomainNames /timetableLaunch

European Commission (1984), *Communication From the Commission to the Council on Telecommunications: Progress Report on the Thinking and Work Done in the Field and Initial Proposals for an Action Programme*, Luxembourg: Office of Official Publications of the EC, Com(84)277, 18.5.84.

European Commission (1985), *White Paper on Completion of the Single European Market*, CEC Luxembourg: Office of Official Publications of the EC, Com(85)658 final, 1985.

European Commission (1988), *Commission Directive of 16th May 1988 on Competition in the Markets in Telecommunications Terminal Equipment*, Luxembourg: Office of Official Publications of the EC, 88/301/EEC, 27.5.88.

European Commission (1990), *Directive of 28 June 1990 on Competition in the Markets for Telecommunications Services*, Luxembourg: Office of Official Publications of the EC, OJL192/10, 90/388/EEC, 24. 07.90.

European Commission (1992), *Review of the Situation in the Telecommunications Sector*, SEC(92) 1048 final. 21.10.92.

European Commission (1994a), *Europe and the Global Information Society: Recommendations to the EC*, Brussels: European Commission, the 'Bangemann Report'.

European Commission (1994b), 'Europe's Way to the Information Society: An Action Plan'. Luxembourg: European Commission', Com(94) 347, 19 July.

European Commission (1997a), *Green Paper on the Convergence of the Telecommunications, Media and Information Technology Sectors, and the Implications for Regulation: Towards an Information Society Approach*, Brussels, Com(97)623, 3.12.98.

European Commission (1997b), 'A European Initiative in E-Commerce – Communication to the European Parliament, the Council, the Economic and Social Committee and the Committee of the Regions' Brussels, Com(97)157, 15.04.97.

European Commission (1998a), 'Proposal for a European Parliament and Council Directive on Certain Legal Aspects of Electronic Commerce in the Internal Market'. Brussels, Com(1998)586 final, 18 November.

European Commission (1998b), 'Transparency Directive', OJL 204 21 July.

European Commission (1998c), 'Commission Recommendation of 30 March 1998 on the Principles Applicable to the Bodies Responsible for Out-of-Court Settlement of Consumer Disputes', Brussels, 98/257/EC, OJL 115 17 April, pp.0031-0034.

European Commission (1999), 'Towards a New Framework for Electronic Communications Infrastructure and Associated Services', *The 1999 Communications Review*, Brussels, Com(1999)539.

European Commission (2000a), 'Europe – An Information Society for All, Communication on a Commission Initiative for the Special European Council of Lisbon, (23 and 24 March 2000).

European Commission (2000b), 'Commission Recommendation of 25 May 2000 on Unbundled Access to the Local Loop: Enabling the Competitive Provision of a Full Range of Electronic Communications Services including Broadband Multimedia and High-Speed Internet', 2000/417/EC.

European Commission (2000c), 'Internet Domain Name System: Creating the .EU Top Level Domain', Communication from the Commission to the European Parliament and the Council, Com(2000)421.

European Commission (2000d), 'The Creation of the .eu Internet TLD', Commission Working Paper, 2 February.

European Commission (2000e), 'Communication from the Commission to the Council, the European Parliament, The Organisation and Management of the Internet – International and European Policy Issues 1998–2000', Com(2000)202, 11 April.

European Commission (2001a), 'Commission Recommendation of 4 April 2001 on the Principles for Out-of-Court Bodies Involved in the Consensual Resolution of Consumer Disputes, Brussels, 19 April 2001/310/EC, OJL 109/56.

European Commission (2001b), 'Communication from the Commission on the Application of State Aid Rules to Public Service Broadcasting', Official Journal of the European Communities, 2001/C 320/04.

European Commission (2001c), *Communication From the Commission to the Council and the European Parliament. E-Commerce and Financial Services,* Com(2001)yyy final (no available code or date).

European Commission (2002), 'Communication From the Commission to the Council, the European Parliament, the Economic and Social Committee and the Committee of the Regions. eEurope: An Information Society for All. An Action Plan to be Presented in View of the Sevilla European Council', *21/22 June 2002,* Brussels, Com(2002)263 final, 28 May.

European Commission (2003a), 'Report from the European Commission. First Report on the Implementation of the Data Protection Directive', (95/46/EC), Brussels, Com(2003)265 final, 15 May.

European Commission (2003b), 'Communication From the Commission to the Council, the European Parliament and the European Central Bank. Application to Financial Services of Article 3(4) to (6) of the Electronic Commerce Directive', Brussels, Com(2003)259 final, 14 May.

European Commission (2003c), 'Communication from the Commission to the Council, the European Parliament, the European Economic and Social Committee and the Committee of the Regions, Towards a Global Partnership in the Information Society: EU Perspective in the Context of the United Nations World Summit on the Information Society', Com(2003)271 final, 19 May.

European Commission (2004a), 'Commission Regulation of 28 April 2004 Laying down Public Policy Rules Concerning the Implementation and Functions of the .eu Top Level Domain and the Principles Governing Registration', EC No 874/2004, OJL162/40, April 30.

European Commission (2004b), Commission Staff Working Paper. Annex to the European Electronic Communication Regulation and Markets 2004 (10th Report), Volume 2, Brussels, 2.12.2004 (SEC (2004) 1535.

European Commission (2004c), 'Communication from the Commission to the Council, the European Parliament, the European Economic and Social Committee and the Committee of the Regions, Towards a Global Partnership in the Information Society: Translating the Geneva Principles into Actions. Commission Proposals for the Second Phase of the World Summit on the Information Society', Brussels, Com(2004)480 final, 13 July.

European Commission (2004d), 'Communication from the Commission to the Council, the European Parliament, the European Economic and Social Committee and the Committee of the Regions. Challenges for the European Information Society Beyond 2005', Brussels, Com(2004)757 final.

European Commission (2005a), 'Commission Outlines EU Negotiation Principles for the World Summit on the Information Society in Tunis', Press Release, IP/05/672, 5 June.

European Commission (2005b), 'Communication from the Commission to the Council, the European Parliament, the European Economic and Social Committee and the Committee of the Regions, Towards a Global Partnership in the Information Society: The Contribution of the European Union to the Second Phase of the World Summit on the Information Society', Brussels, Com(2005)234 final, 2 June.

European Commission (2005c), 'EU Brokers Deal on Progressive Internationalisation of Internet Governance at Tunis World Summit', Press Release, IP/05/1433, 16 November.

European Commission (2005d), 'Communication from the Commission to the Council, the European Parliament, the European Economic and Social Committee and the Committee of the Regions, i2010 – A European Information Society for Growth and Employment', Brussels, Com(2005)229 final, SEC(2005)717, 1 June.

European Commission (2005e), 'EU Regulators Favour Pro-Competitive Approach to Internet Telephony', IP/05/167, 11 February.

European Council of Ministers (1993), *Council Resolution of 22nd July 1993 on the Review of the Situation in the Telecommunications Sector and the Need for Further Development in that Market,* Luxembourg, Office of Official Publications of the EC, 93/C213/01, 06.08.1993.

European Council of Ministers (1994), 'Council Resolution of 22nd December 1994 on the Principles and Timetable for the Liberalisation of Telecommunications Infrastructures', Luxembourg, Office of Official Publications of the EC, OJ No C 379, 31.12.94.

European Council of Ministers (1997), 'Global Information Networks: Ministerial Declaration', Ministerial Conference, Bonn, http://europa.eu.int/ISPO/bonn/Min_declaration/i_finalen.html

European Council of Ministers (2000a), 'Council Regulation (EC) No 44/2001 of 22nd December 2000 on Jurisdiction and the Recognition and

Enforcement of Judgments in Civil and Commercial Matters' Brussels, OJ L12/1, 16 January, 2001.

European Council of Ministers (2000b), 'Council Resolution on a Community Wide Network of National Bodies for the Extra Judicial Settlement of Consumer Disputes', Brussels, 7876/00, 11 May.

European Council of Ministers (2000c), 'Council Resolution of 3 October 2000 on the Organisation and Management of the Internet', 2000/C 293/02, 14 October.

European Council of Ministers (2003a), 'Council Resolution on the Implementation of the eEurope 2005 Action Plan', Brussels, 5197/03, 28 January.

European Council of Ministers (2003b), 'Council Resolution of 18 February 2003 on a European Approach Towards a Culture of Network and Information Security', Brussels, 2003/C 48/01, 28 February.

European Council of Ministers (2004), 'World Summit on the Information Society: Council Conclusions', 15504/04, 2 December.

European Council of Ministers (2005), 'Draft Council Conclusions on WSIS: Financial Mechanisms', Brussels, 5945/05, 4 February.

European Data Protection Working Party (2003a), 'Opinion 2/2003 on the Application of the Data Protection Principles to the Whois Directories', 10972/03/EN final WP 76, 13 June.

European Data Protection Working Party (2003b), 'Working Document: Transfers of Personal Data to Third Countries: Applying Article 26(2) of the EU Data Protection Directive to Binding Corporate Rules for International Data Transfers', 11639/02/EN, WP 74, 3 June.

European Ministerial Declaration (Bonn) (1997) 'Europe Paves the Way for Rapid Growth of Global Information Networks', Press Release, 8 July.

European Parliament and Council (1995) 'Directive 95/46/EC of the European Parliament and of the Council of 24 October 1995 on the Protection of Individuals with Regard to the Processing of Personal Data and on the Free Movement of Such Data', Brussels, OJL281/31, 23 November.

European Parliament and Council (1997), *Directive 97/7/EC of the European Parliament and of the Council of 20 May 1997 on the Protection of Consumers in Respect of Distance Contracts*, Brussels, 4.06.97, OJL 144.

European Parliament and Council (1998), *Directive 98/34/EC of the European Parliament and of the Council Laying Down a Procedure for the Provision of Information in the Field of Technical Standards and Regulation and of Rules on Information Society Services*, Brussels, 29 June.

European Parliament and Council (1999), *Directive 1999/93/EC of the European Parliament and of the Council of 13 December 1999 on a Community Framework for Electronic Signatures*, Brussels, OJL 13/12, 19 January 2000.

European Parliament and Council (2000a), *Regulation (EC) No 2887/2000 of the European Parliament and of the Council of 18 December 2000 on*

Unbundled Access to the Local Loop, Official Journal of the European Communities, 30.12.2000, L 336/4–8.

European Parliament and Council (2000b), *Directive 2000/31/EC of the European Parliament and of the Council of 8th June 2000 on Certain Legal Aspects of Information Society Services, in Particular Electronic Commerce, in the Internal Market (Directive on Electronic Commerce)*, OJ L178/1, 17.7.2000.

European Parliament and Council (2001), *Directive 2001/29/EC of the European Parliament and of the Council of 22nd May 2001 on the Harmonisation of Certain Aspects of Copyright and Related Rights in the Information Society*, Brussels, OJL 167/10, 26 June.

European Parliament and Council (2002a), *Directive of the European Parliament and Council on Competition in the Markets of Electronic Communications Services*, Brussels, 2002/77/EC, OJL249, 17 September.

European Parliament and Council (2002b), *Directive of the European Parliament and Council on a Common Regulatory Framework for Electronic Communications Networks and Services (Framework Directive)*, Brussels, PE-CONS 3672/01, 4 February.

European Parliament and Council (2002c), *Directive 2002/19/EC of the European Parliament and of the Council of 7th March 2002 on Access to and Interconnection of, Electronic Communications Networks and Associated Facilities (Access Directive)*, Brussels, OJL 108/7-20, 24 April.

European Parliament and Council (2002d), *Directive of the European Parliament and Council on the Authorisation of Electronic Communications Networks and Services*, Brussels, 2002/20/EC, OJL108, 24 April.

European Parliament and Council (2002e), *Directive of the European Parliament and of the Council on Universal Service and User's Rights relating to Electronic Communication Networks and Services (Universal Services Directive)*, Brussels, PE-CONS 3673/01, 4 February.

European Parliament and Council (2002f), *Directive 2002/58/EC of the European Parliament and of the Council of 12 July 2002 Concerning the Processing of Personal Data and the Protection of Privacy in the Electronic Communications Sector (Directive on Privacy and Electronic Communications)*, Brussels, OJL201/37, 31 July.

European Parliament and Council (2002g), *Regulation on the Implementation of the .eu Top Level Domain*, (EC) No.733/2002, OJL133/1, 30 April.

European Parliament and Council (2003), 'Decision No 2256/2003/EC of the European Parliament and of the Council of November 17 2003 adopting a Multiannual Programme (2003–2005) for the Monitoring of the eEurope 2005 Action Plan, Dissemination of Good Practices and the Improvement of Network and Information Security (MODINIS)', Brussels, OJ L336/1, 23 December.

European Union Committee of the American Chamber of Commerce (2002) *Alternative Regulatory Models: Towards Better Regulation*, Brussels: EU Committee of the American Chamber of Commerce.

Eurostat (2004), *Information Society: Computers and the Internet in Households and Enterprises*, 1 October.

Eurostat (2005a), *The Digital Divide in Europe*, 38/2005, 10 October.

Eurostat (2005b), *Internet Activities in the European Union*, 40/2005, 11 August.

Eyre, Sebastian and Nick Sitter (1999), 'From PTT to NRA: Towards a New Regulatory Regime' in Kjell A. Eliassen and Marit Sjovaag (eds) *European Telecommunications Liberalisation*, Routledge: London and New York, pp.55–73.

Farrell, Henry (2003), 'Constructing the International Foundations of E-Commerce: The EU-US Safe Harbor Arrangement', *International Organization*, **57** (2), 277–306.

Federal Government of Germany, 'Information Society Germany 2006. Action Programme. A Master Plan for Germany's Road to the Information Society', http://www.bmbf.de/pub/aktionsprogramm_2006_gb.pdf

Finland (2001), 'Opinion of the Constitutional Law Committee of the Parliament', PeVL 60/2001 vp, p.3. Available in Finnish and Swedish at www.eduskunta.fi

Finnish Constitution: http://www.finlex.fi/pdf/saadkaan/E9990731.pdf

Finnish Council of State (1995): http://www.uta.fi/~ttanka/finland.htm#

Finnish Telecoms Policy Report (2003), Ministry of Transport and Communications, Finland, Programmes and Strategies, 1/2003.

Franda, Marcus (2001), *Governing the Internet: The Emergence of an International Regime*, Boulder, CO: Lynne Rienner Publishers.

Fredebul-Krein, Markus and Andreas Freytag (1999), 'The Case for a More Binding WTO Agreement on Regulatory Principles in Telecommunications Markets', *Telecommunications Policy*, **23**, 625–44.

Froomkin, Michael, (2001) 'Wrong Turn in Cyberspace: Using ICANN to Route around the APA and the Constitution', http://www.law.duke.edu/journals/dlj/articles/dlj50p17.htm

Froomkin, Michael and Mark Lemley (2001), 'ICANN and Antitrust'. Paper presented at the 29th Telecommunications Policy Research Conference, 'Communication, Information and Internet Policy', Alexandria, Virginia, US, 27–29 October 2001, www.tprc.org

Frykman Henrik and Ulrika Morth (2004), 'Soft Law and Three Notions of Democracy: the Case of the EU' in Ulrika Morth (ed.) *Soft Law in Governance and Regulation: An Interdisciplinary Analysis*, Cheltenham, UK and Northampton, MA, USA: Edward Elgar, pp.155–70.

'Generic Top Level Domain Memorandum of Understanding', http://www.gtld-mou.org/docs/faq.html

German Federal Government, *Information and Communications Services Act* (1997), http://www.iid.de/iukdg/iukdge.html

Germany: Doing E-Commerce in Europe, http://www.bakernet.com/ ecommerce/germany-t.htm

Gilardi, Fabrizio (2002), 'Policy Credibility and Delegation to Independent Regulatory Agencies: A Comparative Empirical Analysis', *Journal of European Public Policy,* **9** (6), 873–93.

Grabosky, Peter (1994), 'Beyond the Regulatory State', *Australian and New Zealand Journal of Criminology*, **27**, 192–97.

Grabosky, Peter (1995), 'Using Non-governmental Resources to Foster Regulatory Compliance', *Governance*, **8**, 527–50.

Graham, Andrew (2000), 'The Future of Communications: Public Service Broadcasting. Discussion Document', http://www.culture.gov.uk/creative /dti-dcms_graham.PDF

Green-Cowles, Maria (2001), 'The Global Business Dialogue on e-commerce (GBDe): Private Firms, Public Policy, Global Governance', http://www.itas.fzk.de/deu/tadn/tadn014/gree01a.htm

Green-Cowles, Maria (2004), 'Non-state Actors and False Dichotomies: Reviewing IR/IPE Approaches to European Integration' in Erik Jones and Amy Verdun (eds) *The Political Economy of European Integration: Theory and Analysis*, Aldershot: Ashgate, pp.25–38.

Guice, Jon (1998), 'Looking Backward and Forward at the Internet', *The Information Society*, **14**, 201–11.

Gunningham, Neil and Peter Grabosky (1998), *Smart Regulation: Designing Environmental Policy*, Oxford: Oxford University Press.

Hall, Peter A and Davis Soskice (2001), *Varieties of Capitalism,* Oxford: Oxford University Press.

Halpin, Edward and Seamus Simpson (2002), 'Between Self-regulation and Intervention in the Networked Economy: the European Union and Internet Policy', *Journal of Information Science*, **28** (4), 285–96.

Harcourt, Alison (2005), *The European Union and the Regulation of Media Markets*, Manchester: MUP.

Held, David and Anthony McGrew (2002), *Governing Globalization: Power, Authority and Global Governance*, Cambridge: Polity.

Héritier, Adrienne (2001), 'Differential Europe: The European Union Impact on National Policymaking', in A Héritier et al., *Differential Europe. The EU Impact on National Policymaking*, Boulder Colorado: Rowman and Littlefield, pp.44–59.

Héritier, Adrienne (2002), 'New Modes of Governance in Europe: Policy-Making without Legislation?' in Adrienne Héritier (ed.) *The Provision of Common Goods: Governance Across Multiple Arenas*, Boulder, CO: Roman and Littlefield, pp.185–206

Héritier, Adrienne (2003), '5 New Modes of Governance in Europe: Increasing Political Capacity and Policy Effectiveness', in Börzel, T.A and

Cichowski, R.A (eds.) *The State of the European Union 6,* Law, Politics and Society, pp.105–127.

Hills, Jill (1986), *Deregulating Telecoms: Competition and Control in the United States, Japan, and Britain,* Westport, CT: Quorum.

Hofmann, Jeanette (2005), 'Internet Governance: A Regulative Idea in Flux', http://duplox.wz-berlin.de/people/jeanette/texte/Internet%20Governance%20english%20version.pdf

Hulsink, Willem (1999), *Privatisation and Liberalisation in European Telecommunications: Comparing the Netherlands and France,* London and New York: Routledge.

Humphreys, Peter (1990), 'The Political Economy of Telecommunications in France: A Case Study of "Telematics"', in Kenneth Dyson and Peter Humphreys (eds) *The Political Economy of Communications: International and European Dimensions,* London and New York: Routledge, pp.198–228.

Humphreys, Peter (1992), 'The Politics of Regulatory Reform in German Telecommunications', in Kenneth Dyson (ed.) *The Politics of German Regulation,* Aldershot: Dartmouth, pp.105–36.

Humphreys, Peter (1996), *Mass Media and Media Policy in Western Europe,* Manchester: Manchester University Press.

Humphreys, Peter (1999), 'Regulating for pluralism in the era of digital convergence', paper presented at the ECPR Joint Research Sessions, Mannheim, Workshop 24: 'Regulating Communications in the Multimedia Age', 26-31 March.

Humphreys, Peter (2002), 'Europeanisation, Globalisation and Policy Transfer in the European Union' in Peter Humphreys (ed.) Special Issue on Telecommunications in Europe, *Convergence: The Journal of Research into New Media Technologies,* **8** (2), 52–79.

Humphreys, Peter and Seamus Simpson (1996), 'European Telecommunications and Globalization' in Philip Gummett (ed.) *Globalization and Public Policy,* Cheltenham, UK and Brookfield, USA: Edward Elgar, pp.105–24.

Humphreys, Peter and Seamus Simpson (2005), *Globalisation, Convergence and European Telecommunications,* Cheltenham, UK and Northampton MA, USA: Edward Elgar.

Hussein Kassim and Anand Menon (2004), 'The Principal-Agent Approach and the Study of the European Union' in Erik Jones and Amy Verdun (eds) *The Political Economy of European Integration–Theory and Analysis,* Aldershot: Ashgate, pp.39–53.

IAHC (1997) 'Final Report of the International Ad Hoc Committee: Recommendations for Administration and Management of gTLDs' available at: http://www.iahc.org/draft-iahc-recommend-00.html.

Ibanez, Josep (2005), 'Who Governs the Internet: The Emerging Regime of E-Commerce' paper presented at European Consortium for Political Research

Joint Sessions, workshop 23: Transnational Private Governance in the Global Political Economy Granada, Spain 14–19 April.

ICANN GAC (1999), 'ICANN GAC Executive Minutes – inaugural Meeting, Singapore', 2 March, http://www.gacsecretariat.org/web/meetings/mtg1/gac1min.htm

ICANN GAC (2001a), 'ICANN GAC Executive Minutes – Meeting at Melbourne'. 9–10 March, http://www.gacsecretariat.org/web/meetings/mtg8/gac8min.htm

ICANN GAC (2001b), 'ICANN GAC Executive Minutes – Meeting at Stockholm', 1–2 June, http://www.gacsecretariat.org/web/meetings/mtg9/gac9min.htm

ICANN GAC (2002) 'ICANN GAC Executive Minutes – Meeting at Accra'. 11–12 March. Available at: http://www.gacsecretariat.org/web/meetings/mtg12/gac12min.htm

ICANN GAC (2003), 'ICANN GAC Communique – Meeting at Rio De Janeiro', 23–25 March, http://www.gacsecretariat.org/web/meetings/mtg15/CommuniqueRioDeJaneiro.htm

ICANN GAC (2004), 'Executive Minutes – GAC Meeting XVIII Rome', 4 February to 3 March', GAC/Rome/003, 29 July.

ICANN GAC (2005), 'GAC Communique – Mar del Plata, Argentina, 2—5 April', 5 April.

ICSTIS: The Independent Committee for the Supervision of Standards of Telephone Information Services: http://www.icstis.org.uk/icstis2002/default.asp?Node=61

ICSTIS, 'ICSTIS takes first action under e-commerce regulations', http://www.legal500.com/devs/uk/it/ukit_119.htm

ICT: Activity of UK businesses, 2004, http://www.statistics.gov.uk/downloads/theme_economy/ecommerce_report_2004.pdf

Information Society Programme, Finland, http://www.infosoc.fi

International Forum on the White Paper, http://www.domainhandbook.com/ifwp.html

Jayasuriya, Kanishka (2001), 'Globalisation and the Changing Architecture of the State: The Regulatory State and the Politics of Negative Co-ordination', *Journal of European Public Policy*, 8 (1), 101–23.

Johnson, Davis and David Post (1997), 'And how shall the Net be Governed? A Mediation in the Relative Virtues of Decentralized, Emergent Law' in Brian Kahin and James Keller (ed.) *Coordinating the Internet*, Cambridge: Cambridge University Press pp. 62–91.

Jordana, Jacint (2002) (ed.), *Governing Telecommunications and the New Information Society In Europe*, Cheltenham, UK and Northampton, MA, USA: Edward Elgar.

Jordana, Jacint, David Levi-Faur and Puig Imma (2003), 'The Limits of Europeanization: Telecommunications and Electricity Liberalisation in

Spain and Portugal', paper presented at the 2nd *ECPR General Conference*, Marburg, Germany, 18–21 September.

Jordana, Jacint and David Levi-Faur (eds) (2004), *The Politics of Regulation: Institutions and Regulatory Reforms in the Age of Governance*, Cheltenham, UK and Northampton, MA, USA: Edward Elgar.

Kassim, Hussein and Anand Menon (2005) 'The Principal Agent Approach and the Study of the European Union – Promise Unfulfilled?' in Erik Jones and Amy Verdun *The Political Economy of European Integration – Theory and Analysis*, London: Routledge, pp.39–53.

Kielbowicz, Robert B, (2002), 'Regulating the Internet: EU and US Perspectives', *Telematics and Informatics*, **19** (2), 67–68.

Kirton, John and Michael Trebilcock, (2004) 'Introduction: Hard Choices and Soft Law in Sustainable Global Governance' in John Kirton and Michael Trebilcock (eds) *Hard Choices, Soft Law – Voluntary Standards in Global Trade, Environment and Social Governance*, Aldershot: Ashgate, pp.3–30.

Kleinwachter, Wolfgang (2004) 'WSIS and Internet Governance: Towards a Multistakeholder Approach' paper presented to the International Telecommunications Union Workshop on Internet Governance, Geneva, 26–27 February.

Knill, Christoph and Andrea Lenschow (2000), *Implementing EU Environmental Policy: New Directions and Old Problems*, Manchester: Manchester University Press.

Knill, Christoph and Andrea Lenschow (2004), 'Modes of Regulation in the Governance of the European Union: Towards a Comprehensive Evaluation', in Jacinct Jordana, and David Levi-Faur (2004) (eds), *The Politics of Regulation*, Cheltenham, UK and Northampton, MA, USA: Edward Elgar, pp.218–244.

Koenig, Christian and Ernst Röder (1998), 'Converging Communications, Diverging Regulators: Germany's Constitutional Duplication in Internet Governance', *International Journal of Communications Law and Policy*, IJCLP Web-doc 1-1-1998. http://www.ijclp.org/1_1998_webdoc_1_1 .html

Kogut, Bruce (2002). *The Global Internet Economy*, Cambridge, MA: MIT Press.

Kummoinen, Katri (2002), 'Regulating E-Commerce in Finland – Especially on Service Providers Acting as Intermediaries' unpublished legal document, Ministry of Justice, Finland.

Ladeur, Karl-Heinz (2004), 'Globalisation and Public Governance – a Contradiction' in Karl-Heinz Ladeur (ed.), *Public Governance in the Age of Globalisation*, pp.1–24.

Leib, Volker (2002), 'ICANN – EU can't: Internet Governance and Europe's role in the formation of ICANN', *Telematics and Informatics*, **19**, 159–71.

Levi-Faur, David (1999), 'The Governance of Competition: The Interplay of Technology, Economics, and Politics in European Union Electricity and Telecom regimes', *Journal of Public Policy*, **19** (2), 175–207.

Levy, David (1997), 'Regulating Digital Broadcasting in Europe: the Limits to Policy Convergence', *West European Politics*, **20** (4), 24–42.

Levy, David (1999), *Europe's Digital Revolution: Broadcasting Regulation, the EU and the Nation State*, London and New York: Routledge.

Liikanen, Erkki (2004) 'Internet Governance – the Way Ahead' speech made at SIDN event, Hague, 15 April.

Lodge, Martin (2002), *On Different Tracks: Designing Railways Regulation in Britain and Germany,* Westport: Praeger.

Luff, David (2004), 'Current International Trade Rules Relevant to Telecommunications Services', in D. Luff and D. Geradin (eds) *The WTO and Global Convergence in Telecommunications and Audiovisual Services*, Cambridge: Cambridge University Press, 34–50.

Majone, Giandomenico (1994), 'The Rise of the Regulatory State in Europe', *West European Politics*, **17** (3), 77–101.

Majone, Giandomenico (1996), *Regulating Europe*, London and New York: Routledge.

Majone, Giandomenico (1997), 'The New European Agencies: Regulation by Information', *Journal of European Public Policy*, **4** (2), 262–75

Majone, Giandomenico (2000), 'The Credibility Crisis of Community Regulation', *Journal of Common Market Studies*, **38** (2), 273–302.

Mann, Michael (1997), 'Has Globalization Ended the Rise and Rise of the Nation State?' *Review of International Political Economy*, 4, 472–96.

Marcussen, Martin (2004) 'OECD Governance Through Soft Law' in Ulrika Morth (ed.) *Soft Law in Governance and Regulation: An Interdisciplinary Analysis*, Cheltenham, UK and Northampton, MA, USA: Edward Elgar, pp.103–25.

McGowan, Francis and Wallace Helen (1996), 'Towards a European Regulatory State', *Journal of European Public Policy*, **3** (4), 560—76.

Michalis, Maria (1999), 'European Union Broadcasting and Telecoms: Towards a Convergent Regulatory Regime?', *European Journal of Communication*, **14** (2), 141–71.

Minogue, Martin (2002), 'Governance-Based Analysis of Regulation', *Annals of Public and Cooperative Economics,* **73** (4), 649—666.

Moran, Michael (2002), 'Understanding the Regulatory State', *British Journal of Political Science*, **32**, 391–413.

Moran, Michael (2003), *The British Regulatory State: High Modernism and Hyper-Innovation*, Oxford: Oxford University Press.

Morgan, Kevin and Douglas Webber (1986), 'Divergent Paths: Political Strategies for Telecommunications in Britain, France and West Germany' in Kenneth Dyson and Peter Humphreys (eds) *The Politics of the*

Communications Revolution in Western Europe, London: Frank Cass, pp.56–79.

Morth, Ulrika (2004), 'Introduction' in Ulrika Morth (ed.) *Soft Law in Governance and Regulation: An Interdisciplinary Analysis*, Cheltenham, UK and Northampton, MA, USA: Edward Elgar, pp.1–7.

Mosher, Jim (2000), 'Open Method of Coordination: Functional and Political Origins' *ECSA Review*, **13** (3), http://eucenter.wisc.edu/OMC/Papers /EUC/MosherECSA.doc

Mueller, Milton (2002), *Ruling the Root: Internet Governance and the Taming of Cyberspace*, Cambridge: MIT Press.

Mueller, Milton, John Mathiason and Lee McKnight (2004), 'Making Sense of 'Internet Governance': Defining Principles and Norms in a Policy Context', Internet Governance Project, Syracuse University, The Convergence Center, 26 April, http://dcc.syr.edu/misarticles/SU-IGP-rev2.

Natalicchi, Giorgio (2001), *Wiring Europe: Reshaping the European Telecommunications Regime*, Lanham, Boulder, CO, New York, and Oxford: Rowman and Littlefield.

Newman, Abraham and Bach, David (2001), 'In the Shadow of the State: Self-Regulatory Trajectories in a Digital Age' paper presented at the 2001 Annual Convention of the American Political Science Association, San Francisco, CA, 30 August–2 September 2001.

Ohmae, Kenichi (1996), *The End of the Nation State: The Rise of Regional Economies*, London: HarperCollins.

Ohmae, Kenichi (1999), *The Borderless World: Power and Strategy in the Interlinked Economy*, New York: Harper Business.

Ostry, Silvia (2004) 'The Future of the World Trading System: Beyond Doha', in John Kirton and Michael Trebilcock (eds.) *Hard Choices, Soft Law – Voluntary Standards in Global Trade, Environment and Social Governance*, Aldershot: Ashgate, pp. 270–87.

Paris, Roland (2003), 'The Globalization of Taxation? Electronic Commerce and the Transformation of the State', *International Studies Quarterly*, **47** (3), 153–182.

Pauwels, Caroline (1998), 'Integrating Economies, Integrating Policies: the Importance of Antitrust and Competition Policies Within the Global Audiovisual Order', *Communications and Strategies*, **30**, 103–32.

Payne, Anthony (2000), 'Globalization and Modes of Regionalist Governance' in J. Pierre (ed.), *Debating Governance: Authority, Steering and Democracy* , Oxford: Oxford University Press.

Price, Monroe E. and Verhulst, Simon (2000), 'In Search of the Self: Charting the Course of Self-Regulation on the Internet in a Global Environment', in Christopher T. Marsden, (ed.), *Regulating the Global Information Society*, London and New York: Routledge, pp.57–78.

Price, Monroe E. and Verhulst, Simon (2005), *Self-regulation and the Internet*, The Hague: Kluwer Law International.

Reding, Viviane (2005a) 'Speech Made to a Conference of the Internet Corporation for Assigned Names and Numbers', Luxembourg, speech 05/457, 11 July.

Reding, Viviane (2005b) 'Opportunities and Challenges of the Ubiquitous World and Some Words on Internet Governance', speech made at the 2005 Summit of the Global Business Dialogue on Electronic Commerce, 17 October.

Report of the Expert Group on B2B trading Platforms: Final Report, http://europa.eu.int/comm/enterprise/ict/policy/b2b/wshop/fin-report.pdf

Ronit, Karsten (2005), 'Self-regulation and Public Regulation: Financial Services and the Out-of-Court Dispute Services', paper presented to the European Consortium for Political Research Joint Sessions, workshop 23: 'Transnational Private Governance in the Global Political Economy', Granada, Spain, 14–19 April.

Roy, Simon (2002), 'Telecommunications Policy in the European Union', in Peter Humphreys (ed.), Special Issue on Telecommunications in Europe, *Convergence: the Journal of Research into New Media Technologies*, **8** (2), 100–13.

Sandholtz, Wayne (1993), 'Institutions and Collective Action. The New Telecommunications in Western Europe', *World Politics*, **45** (2), 242–70.

Sandholtz, Wayne (1998), 'The Emergence of a Supranational Telecommunications Regime', in Wayne Sandholtz and Alexander Stone Sweet (eds), *European Integration and Supranational Governance*, Oxford: Oxford University Press, pp.134–63.

Sassen, Saskia (2004), 'De-nationalized State Agendas and Privatized Norm-Making' in Karl-Heinz Ladeur (ed.) *Pubic Governance in the Age of Globalisation*, Aldershot: Ashgate, pp.51–70.

Schaede, Ulrike (2000), *Cooperative Capitalism: Self-regulation, Trade Associations and the Antimonopoly Law in Japan,* Oxford: Oxford University Press

Scharpf, Fritz W. (1993), 'Coordination in Hierarchies and Networks', in Fritz Scharpf (ed.), *Games in Hierarchies and Networks*, Boulder CO: Westview Press.

Scharpf, Fritz W. (1994), 'Games Real Actors Could Play: Positive and Negative Coordination in Embedded Negotiations', *Journal of Theoretical Politics*, **61**, 27–53.

Scharpf, Fritz W. (1996), 'Negative and Positive Integration in the Political Economy of European Welfare States', in Gary Marks et al. (eds), *Governance in the European Union*, London: Sage, pp.15–39.

Scharpf, Fritz W. (1997), *Games Real Actors Play*, Boulder: Westview Press.

Schelke, Waltraud (2004), 'Understanding New forms of European Integration – a Study in Competing Political Economy Explanations' in Erik Jones and Amy Verdun (eds) *The Political Economy of European Integration: Theory and Analysis*, Aldershot: Ashgate, pp.149–69.

Schiller, Dan (1999), *Digital Capitalism: Networking the Global Market System,* Cambridge, MA: MIT Press.

Schmidt, Patrick (2004), 'Law in the Age of Governance' in Jacinct Jordana, David Levi-Faur (eds.) *The Politics of Regulation: Institutions and Regulatory Reforms in the Age of Governance,* Cheltenham, UK and Northampton, MA, USA: Edward Elgar pp. 273–95.

Schmidt, Susanne K. (1996), 'Sterile debates and dubious generalisations: European integration theory tested by telecommunications and electricity', *Journal of Public Policy,* **16** (3), 233-71.

Schmidt, Vivien A. (1996), *From State to Market? The Transformation of French Business and Government,* Cambridge: Cambridge University Press.

Schmidt, Vivien, A. (2002), *The Futures of European Capitalism,* Oxford: Oxford University Press.

Schneider, Volker and Raymund Werle (1990), 'International Regime or Corporate Actor? The European Community in Telecommunications Policy', in Kenneth Dyson and Peter Humphreys (eds) *The Political Economy of Communications: International and European Dimensions,* London and New York: Routledge, pp.77–106.

Schulz, Wolfgang and Thorsten Held, (2001), 'Regulated Self-regulation as a Form of Modern Government', Hans-Bredow-Institute, Interim Report (October), Study Commissioned by the German Federal Commissioner to Cultural and Media Affairs.

Scott, Colin (2002), 'Private Regulation of the Public Sector: A Neglected Facet of Contemporary Governance', *Journal of Law and Society,* **29**, 56–76.

Scott, Colin (2004), 'Regulation in the Age of Governance: The Rise of the Post-regulatory State', in Jacint Jordana and David Levi-Faur (eds) *The Politics of Regulation,* Cheltenham: Edward Elgar, pp. 145–74.

Seidman, Harold and Robert Gilmour (1986), *Politics, Position, and Power: From the Positive to the Regulatory State,* 4th edition, New York: Oxford University Press.

Self-regulation of Digital Media Converging on the Internet: Industry Codes of Conduct in Sectoral Analysis (2004), Programme in Comparative Media Law and Policy, Oxford University Centre for Social Legal Studies, http://pcmlp.socleg.ox.ac.uk/text/IAPCODEfinal.pdf

Serot, Alexandre (2002), 'When National Institutions do not Matter. The Importance of International Factors: Pricing Policies in Telecoms', *Journal of European Public Policy,* **9** (6), 973–994.

Simpson, Seamus (1999), 'Regulating ICT Convergence', *Javnost: The Public,* **6** (3), 49–66.

Simpson, Seamus (2000), 'Intra-institutional Rivalry and Policy Entrepreneurship in the European Union: the politics of Information and

Communications Technology Convergence', *New Media and Society*, **2** (4), 445–66.

Simpson, Seamus (2002) 'Harmony, Hegemony and the Internet: a Neo-Gramscian Perspective'. Proceedings of the Fifth Annual International Business and Economics (IBEC) Conference, 11-12 October, St Norbert's College, Green Bay, Wisconsin, USA, pp. 22–36.

Simpson, Seamus (2004), 'Explaining the Commercialisation of the Internet: a Neo-Gramscian Contribution', *Information, Communications and Society*, **7** (1), 50–69.

Simpson, Seamus and Rorden Wilkinson (2003a), 'Governing E-commerce: Prospects and Problems', paper presented to the 31st Telecommunications Policy Research Conference, 'Communication, Information and Internet Policy', National Center for Technology and Law, George Mason University School of Law, Arlington, Virginia, USA, 19—21 September, http://www.tprc.org

Simpson, Seamus and Rorden Wilkinson (2003b), 'First-mover Preferences, Structural Power and Path Dependency: the World Trade Organization and E-commerce' paper presented to the International Research Foundation for Development, World Forum on the Information Society, Geneva, Switzerland, 8–10 December.

Siune, Karen and Wolfgang Truetzschler (1993) (eds), *Dynamics of Media Politics: Broadcast and Electronic Media in Western Europe*, London: Sage.

Slaughter, Anne-Marie (2004), 'Global Government Networks, Global Government Agencies, and Disaggregated Democracy' in Karl-Heinz Ladeur (ed.) *Pubic Governance in the Age of Globalisation*, Aldershot: Ashgate, pp.121–56.

Slevin, James (2000), *The Internet and Society,* Cambridge: Polity Press.

Smith, Martin J. and David Richards (2002), *Governance and Public Policy in the UK*, Oxford: Oxford University Press.

Statistics Finland (2003) 'Internet Use and E-commerce in Enterprises', http://www.stat.fi/index_en.html

E-commerce and paying by mobile phone:
http://www.stat.fi/tk/yr/tietoyhteiskunta/verkkokauppa_en.html

Finland: E-commerce to increase in 2005

http://e.finland.fi/netcomm/news/showarticle.asp?intNWSAID=40620

Stoker, Gerry (1998), 'Governance as a Theory: Five Propositions', *International Social Science Journal*, **155**, 17–27.

Strange, Susan (1996), *The Retreat of the State: The Diffusion of Power in the World Economy*, Cambridge: Cambridge University Press.

Streeck, Wolfgang and Philippe C. Schmitter (ed.), *Private Interest Government. Beyond Market and State,* London: Sage.

Teixeira, Pedro Gustavo (2004) 'Public Governance and the Co-operative Law of Transnational Markets: The Case of Financial Regulation' in Karl-

Heinz Ladeur (ed.) *Pubic Governance in the Age of Globalisation* Aldershot: Ashgate, pp. 305–35.

Telecom Markets (31.07.2001), 'European Regulators Make Flat-rate Internet Progress', **411**, 4–6.

Teubner, Gunther (2004), 'Global Private Regimes: Neo-Spontaneous Law and Dual Constitution of Autonomous Sectors' in Karl-Heinz Ladeur (ed.) *Pubic Governance in the Age of Globalisation*, Aldershot: Ashgate, pp. 71–88.

Thatcher, Mark (1999), *The Politics of Telecommunications: National Institutions, Convergence, and Change*, Oxford: Oxford University Press.

Thatcher, Mark (2001a), 'The Commission and National Governments as Partners: EC Regulatory Expansion in Telecommunications 1979-2000', *Journal of European Public Policy*, **8** (4), 558–84.

Thatcher, Mark (2001b), 'European Regulation' in Jeremy Richardson (ed.) *European Union: Power and Policy-making,* London: Routledge, pp. 303–18.

Thatcher, Mark (2002a), 'Analysing Regulatory Reform in Europe', *Journal of European Public Policy*, **9** (6), 859–872.

Thatcher, Mark (2002b), 'Regulation after Delegation: Independent Regulatory Agencies in Europe', *Journal of European Public Policy*, **9** (6) 202, 954–72.

Thatcher, Mark (2004), 'Varieties of Capitalism in an Internationalized World: Domestic Institutional Change in European Telecommunications', *Comparative Political Studies*, **37** (7), 1–30.

Tsakalotos, Euclid (2003) 'Social Norms and Endogenous Preferences: the Political Economy of Market Expansion' in Nicholas Bayne and Stephen Woolcock (eds.) *The New Economic Diplomacy: Decision-making and Negotiation in International Economic Relations,* Aldershot: Ashgate, pp.5–37.

Tsingou, Eleni (2005), 'Transnational Private Governance and the Basel Process: Banking Regulation and Supervision, Private Interests and Basel II', paper presented to the European Consortium for Political Research Joint Sessions, workshop 23: 'Transnational Private Governance in the Global Political Economy', Granada, Spain, 14-19 April.

UK Government (1998), 'Competitiveness White Paper: Building the Knowledge Driven Economy', http://www.dti.gov.uk/comp /competitive/main.htm

UK Government (2000), 'Modernising Government. E-Government: A Strategic Framework', http://www.cabinet-office.gov.uk/moderngov/

UK Government (2002), 'The Electronic Commerce Directive (00/31/EC) & The Electronic Commerce (EC Directive) Regulations 2002 (SI 2002 No. 2013)' http://www.dti.gov.uk/industries/ ecommunications /electronic_commerce_directive_0031ec.html

UK Government Performance and Innovation Unit (1999), 'E-Commerce@its.best.uk', September 1999.

UK Treasury, 'Implementation of the E-Commerce Directive', http://www.hm-treasury.gov.uk/Documents/Financial_Services/Regulating _Financial_Services/fin_rsf_edirec.cfm?

United Nations (2001), 'UN General Assembly Resolution 56/183 World Summit on the Information Society', 90th plenary meeting, 56/183, 21 December.

US Government (2005), 'Domain Names: US Principles on the Internet's Domain Name and Addressing system', http://www. ntia.doc .gov/ntia home/ USDNprinciples_06302005.htm

US Department of Commerce (DOC) (1998a), 'A Proposal to Improve Technical Management of Internet Domain Names (Green Paper)', http://www.ntia.doc.gov.ntiahome/domainname/dnsdrft.htm

US Department of Commerce (DOC) (1998b), 'Management of Internet Names and Addresses (White Paper)', http://www.ntia.doc. gov.ntiahome/domainname/6_5_98dns.htm

US Department of Commerce (DOC) (1998c), 'Memorandum of Understanding Between the US Department of Commerce and ICANN', http://www.ntia.doc.gov/ntiahome/domainname/icann-memorandum.htm

Venturelli, Shalini (2002), 'Inventing E-regulation in the US, EU and East Asia: Conflicting Social Visions of the Information Society', *Telematics and Informatics* **19**, 69–90.

Vogel, David (1986), *National Styles of Regulation: Environmental Policy in Britain and the US*, Ithaca: Cornell University Press.

Vesting, Thomas (2004), 'The Network Economy as a Challenge to Create New Public Law (Beyond the State)' in Karl-Heinz Ladeur (ed.) *Public Governance in the Age of Globalisation*, Aldershot: Ashgate, pp.247–88.

Waesche, Niko M. (2003), *Internet Entrepreneurship in Europe: Venture Failure and the Timing of Telecommunications Reform*, Cheltenham, UK and Northampton, MA, USA: Edward Elgar.

Webber, Douglas and Peter Holmes (1985), 'Europe and Technological Innovation', ESRC Newsletter, **55**.

Weinberg, Jonathan (2001), 'ICANN as Regulator', paper presented to the 29th Telecommunications Policy Research Conference, 'Communication, Information and Internet Policy', 27-29 October, Alexandria, Virginia, US, http://www.arxiv.org/abs/cs. CY/0109099.

Werle, Raymond (2002), 'Internet @ Europe: Overcoming Institutional Fragmentation and Policy Failure', in Jacinct Jordana, *Governing Telecommunications and the New Information Society in Europe*, Cheltenham, UK and Northampton, MA, USA: Edward Elgar.

Wilkinson, Christopher (2000) 'The Organisation and Management of the Internet'. Speech at the China Internet Conference and Exhibition, Beijing,

8 June. Available at: http://europa.eu. int/ISPO /eif/InternetPoliciesSite/ ChristopherWilkinson.htm

Wilkinson, Rorden (2000), *Multilateralism and the World Trade Organisation*, London: Routledge.

Wilkinson, Rorden (2001), 'The WTO in Crisis: Exploring the dimensions of institutional inertia", *Journal of World Trade*, **35** (3), pp.397–419.

Winston, Brian (1998) *Media, Technology and Society: a History*. London: Routledge.

WGIG (2005), 'Report of the Working Group on Internet Governance', Château de Bossey, 0541622, June.

Woolcock, Stephen (2003), 'State and Non-State Actors' in Nicholas Bayne and Stephen Woolcock (eds.), *The New Economic Diplomacy: Decision-making and Negotiation in International Economic Relations,* Aldershot: Ashgate, pp.45–64.

Woolcock, Stephen, Michael Hodges and Kristin Schreiber (1992), *Britain, Germany and 1992: The Limits of Deregulation*, London: Royal Institute of International Affairs.

WSIS (2003a), 'Note by the Secretary-General of the Summit: Draft Declaration of Principles', WSIS-03/GENEVA/DOC/4-E, 10 December.

WSIS (2003b), 'Note by the Secretary General of the Summit: Draft Plan of Action', WSIS-03/GENEVA/DOC/5-E, 10 December.

WSIS (2005a), 'President of the PrepCom of the Tunis Phase: Tunis Agenda for the Information Society', document WSIS-05/TUNIS/DOC/6(Rev.1)-E, 15 November.

WSIS (2005b), 'EU Proposal for Addition to Chair's Paper Sub-Com A Internet Governance on Paragraph 5 "Follow-up and Possible Arrangements"', WSIS-II/PC-3/DT/21-E, 30 September.

WTO (1998a), 'Work Programme on Electronic Commerce', 25th September, WT/L/274 (98-3738).

WTO (1998b), 'The Work Programme on Electronic Commerce. Note by the Secretariat of the Council for Trade in Services', 16th November, S/C/W/68 (98-4585),http://docsonline. wto.org/GEN_ viewerwindow .asp? D:/DDFDOCUMENTS/T/S/C/W68.DOC.HTM

WTO (1998c), 'Council for Trade Related Aspects of Intellectual Property Development: Work Programme on Electronic Commerce. Communication from the European Communities and their Member States', WT/GC/W/85, (98-1669), 23 April.

WTO (1999a), 'Preparations for the 1999 Ministerial Conference. Work Programme on Electronic Commerce: Communication from the European Communities and their Member States', WT/GC/W/306 (99-3377), 9 August.

WTO (1999b), 'Council for Trade Related Aspects of Intellectual Property Development: Work Programme on Electronic Commerce. Communication from the European Communities and their Member States', G/C/W/138, (99-0851), 4 March.

WTO (1999c), 'Council for Trade Related Aspects of Intellectual Property Development: Work Programme on Electronic Commerce. Communication from the European Communities and their Member States', IP/C/W/140, (99-1898), 7 May.

WTO (2000), 'Council for Trade Related Aspects of Intellectual Property Development: Work Programme on Electronic Commerce. Communication from the European Communities and their Member States', IP/C/W/224 (00-4901), 17 November.

WTO (2001), 'Electronic Commerce Briefing Note. Work Programme Reflects Growing Importance', http://www.wto.org/english/ tratop_e/com_e/com_briefnote_e.htm

WTO (2003), 'Work Programme on Electronic Commerce: Submission from the European Communities', (03-2480), WT/GC/W/497, 9 May.

WTO (2005), 'Work Programme on Electronic Commerce: Communication from the United States', WT/GC/W/551, (05-5028), 28 October.

Young, Alisdair R. (2002), *Extending European Cooperation: The European Union and the 'New' International Trade Agenda*, Manchester: Manchester University Press.

Young, Alisdair R. and Wallace, Helen (2000), *Regulatory Politics in the European Union*, Manchester: Manchester University Press.

Index

1998 Framework 62

ABT (Agreement on Basic
    Telecommunications) 143–4
accountability and private self-regulation
    22
ADR *see* Alternative Dispute Resolution
Advanced Research Projects Agency
    (ARPA) 28
Agreement on Basic
    Telecommunications (ABT) 143–4
Ahrne, G. 168
Alternative Dispute Resolution (ADR)
    86, 112–13, 163
    and Directive on E-commerce 108
alternative regulation, EU 166–7
ARPANET 28–30
audiovisual communications, role of the
    state, Europe 51–3

Bach, D. 19–20, 137
Baker, A. 165, 173
Bangemann Report 96–7
Belgian model of TLD management 85
Better Regulation Action Plan (EC) 167
Bislev, S. 2
Bolkenstein, F. 117
Brants, K. 66
broadcasting
    policy, EU 67–8
    role of the state, EU 51–3, 65–7
Brunsson, N. 168
BT and local loop unbundling 101
business-to-business e-commerce, EU
    94–5
business-to-consumer e-commerce, EU
    95

Castells, M. 120
Cerny, P.G. 4–5, 161, 172
codes of conduct 163

and Directive on E-commerce 108,
    118–19
for registrars, dot eu Top Level
    Domain 86
commercialisation
    of broadcasting 66–7
    of the Internet 32
communications sector
    governance, EU 48–74
    regulatory framework, EU 70
    trade, global governance 140–44
competition
    broadcasting sector 67
    telecommunications sector 55–8
competitive regulatory state, and
    globalisation 4–7
consumer dispute settlement, EC
    Recommendation 112–13
consumer protection, Finland 121
consumer rights, and country of origin
    principle 106
contract specifications, DEC 107
convergence
    communications sector 68–70
    and ECRF 64–5, 70, 169–70
    and Internet regulation 71–2
    telecommunications sector 63–4
cooperation requirements, DEC 109
coordination within the regulatory state
    6–7, 8
co-regulation 167
counter-notice procedure 125
country of origin principle, and
    e-commerce 105–7
Cutler, C.A. 21

DEC *see* Directive on E-commerce
DGIS (Directorate General Information
    Society) 77
Dickie, J. 106
Die Welt case, Germany 129

Directive on distance selling, EU
110–11
Directive on E-commerce 102–9, 163–4
and Finland 120–23
and Germany 127–9
and national regulatory systems
116–31
transposition and implementation
117–19
and UK 123–7
Directorate General Information Society
(DGIS) 77
dispute resolution *see* Alternative
Dispute Resolution
distance selling Directive, EU 110–11
Domain Name System (DNS) 30, 33–6
and EU position 155
dot eu Top Level Domain 75–91
development 76–9
public policy rules 82–6, 89
regulation 79–91, 163, 166
self-regulation 87–8, 89
Drake, W. 2, 144
Drezner, D.W. 171

EC *see* European Commission
e-commerce
Finland 120–23
Germany 127–9
governance, EU 161–70
regulation, EU 93–115
UK 123–7
WTO and EU 144–8
ECRF (Electronic Communications
Regulatory Framework) 64–5, 70,
169–70
eEurope 102
e-financial services regulation 113–14
Electronic Commerce Directive *see*
Directive on E-Commerce
Electronic Commerce (EC Directive)
Regulation, UK 124
electronic commerce work programme,
WTO 145
Electronic Communications Regulatory
Framework (ECRF) 64–5, 70,
169–70
electronic contracting and DEC 118
electronic network communications,
Europe, role of the state 50–54

Eliassen, K.A. 116
Ethernet 31
EU *see* European Union
Eurid (European Registry for Internet
Domains) 82–6
Policy Council 88
*Europe and the Global Information
Society* (Bangemann Report) 96–7
European Commission
Better Regulation Action Plan 167
DGIS 77
Directive on E-Commerce *see*
Directive on E-Commerce
and dot eu Top Level Domain
regulation 81–6
recommendations to WSIS 153–4
report on e-commerce regulation
97–100
*European Initiative in Electronic
Commerce* (EC) 97–100
European Registry for Internet Domains
see Eurid
European Union
and broadcasting policy 65–8
and communications sector
governance 48–74
distance selling Directive 110–11
and global governance of
communications trade 140–44
and global Internet governance
133–59, 171–3
and ICANN 42–4, 45, 135–40
and Internet commerce 93–115,
161–70
regulatory state 7–10, 14–18
telecommunications policy 58–65
and WSIS 152–7
and WTO negotiations on e-commerce
144–8
Europeanisation of telecommunications
policy 58–63

FICORA (telecommunications regulator,
Finland) 121
financial services regulation 113–14
Finland and Directive on E-commerce
120–23
Flyverbom, M. 2
frameworks for Internet governance 2
France, telecommunications sector 57

GAC (Governmental Advisory
    Committee) and ICANN 43–4,
    135–40
GATS
    and e-commerce 147
    and telecommunications 142–3
GATT (General Agreement on Tariffs
    and Trade) 141
    and e-commerce 147
Generic Top-Level Domain
    Memorandum on Understanding 37
Germany
    and Directive on E-commerce 127–9
    telecommunications sector 57
global governance of communications
    trade, and EU 140–44
Global Internet Council (GIC) 151
global Internet governance
    and the EU 133–59
    recommendations for future 171–3
Global Internet Policy Council (GIPC)
    152
Global Internet Project (GIP) 39
globalisation
    and the competitive regulatory state
        4–7
    and Internet growth 161
governance, Internet *see* Internet
    governance
governance modalities, Internet
    commerce, EU 165–8
governance models, Internet, WGIG
    151–2
Governmental Advisory Committee
    (GAC), ICANN 43–4, 135–40
Grabosky, P. 9
Green-Cowles, M. 163, 165
Green Paper on convergence (EC) 69
Green Paper on domain name
    management (US) 37–9
gTLD-MOU, US opposition to 37

Heise case, Germany 129
Held, T. 20
Himanen, P. 120
Hofmann J. 31–2, 37
horizontal policy areas 99–100
host provider liability for content,
    Finland 122–3
Humphreys, P. 5, 58, 60, 66

hyperlinkers, liability
    Germany 129
    UK 125

IAHC (International ad hoc Committee),
    ISOC 36
IANA (International Assigned Number
    Authority) 32, 34
Ibanez, J. 2
ICANN (Internet Corporation for
    Assigned Names and Numbers)
    37–44, 76–7, 134–40
    and dot eu Top Level Domain 78–9,
        81
    and the EU 42–4
    and GAC 43–4, 135–40, 151
    and US government 41, 155, 157
ICSTIS (Independent Committee for the
    Supervision of Telephone
    Information Service) 125–6
IETF (Internet Engineering Task Force)
    31–2, 46
information provision to customers,
    DEC 107
Information Society (IS) and the EU
    95–6
    Finland 120
intermediate service providers liability,
    DEC 108, 119
    Finland 122
    Germany 129
    UK 124–5
internal market clause, DEC 104–5,
    117–18
    Germany 129
    UK derogation 125–6
International Forum on the White Paper
    (IFWP) 39–40
International Internet Council, proposed
    151–2
international regime analysis,
    e-commerce 2
International Telecommunications Union
    and WSIS 148–9
Internet
    commercialisation 30–32
    development of 28–32
Internet Assigned Numbers Authority
    (IANA) 32, 34
Internet commerce *see* e-commerce

Internet Corporation for Assigned Names and Numbers *see* ICANN
Internet Domain Name System *see* Domain Name System
Internet Engineering Task Force (IETF) 31–2, 46
Internet governance 1–2
  and convergence 71–2
  development 27–45
  and EU 10, 133–59, 171–3
  WGIG recommendations 149–52
  see also ICANN
Internet Governance Forum (IGF) 156, 172
Internet Informal Group (IIG) 77–8
Internet intermediaries *see* intermediate service providers
Internet naming and addressing *see* Domain Name System; ICANN
Internet Society (ISOC) 46
ISO and dot eu Top Level Domain accreditation 78–9
ISOC (Internet Society) 46
ITU (International Telecommunications Union) and WSIS 148–9

Jayasuriya, K. 5–6, 6–7, 10
Jordana, J. 9
jurisdiction country and e-commerce 106

Kirton, J. 166
Kleinwachter, W. 1
Knill, C. 16–18
Kummoinen, K. 122, 123

Ladeur, K.-H. 173
language issues, dot eu Top Level Domain 84
legislation, EU and Internet commerce 109–14
legitimacy of self-regulation 21–2
Lenschow, A. 16–18
Levi-Faur, D. 9
liability of intermediate service providers, DEC 108, 119
  Finland 122
  Germany 129
  UK 124–5
liberalisation, telecommunications sector 55–8

and WTO 142–3
Liikanen, E. 18–19
local loop unbundling 64, 100–101
location tool services liability
  Germany 129
  UK 125

Majone, G. 14–16
Mandelkern Group 167
Marcussen, M. 168
media pluralism, lack of policy, EU 68
Menzel 171
meta-regulation 13
Metcalfe, R. 31
modalities of Internet commerce governance, EU 165–8
modes of regulation 14–18
Moran, M. 9
Morth, U. 172
Mueller, M. 29, 34, 40, 41, 44

national regulatory systems and DEC 116–31
National Science Foundation *see* NSF
negative coordination 6–7, 8
neo-liberal ideology and telecommunications, Europe 55–8
Network Solutions *see* NSI
Newman, A. 19–20, 137
Nicolaidis, K.144
notice and take down procedures, DEC 119
  UK 125
NSF (National Science Foundation) 30
  and domain name registrations 34
NSFNET 30
  privatisation and commercialisation 32
NSI (Network Solutions)
  and domain name registration 34–5
  and ICANN 41

online contracts and DEC 107
online financial services regulation 113–14
Open Method of Coordination (OMC) 17–18, 172–3
Open Network Provision compromise 61
out-of-court dispute settlement, Recommendation on 112–13

policy, EU, Internet commerce
    regulation 109–14
Policy Council, Eurid 88
positive coordination 6, 8
post-regulatory state 10–14, 163
Postel, J. 34, 35
PPR (Public Policy Rules) and dot eu
    TLD 82–6
premium rate numbers, UK action
    against foreign companies 125–6
Prepcom 153
Price, M.E. 21
private authority governance 165
private-public interests and
    self-regulation 21
private self-regulation 18, 21–2
Public Policy Rules and dot eu TLD
    82–6
public-private governance 173
public-private interests and
    self-regulation 21

Recommendation on out-of-court dispute
    settlement 112–13
Reding, V. 155–6, 157, 170
regulated self-regulation 20–21
regulation of Internet commerce, EU
    93–115
regulatory credibility problems, EU 15
regulatory framework for
    communications, EU 70
regulatory modes 14–18
regulatory-networked agency model 16
regulatory state 7–10
    and e-commerce governance 162
    modes of regulation 14–16
responsive regulation 11–13
Ronit, K. 21
root zone file, DNS 33
    control and ownership 35–6

Sassen, S. 165
Schaede, U. 9
Scharpf, F. 6
Schiller, D. 29, 30, 31
Schmidt, P. 166
Schmidt, V. 58
Schultz, W. 20
Scott, C. 10–11, 12, 13–14
self-regulation

and Directive on E-commerce 118–19
domain names 137–8
dot eu Top Level Domain 87–8, 89,
    163
enforcement 19–20
and EU 18–23, 166
Simpson, S. 5, 27, 31, 58, 60
Single European Information Space 169
Siune, K. 66
Sjøvaag, M. 116
Slaughter, A.-M. 173
Slevin 27, 28, 29, 30
soft law 13, 172
spam, and Directive on E-commerce 107
state
    and audiovisual sector 51–3
    and broadcasting 51–3, 65–7, 68
    and dot eu Top Level Domain
        regulation 82–6
    and globalisation 4–7
    post-regulatory 10–14, 163
    regulatory 7–10
    and telecommunications 50–51
Stoker, G. 10
substantive and regulatory standards 16
sunrise period, dot eu Top Level Domain
    84, 85

TCP/IP (Transmission Control
    Protocol/Internet Protocol) 29
Telecommunications Annex, GATS
    142–3
telecommunications sector
    governance, EU 58–63
    liberalisation 55–8, 142–4
    state role 50–51
    and technological change 54–8
television *see* broadcasting
Television Without Frontiers Directive
    67
Teubner, G. 171
Top Level Domains (TLD) 35
    EC criticism of market 136–7
    see also dot eu Top Level Domain;
        ICANN
trade, international, and communications
    140–44
trademark protection, domain names 34
trans-European regulatory network
    concept 14–16

transgovernmental regulatory networks 173

Transmission Control Protocol/Internet Protocol (TCP/IP) 29

Transparency Directive, EU 111–12

transposition and implementation, DEC 117–19
Finland 120–23
Germany 127–9
UK 123–7

Trebilcock, M. 166

unbundling telecommunications local loop 64, 100–101

United Kingdom
Directive on E-commerce implementation 123–27
local loop unbundling 101
telecommunications sector liberalisation 56

United States
Green Paper on domain name management 37–9
and ICANN 41, 155, 157
and Internet governance 36–42
and self-regulation, domain names 137–8
White Paper on Internet name management 37, 39–40

unsolicited commercial communications (spam) and DEC 107

Uruguay Round and telecoms liberalisation 141–2

Value Added Network Services (VANS) 54

Venturelli, S. 2

Verhulst, S. 21

Vesting, T. 94, 173, 174

Voice over Internet Protocol (VoIP) 170

Weinberg, J. 34, 35, 41

Werle, R. 42

WGIG (Working Group on Internet Governance) 149–52

White Paper on management on Internet names and addresses (US) 37, 39–40

WICANN (World Internet Corporation for Assigned Names and Numbers) 152

Wilkinson, C. 77, 78

Work Programme on electronic commerce, WTO 145

Working Group on Internet Governance (WGIG) 149–52

World Internet Corporation for Assigned Names and Numbers (WICANN) 152

World Summit on the IS *see* WSIS

World Wide Web (WWW) 32

WSIS (World Summit on the IS) 148–57
EU role 152–7

WTO
and e-commerce 144–8
and trade liberalisation 141–2